Shouting Softly

Other Books of Interest from St. Augustine's Press

Joseph Bottum, *The Decline of the Novel*

David Ramsay Steele, *The Mystery of Fascism*

James V. Schall, *On the Principles of Taxing Beer:
And Other Brief Philosophical Essays*

James V. Schall, *The Praise of 'Sons of Bitches':
On the Worship of God by Fallen Men*

Rémi Brague, *The Anchors in the Heavens*

Roger Kimball, The Fortunes of Permanence:
Culture and Anarchy in an Age of Amnesia

Marvin R. O'Connell, *Telling Stories that Matter: Memoirs and Essays*

Josef Pieper, *Traditional Truth, Poetry, Sacrament:
For My Mother, on her 70th Birthday*

Peter Kreeft, *Summa Philosophica*

Peter Kreeft, *Ethics for Beginners: Big Ideas from 32 Great Minds*

John von Heyking, *Comprehensive Judgment and Absolute Selflessness:
Winston Churchill on Politics as Friendship*

Gerard V. Bradley, *Unquiet Americans:
U. S. Catholics and America's Common Good*

David Lowenthal, *Slave State: Rereading Orwell's 1984*

Gene Fendt, *Camus' Plague: Myth for Our World*

Nathan Lefler, *Tale of a Criminal Mind Gone Good*

Nalin Ranasinghe, *The Confessions of Odysseus*

Will Morrisey, *Herman Melville's Ship of State*

Roger Scruton, *The Politics of Culture and Other Essays*

Roger Scruton, *The Meaning of Conservatism: Revised 3rd Edition*

Roger Scruton, *An Intelligent Person's Guide to Modern Culture*

Stanley Rosen, *The Language of Love: An Interpretation of Plato's Phaedrus*

Winston Churchill, *The River War*

Shouting Softly
Lines on Law, Literature, and Culture
ALLEN MENDENHALL

ST. AUGUSTINE'S PRESS
South Bend, Indiana

Manufactured in the United States of America.

1 2 3 4 5 6   26 25 24 23 22 21

Library of Congress Control Number: 2021944213

∞ The paper used in this publication meets the minimum
requirements of the American National Standard for Information Sciences –
Permanence of Paper for Printed Materials, ANSI Z39.48-1984.

St. Augustine's Press
www.staugustine.net

Table of Contents

Part One: Law 1
Nomocracy and Nomocratic Jurisprudence 1
What of Richard Posner? 18
Justice Stephen Breyer, the Anti-Nomocratic Judge 31
Against Centralizing, Nationalist Jurisprudence 45
Nomocracy and the Rule of Law 55
How to Achieve Nomocracy? 58
Remember Russell Kirk 71

Part Two: Literature 77
Influence with or without Anxiety 80

Part Three: Culture 128
Phantoms of Terror 128
Boswell Gets His Due 131
Donald Trump the Cowboy 134
Teaching Humbly and without Malice 137
Sex with the Dead 140
Flourishing and Synthesis 148
Debunking the Demographers 152
Ideas Make Us Rich 155
The Dirty Business of Government Trash Collection 161
Make America Mobile Again 164
Pragmatists versus Agrarians? 168
Socialism: World's Greatest Generator of Poverty 174
The Antiwar Tradition in American Letters 176
Glory and Indignity 179
Dixie Bohemia 183
Buckley for the Masses 185
In Search of Fascism 187

The Conservative Mindset 191
Sanctifying the Individual 196
Illiberal Arts 200
Ron Paul's Education Revolution 203
No One Knows What "Change" and "Equality" Mean 206
Learning What We Don't Know 209

Acknowledgments 214

Endnotes 220

PART ONE: LAW

Nomocracy and Nomocratic Jurisprudence

Saying anything celebratory or positive about former United States Supreme Court Justice Oliver Wendell Holmes Jr. will invariably provoke the ire of commentators on both the left and the right. Few jurists are as controversial or confusing. Few scholars are able to write about him without passing judgment on him or his jurisprudence, without praising or condemning his judicial opinions. Most educated readers interested in the law carry with them a bundle of presuppositions about Holmes that are difficult to see beyond or overcome. There are good reasons, however, why figures as wide-ranging as Robert H. Bork,[1] William H. Rehnquist,[2] Thomas Sowell,[3] and J. Harvie Wilkinson III[4] have celebrated Holmes, whose jurisprudence has been compared to the philosophy of Michael Oakeshott.[5] His methodology challenges constructivist and rationalistic jurisprudence that overstates the capacity of human reason and the universalizability of binding rules and normative orders. Holmes exposits a pragmatic jurisprudence that finds its place alongside Oakeshott, Sir Matthew Hale, Edmund Burke, Adam Smith, David Hume, Bernard Mandeville, F. A. Hayek, Michael Polanyi, and Frederic William Maitland, who, in various ways, account for spontaneous ordering and bottom-up rulemaking in their formulations of civil society.

Holmes's jurisprudence is nomocratic in that it treats the rule of law as a condition for liberty, respects the emergent processes and procedures present in the common-law system, confines judges to fields of inquiry grounded in situated or embedded norms while leaving speculation and conjecture to the philosophers, restrains and divides central power, embraces the historical over the ahistorical, limits government authority, defers to local political units, and commits itself to textual givens rather than to *a priori* ideals or abstractions.

Law and nomocracy interact to protect individual liberty through the mediating institutions of small communities within larger political regimes. A jurisprudence of nomocracy recognizes that imperfections in the legal system are inevitable and must be tolerated to some degree to avoid worse tyrannies that result from unrestrained ideology and the centralization or concentration of power. Human beings are fallible creatures with limited knowledge and selective memory whose attempts to realize in the law grand or utopian visions tend to destroy liberty and institutionalize tyranny. Disagreement among humans is unavoidable; conflict is inescapable. The law, guided by prudence and practical reasoning, must therefore, according to nomocratic jurisprudence, maintain disagreement and conflict at the level of rhetoric and discourse to prevent physical violence and coercion. Nomocracy balances prudence and liberty to ensure that time-tested principles and practices preserve the wisdom of the past during innovative and disorienting times.

Although I submit that Holmes is nomocratic, I am mindful of Justice Felix Frankfurter's admonition that "[o]nly the shallow would attempt to put Mr. Justice Holmes in the shallow pigeonholes of classification."[6]

A definition is in order. By "nomocratic" and "nomocracy," I mean the opposite of "teleocratic" and "teleocracy." Forrest McDonald explains the difference in this way:

> [The idea behind nomocratic constitutionalism] is that the Constitution was designed to bring government under the rule of law, as opposed to achieving any specific purpose. . . .[T]he Constitution is primarily a structural and procedural document, specifying who is to exercise what powers and how. It is a body of law, designed to govern, not the people, but government itself; and it is written in language intelligible to all, that all might know whether it is being obeyed. The alternative, teleocratic view, is one that has come into fashion the last few decades and has all but destroyed the original Constitution. This is the notion that the design of the Constitution was to achieve a certain kind of society, one based upon abstract principles of natural rights or justice or equality or democracy or all of the above. It holds that the specific provisions of the document are of

secondary importance or none at all; what counts are the "principles" it supposedly embodies, usually principles based upon the Declaration of Independence or Lincoln's Gettysburg Address, neither of which has any standing in the law.[7]

Constitutionalism is important to nomocracy. Designed to limit government power, repurposing both the biblical notion of a covenant and the social contract theory emanating from, among others, Hugo Grotius, Thomas Hobbes, John Locke, and Jean-Jacques Rousseau, and recalling the binding contractual character of monarchical charters, constitutions establish the fundamental framework for all laws and institutions within the jurisdiction. They posit general principles and practical ideals that guide and restrain legislators, executive officials, and judges. They define and delineate the balance between liberty and authority, freedom and order, leaving the political processes to determine procedural technicalities and subsidiary rules. Unwritten constitutions are bodies of rules containing the usages, customs, practices, and norms that have for long periods governed the lived experience in a particular political territory.

Marshall L. DeRosa, working out of McDonald's paradigm, clarifies the difference between nomocratic and teleocratic constitutional schemes in this way:

> If the Constitution is essentially nomocratic, then the federal courts would be restricted to the enforcement of constitutionally established procedures through which participants in the political process compete against one another in the attempt to have their respective interest prevail in the public policy-making process, whether those interests are economic, social, cultural, religious, regional, and/or political. Judicial review would be invoked when the procedures are allegedly breached, with the courts being responsible for upholding the constitutional integrity of the political process. Under this model political questions are nonjusticiable. This does not mean that the Constitution fails to place limits on nomocratic procedures for making public policy. It certainly does (see Art. I, sections nine and ten and the Bill of Rights), but these limits were nomocratically produced through

3

the drafting and ratifying of constitutional provisions. . . .Nevertheless, if the U.S. Constitution is construed to be a teleocratic a priori embodiment of truth, justice, and righteousness, with U.S. Supreme Court justices serving as its privileged interpreters, then popular control over important areas of public policy becomes precarious and subject to the domination of exclusive interests—usually ideological in nature—which at any particular period of constitutional development may exercise control over the policy-making process through the institutional Supreme Court.[8]

Holmes favored a nomocratic approach to constitutionalism that is in keeping with these descriptions. His preference for nomocracy is evident in his judicial restraint in the form of deference to legislatures, his admiration for the common-law system in which rules evolve incrementally while always retaining and reflecting the values of our predecessors, and his skepticism that natural law and natural rights theorizing is appropriate for judges, who, after all, are lawyers in robes, not philosophers.

While considering whom to nominate to succeed Justice David H. Souter on the United States Supreme Court, President Barack Obama alleged that "empathy" was a suitable criterion for evaluating the merits of a judge. He did not clarify what it meant to be an empathetic justice or how an empathetic justice was supposed to rule. During this time, Sowell penned an op-ed that presented empathy as antithetical to the law and referred to Holmes as a "great Supreme Court justice" who would not have been "appointed under Pres. Barack Obama's criterion of 'empathy' for certain groups."[9] Sowell explained that Holmes "had empathy for some and antipathy for others, but his votes on the Supreme Court often went against those for whom he had empathy and in favor of those for whom he had antipathy."[10] He then recalled Holmes's own words: "I loathed most of the things in favor of which I decided."[11] Sowell might have added Holmes's remark to John T. Morse that "[i]t has given me great pleasure to sustain the Constitutionality of laws that I believe to be as bad as possible, because I thereby helped to mark the difference between what I would forbid and what the Constitution permits."[12]

What makes a judge rule against his beliefs? The answer is the preempting belief that his other beliefs are irrelevant to the job at hand. Holmes explained that a judge's "first business is to see that the game is played according to the rules whether [he] like[s] them or not."[13] This remark anticipates Chief Justice John Roberts's umpire analogy, made famous during his confirmation hearings. Holmes's judicial restraint meant deference to state legislatures. "I think the proper course," he said, "is to recognize that a state legislature can do whatever it sees fit to do unless it is restrained by some express prohibition in the Constitution of the United States or of the State, and that Courts should be careful not to extend such prohibitions beyond their obvious meaning by reading into them conceptions of public policy that the particular Court may happen to entertain."[14] The judge or justice should respect the will of the people (as expressed through legislation enacted by elected representatives) so long as it fits within the fixed parameters of the United States Constitution and the applicable state constitution. No matter how bad or offensive the legislation appears to be, the judge is not to disturb it absent obvious constitutional authority to do so. "If my fellow citizens want to go to Hell," Holmes said, "I will let them. It's my job."[15] On this theory, Holmes, controversially, opined to uphold an Alabama law disqualifying blacks from voting[16] and an Iowa prohibition against the teaching of foreign languages.[17] Justice Frankfurter most likely had cases like these in mind when he said that Holmes "has ever been keenly conscious of the delicacy involved in reviewing other men's judgment not as to its wisdom but as to their right to entertain the reasonableness of its wisdom."[18] In the 1990s, Thomas Grey echoed Frankfurter, remarking that Holmes "believed that his public duty was to subordinate his own views to the dominant opinion of the community, that of his masters, the people. He did not respect the substance of those views, but he respected their source."[19]

In Holmes's opinions and dissents, there are two glaring exceptions to this default position that a state law must be upheld so long as it is constitutional. These are in the areas of free speech and habeas corpus. So much has been made of the former that there is now an entire book on the subject: *The Great Dissent: How Oliver Wendell Holmes Changed His Mind—And Changed the History of Free Speech in America* (2013) by Thomas Healy. This book shows that Holmes was inclined to defer to state legislatures but evolved to support more vigorous protections of free speech. As for habeas corpus, his opinion in *Moore v. Dempsey*[20] and his dissent in *Frank v.*

Mangum[21] reveal an unwillingness to go along with state law. His deference to state legislatures led him to despise the Fourteenth Amendment, or at least its increasingly robust application against the states. His dissent in *Baldwin v. Missouri* lambasted such an expansive application:

> I have not yet adequately expressed the more than anxiety that I feel at the ever increasing scope given to the Fourteenth Amendment in cutting down what I believe to be the constitutional rights of the States. As the decisions now stand I see hardly any limit but the sky to the invalidating of those rights if they happen to strike a majority of this Court as for any reason undesirable. I cannot believe that the Amendment was intended to give us carte blanche to embody our economic or moral beliefs in its prohibitions. Yet I can think of no narrower reason that seems to me to justify the present and the earlier decisions to which I have referred. Of course the words "due process of law[,]" if taken in their literal meaning[,] have no application to this case; and while it is too late t[o] deny that they have been given a much more extended and artificial signification, still we ought to remember the great caution shown by the Constitution in limiting the power of the States, and should be slow to construe the clause in the Fourteenth Amendment as committing to the Court, with no guide but the Court's own discretion, the validity of whatever laws the States may pass.[22]

Elsewhere he was even more pointed in his reproach of the Fourteenth Amendment: "There is nothing that I more deprecate than the use of the Fourteenth Amendment beyond the absolute compulsion of its words to prevent the making of social experiments that an important part of the community desires, in the insulated chambers afforded by the several states."[23] He added that he would uphold state laws even if they "may seem futile or even noxious to me and to those whose judgment I most respect."[24]

In his most famous dissent in *Lochner v. N.Y.*,[25] Holmes stood against the judicial activism of the majority and dissented in colorful language. Appealed from the Court of Appeals of New York, which ruled that a bakery owner had violated a New York labor statute restricting the working hours of bakers, *Lochner* held that the right to contract was protected from state government interference under the Fourteenth Amendment. The Supreme Court thereby ensured that the Fourteenth Amendment, which had been ratified to protect the rights of freed slaves, applied against the states even in cases having nothing to do with freed slaves. Bork would later describe this decision as a "judicial usurpation of power."[26] Justice Antonin Scalia employed the word "usurpation" to describe capacious interpretations of the Fourteenth Amendment at the expense of state and local autonomy.[27] Bork and Scalia appear, then, to have agreed with Holmes.

Although Holmes adored titans of industry and praised business interests in his private correspondence, he dissented against his own personal preferences in *Lochner*, reasoning that the New York statute was not unconstitutional. He claimed that the majority opinion was "decided upon an economic theory which a large part of the country does not entertain,"[28] even if Holmes himself, for aught that appears, entertained this very theory. Rather than imposing a set of beliefs on the citizens, the United States Constitution, he said, was "made for people of fundamentally differing views."[29] Accordingly, the Supreme Court ought not to read into the Constitution restrictions on state sovereignty that are not there.

Much more could be said about Holmes's deference to state law. Those interested in a full treatment of Holmes's judicial restraint should consult Francis R. Kellogg's Oliver Wendell Holmes, Jr., *Legal Theory, and Judicial Restraint* (Cambridge University Press, 2007) or David Luban's *"The Metaphysics of Judicial Restraint"* in volume 44 of the *Duke Law Journal* (1994). Let us consider now Holmes's admiration for the spontaneous order (as against a rationally and centrally planned order) produced by the evolutionary common-law system.

While serving as Chief Justice on the Massachusetts Supreme Judicial Court, Holmes penned the following about the common-law doctrine of stare decisis:

> We may agree that. . .it may be desirable that the courts should have the power in dispute. We appreciate the ease with which, if we were careless or ignorant of precedent, we might deem it enlightened to assume that power. . . [,] [b]ut the improvements made by the courts are made, almost invariably, by very slow

degrees and by very short steps. Their general duty is not to change but to work out the principles already sanctioned by the practice of the past.[30]

This was, in effect, his thesis for *The Common Law*, which was published around twenty years earlier. This theme recurred and resounded in his many judicial opinions and essays. Contrary to conservative criticism, Holmes was not anxious to dispense with rules and principles that had enjoyed a long career in the Anglo-American legal tradition. He did "not expect or think it desirable that the judges should undertake to renovate the law. That is not their province."[31] What was expected, desirable, and within the judges' province was following precedent, i.e., adhering to established traditions, practices, procedures, and norms embodied in accumulated case decisions. Here is his explanation for why he himself followed precedent:

> [P]recisely because I believe that the world would be just as well off if it lived under laws that differed from ours in many ways, and because I believe that the claim of our especial code to respect is simply that it exists, that it is the one to which we have become accustomed, and not that it represents an eternal principle, I am slow to consent to overruling a precedent, and think that our important duty is to see that the judicial duel shall be fought out in the accustomed way.[32]

The common-law practice of abiding by residual precedents revealed, to him, that the legal branch of government (as against the executive and legislative branch) is better off trusting tested and tried principles than it is generating untested and untried principles. Experimentation, when the people deem it necessary, must take place in the halls of legislatures where it is less likely to be radical because of the difficulty of achieving consensus among disparate politicians and competing interest groups. By contrast, the relative ease of securing concurrences among a small group of like-minded judges or justices leads to dangerous concentrations of power. In the United States and in many if not most developed countries, legislators may be voted out of office if their experiments fail whereas judges (e.g., federal judges and many state court judges in the United States) enjoy life tenure. Because experimentation originates in the legislature and the courts are merely responsive to legislation, "in substance the growth of the law is legislative."[33]

Philosophy without history is also dangerous. Because the common law is old (just how old is disputed), a judge must understand and fall back on history to contextualize and resolve present conflicts. Holmes's own words, which appear in an 1880 review of a contracts casebook by Christopher Columbus Langdell, then dean of Harvard Law School, capture this sentiment:

> No one will ever have a truly philosophic mastery over the law who does not habitually consider the forces outside of it which have made it what it is. More than that, he must remember that as it embodies the story of a nation's development through many centuries, the law finds its philosophy not in self-consistency, which it must always fail in so long as it continues to grow, but in history and the nature of human needs.[34]

Similar words appear in the opening lines to *The Common Law*:

> The object of this book is to present a general view of the Common Law. To accomplish this task, other tools are needed besides logic. It is something to show that the consistency of a system requires a particular result, but it is not all. The life of the law has not been logic: it has been experience. The felt necessities of the time, the prevalent moral and political theories, intuitions of public policy, avowed or unconscious, even the prejudices which judges share with their fellow-men, have had a good deal more to do than the syllogism in determining the rules by which men should be governed. The law embodies the story of a nation's development through many centuries, and it cannot be dealt with as if it contained only the axioms and corollaries of a book of mathematics. In order to know what it is, we must know what it has been, and what it tends to become. We must alternatively consult history and existing theories of

legislation. But the most difficult labor will be to understand the combination of the two into new products at every stage.[35]

These lengthy passages are summed up by one line in *New York Trust Co. v. Eisner*: "A page of history is worth a volume of logic."[36]

Such lines provide glimpses into Holmes's complex jurisprudence that prizes history, incrementalism, gradualism, meliorism, and restraint—all elements of nomocracy. His occasional comments about how law adapts over time and in response to changing social settings reflect his immersion in British common-law theory that had little bearing on American public law or constitutional jurisprudence. Holmes's vision of the common law was not new: it was, if anything, anachronistic in an increasingly nationalized public law system governed by a federal constitution and regulated by federal judges. For guidance and methodology, Holmes looked back to when courts were divided into smaller jurisdictions with more limited scope over subject matter, when lawsuits were fewer, when courts at law and equity were separated, when statutory or codified law was more restricted in range and application, when bureaucratic agencies were not as numerous or large, and when judges themselves were better educated in legal custom and doctrine.

Holmes served nearly 30 years as an Associate Justice of the United States Supreme Court and nearly 20 years before that on the Massachusetts Supreme Judicial Court. He has been the subject of numerous biographies since his death in 1935. We have not discovered new details about him since Harvard made his papers available to researchers in 1985, yet the biographer Stephen Budiansky recently decided to tell Holmes's story in a detailed biography. Why?

The answer may have to do with something Holmes said in *The Common Law*: "If truth were not often suggested by error, if old implements could not be adjusted to new uses, human progress would be slow. But scrutiny and revision are justified."[37] Indeed, they are—both in the law and in the transmission of history. Holmes has been so singularly misunderstood by jurists and scholars that his life and thought require scrutiny and revision. Because his story is bound up with judicial methods and tenets—his opinions still cited regularly, by no less than the United States Supreme Court—we need to get him right, or at least "righter," lest we fall into error, sending the path of the law in the wrong direction.

A veritable cottage industry of anti-Holmes invective has arisen on both the left and the right side of the political spectrum. No one, it seems, of any political persuasion, wants to adopt Holmes. He's a giant of the law with no champions or defenders. For some critics, Holmes is the paragon of states' rights and judicial restraint who upheld local laws authorizing the disenfranchisement of blacks (*Giles v. Harris*, 1903) and the compulsory sterilization of individuals whom the state deemed unfit (*Buck v. Bell*, 1927). This latter decision he announced with horrifying enthusiasm: "Three generations of imbeciles are enough."[38] For other critics, he's the prototypical progressive, decrying natural law, deferring to legislation that regulated economic activity, embracing an evolutionary view of law akin to living constitutionalism, and bequeathing most of his estate to the federal government. The truth, as always, is more complicated than tendentious caricatures. Budiansky follows Frederic R. Kellogg—in *Oliver Wendell Holmes Jr. and Legal Logic*—in reconsidering this irreducible man who came to be known as the Yankee from Olympus.

Not since Mark DeWolfe Howe's two-volume (but unfinished) biography, *The Proving Years* and *The Shaping Years*, has any author so ably rendered Holmes's wartime service. Budiansky devotes considerable attention to this period perhaps because it fundamentally changed Holmes. Before the war, Holmes, an admirer of Ralph Waldo Emerson, gravitated toward abolitionism and volunteered to serve as a bodyguard for Wendell Phillips. He was appalled by a minstrel show he witnessed as a student. During the war, however, he "grew disdainful of the high-minded talk of people at home who did not grasp that any good the war might still accomplish was being threatened by the evil it had itself become."[39]

Holmes had "daddy issues"—who wouldn't with a father like Oliver Wendell Holmes Sr., the diminutive, gregarious, vainglorious, and sometimes obnoxious celebrity, physician, and author of the popular "Breakfast Table" series in *The Atlantic Monthly?*—that were exacerbated by the elder Holmes's sanctimonious grandstanding about his noble, valiant son. For the aloof father, the son's military service was a status marker. For the son, war was gruesome, fearsome, and real.[40] The son despised the father's flighty ignorance of the on-the-ground realities of bloody conflict.

Holmes fought alongside Copperheads as well, a fact that might have contributed to his skepticism about the motives of the war and the patriotic fervor in Boston. His friend and courageous comrade Henry Abbott—no fan of Lincoln—died at the Battle of the Wilderness in a manner that Budiansky calls "suicidal" rather than bold. The war and its carnage raised Holmes's doubts regarding "the morally superior certainty that often went hand in hand with belief: he grew to distrust, and to detest, zealotry and causes of all kinds."[41]

This distrust—this cynicism about the human ability to know anything with absolute certainty—led Holmes as a judge to favor decentralization. He did not presume to understand from afar which rules and practices optimally regulated distant communities. Whatever legislation they enacted was for him presumptively valid, and he would not impose his preferences on their government. His disdain for his father's moralizing, moreover, may have contributed to his formulation of the "bad man" theory of the law. "If you want to know the law and nothing else," he wrote, "you must look at it as a bad man, who cares only for the material consequences which such knowledge enables him to predict, not as a good one, who finds his reasons for conduct, whether inside the law or outside of it, in the vaguer sanctions of conscience."[42]

Budiansky's treatment of Holmes's experience as a trial judge—the Justices on the Massachusetts Supreme Judicial Court in those days presided over trials of first instance—is distinctive among the biographies. Budiansky avers,

> [I]n his role as a trial justice, Holmes was on the sharp edge of the law, seeing and hearing firsthand all of the tangled dramas of the courtroom, sizing up the honesty of often conflicting witnesses, rendering decisions that had immediate and dramatic consequences — the breakup of families, financial ruin, even death — to the people standing right before him.[43]

Holmes's opinions as a U.S. Supreme Court Justice have received much attention, but more interesting—perhaps because less known—are the salacious divorce cases and shocking murder trials he handled with acute sensitivity to evidence and testimony.

The epigraph to Seth Vannatta's edition *The Pragmatism and Prejudice of Oliver Wendell Holmes Jr.* aptly encapsulates the complexity of Holmes's thought with lines from Whitman's *Song of Myself*: "Do I contradict myself? / Very well then I contradict myself, / (I am large, I contain multitudes.)"[44] Budiansky recognizes, as others haven't, that Holmes was large and contained multitudes. Holmes's contradictions, if they *are* contradictions, might be explained by the famous dictum of his childhood hero, Emerson: "A foolish consistency is the hobgoblin of little minds."

Holmes was consistently inconsistent. His mind was expansive, his reading habits extraordinary. How to categorize such a wide-ranging man? What were the defining features of his belief? Or did he, as Louis Menand has alleged, "lose his belief in beliefs"?[45] Budiansky condenses Holmes's philosophy into this helpful principle: "[T]hat none of us has all the answers; that perfection will never be found in the law as it is not to be found in life; but that its pursuit is still worth the effort, if only for the sake of giving our lives meaning."[46]

Holmes was intellectually humble, warning us against the complacency that attends certainty. Driving his methods was the sober awareness that he, or anyone for that matter, might be incorrect about some deep-seated conviction. During this time of polarized politics, self-righteous indignation, widespread incivility, and rancorous public discourse, we could learn from Holmes. How civil and respectful we could be if we all recognized that our cherished ideas and working paradigms might, at some level, be erroneous, if we were constantly mindful of our inevitable limitations, if we were searchers and seekers who refuse to accept, with utter finality, that we've figured it all out?

What did Holmes have against "the jurist's search for criteria of universal validity which he collects under the head of natural law"?[47] Having fought in the Civil War, during which he was thrice wounded, having transitioned from a young transcendentalist before the war into a disenchanted realist who fraternized with Southern sympathizers during and after the war, Holmes viewed natural law theories as merely philosophical cover for ideological programs. He had seen what happened when two great powers, the Union and the Confederacy, were convinced of the absolute rightness of their position and were willing to fight and die for their beliefs. He, therefore, thought that doubt and humility were necessary to temper the passions and to preserve civilization itself. "Certitude is not the test of certainty," he said, because "[w]e have been cock-sure of many things that were not so."[48] President Ronald Reagan would later parrot that line but substitute "liberals" for the pronoun "we." The point, anyhow, is that, in Holmes's opinion, too many natural law thinkers mistook their personal prejudices (which grow out of community influence) for holy decrees. If one is deluded into believing he is carrying out the will of God when he is not, his convictions quickly lead to tyranny and oppression.

"The prophecies of what the courts will do in fact, and nothing more pretentious," Holmes remarked, "are what I mean by law."[49] Put another way, the laws of nature or of nature's God, to employ Jefferson's phrase, might be one thing, and the laws of man another thing; if the two conflict, and if society does not recognize the conflict, then society will go on applying the laws of man. Both the laws of God and the laws of man are "laws" according to the nomenclature, but one is "true law" and the other not. Nevertheless, they are both "law" insofar as they constitute rules that people follow, and they will be applied as such in whatever society adheres to them. The question is not necessarily which constitutes law and which doesn't, but which law is better. Holmes believed it was up to the people to decide which is better, that is to say, which ought to obtain in society. If the criterion of the people was a perception of divine or natural law, so be it. Perhaps the people would misinterpret scriptural or ordained mandates; perhaps not. Either way, it was important that judges did not legislate.

No matter what we think the absolute truth may be—and we are entitled to think what we wish about absolute truth—we nevertheless "leave to the unknown the final valuation of that which in any event has value to us."[50] Holmes never said that there was no God who designed the universe and demanded our obedience to a prescribed set of rules. What he said was that judges should not presume to be gods or even agents for God with unmediated access to His complete plan for the universe: "If we think of our existence not as that of a little god outside, but as that of a ganglion within, we have the infinite behind us. It gives us our only but our adequate significance."[51] Accordingly, we and our judges should not attempt to make a false idol or heaven-on-earth out of our legal system, for the "common law is not a brooding omnipresence in the sky, but the articulate voice of some sovereign or quasi sovereign that can be identified."[52]

We have seen in the thought of certain Straussians and neoconservatives a presumed universality in legal norms and conventions. We have also seen resistance to alleged universalities, both here and abroad, most notably in the protests and demonstrations against American military intervention in foreign affairs over the last several decades. Viewing Holmes's comments on natural law helps us to put his frustration into a contemporary context. "The jurists who believe in natural law," he says, "seem to me to be in that naïve state of mind that accepts what has been familiar and accepted by them and their neighbors as something that must be accepted by all men everywhere."[53] One does not need to be as skeptical as he to recognize the importance of modesty and restraint in intellectual matters up for debate, especially within the framework of laws that coerce and control people. It is worth remembering that the binding opinions of a judge, however distinguished and applauded they may be during his or her lifetime, are but "the ultimates of a little creature on this little earth [and probably not] the last word of the unimaginable whole."[54]

Holmes leaves room for natural law, but he never explains how. Bork, however, supplies the explanation. He argues that "a judge, no matter on what court he sits, may never create new constitutional rights or destroy old ones. Any time he does so, he violates the limits of his own authority and, for that reason, also violates the rights of the legislature and the people. When a judge is given a set of constitutional provisions, then, as to anything not covered by those provisions, he is, quite properly, powerless. In the absence of law, a judge is a functionary without a function."[55] For a natural rights theorist or a proponent of certain schools of natural law, this statement is absurd on its face: there can never be an absence of law. But for a nomocratic constitutionalist, theological and philosophical inquiries about divine law and natural order are not within the prescribed authority of the judge. He may philosophize on his own time but may not bind the people based on philosophical convictions that find no articulation or representation in established, functioning rules.

Citizens may want their judges to believe in divine law and natural order; yet they might, at the same time, fear the consequences of allowing judges to coerce society into adhering to possibly wrong interpretations about philosophical abstractions. In a nomocratic paradigm, then, natural law and positive law are not mutually exclusive; they interact. The judge, however, does not dictate his personal beliefs about natural law; instead, he follows those beliefs about natural law that are memorialized in positive rules representing the consensus of the citizens. The distinction between primary and secondary rules drawn by H. L. A. Hart is relevant on this score. It is one thing to say that murder is morally bad and should be punished, as natural or divine law so decrees, and quite another to say whether hearsay should be admitted during the prosecution of an alleged murderer, or whether a man committed "'murder'" when he became intoxicated and then struck a young girl with his automobile while she was playing in the street. These examples suggest that positive law in the form of procedural and substantive rules is necessary to carry out divine or natural law. It also shows that what appears to be obvious natural law does not easily obtain in practice because actual events are more complex and unforeseeable than plain generalizations.

Bork explains the interrelation of positive law and divine or natural law by divorcing the office of the judge from the role of the citizen:

> One need not be skeptical about the existence of moral truths and natural rights to think that appeals, by judges, to natural rights, appeals beyond the text of the Constitution, are a pretext for evading the discipline of the Constitution. . . .
>
> The formulation and expression of moral truths as positive law is, in our system of government, a system based on consent, a task confided to the people and their elected representatives. The judge, when he judges, must be, it is his sworn duty to be, a legal positivist. When he acts as a citizen, he, like all other citizens, must not be a legal positivist, but must seek moral truth. Otherwise, there is no way for anybody to say what the law should be, what should be enacted and what repealed.[56]

A judge acting in isolation is prone to error and overconfidence due to the inherent limitations and fallibility of human beings. No matter how learned or righteous or pious the judge may be, the risk of a mistake or oversight is too great for his moral opinion—his alone—to control the everyday operations of the people subject to his jurisdiction. One may wonder whether Justice Kagan or Justice Sotomayor (or the late Justice Ginsburg) ought to dictate what moral rules obtain in our society, or whether a constitution should restrain them from imposing their moral views on communities having different moral views. Consider these questions in the context of more profound thinkers: If Augustine and Aquinas and Luther and Calvin and Jonathan Edwards and John Henry Newman and so on could not achieve consensus on matters of theology that bear upon the law, then who are our judges, untrained in matters of theology or philosophy, to pronounce which laws are "natural" or "divine" and therefore universally binding? The issue is not whether the laws of society should comport with the laws of God—any seriously religious thinker believes that they should—but what those laws are and how they should be brought about as positive law. One individual cannot be trusted to know what God ordains as law, so natural law must be brought about by a consensus of those people acting through elected representatives—and must be articulated as positive law. A society that is virtuous will enact positive laws consistent with scriptural, divine, or natural mandates; a society that is not virtuous will not. Holmes may not have expressed his jurisprudence in these words, but they are implied in what he did express. For more on what he did express, I recommend his essays "Ideals and Doubts" and "The Path of the Law."

Holmes once said that a "word is not a crystal, transparent and unchanged; it is the skin of a living thought, and may vary greatly in color and content according to the circumstances and time in which it is used."[57] This line is neither a call for liberal hermeneutics nor an excuse for broad applications of the law. Rather, it is a modest acknowledgment that language is contextual: what words mean depends on the speaker's (or writer's) intention and on the hearer's (or reader's) anticipated understanding. Only when the speaker's (or writer's) intention corresponds with the hearer's (or reader's) understanding is meaning possible. Therefore, Holmes's remark would suggest that judges ought meticulously to consider all diction and syntax for their precise meaning.

Holmes did just that. It has been said that he "was exacting in construing a statute" and that "once a statute was clearly constitutional and it became a matter of construing it, Holmes put on his most scrupulous spectacles."[58] In the context of the Fourteenth Amendment, and in particular due process, he protested that courts could distort the word "liberty" to mean or justify whatever they wanted. "[L]iberty," he said, "is perverted when it is held to prevent the natural outcome of a dominant opinion."[59] In *U.S. v. Johnson*,[60] he painstakingly analyzed the meaning of "misbranding" pursuant to § 8 of the Food and Drugs Act of 1906. In *Boston Sand & Gravel Co. v. U.S.*,[61] he considered a special act brought by the corporate owner of a steam lighter that had collided with a government destroyer and determined that the act did not permit the collection of interest as damages.

Holmes's own words deserve such high levels of scrutiny. Those of us who embrace nomocratic jurisprudence do not have to like Holmes to admit that he was nomocratic. For my own part, I wince at his callousness in *Buck v. Bell* and despise his comment that "[t]axes are what we pay for civilized society."[62] Many of his other views I find deplorable and indefensible. That makes me all the more grateful that his jurisprudence did not seek to impose those views on me and my society, and intrigued that he made it his business to ensure that judges were not treated as Platonic guardians. Had future Supreme Court justices followed in his footsteps, holdings such as the one in *Roe v. Wade* might not have been possible. He was selfish, vain, and obnoxious, but an impartial jurist. There's much to be said for that.

What of Richard Posner?

"I'm not a typical federal judge," Richard Posner says in *The Federal Judiciary*, which seems designed to affirm that claim.[63] Released in August of 2017, this tome shouldn't be confused with his self-published *Reforming the Federal Judiciary*, released in September of 2017. The latter generated controversy because it includes documents internal to the Seventh Circuit Court of Appeals, including personal emails from Chief Judge Diane Wood and confidential bench memoranda. The former is no less blunt, though one suspects its editors at Harvard University Press ensured that it excluded improper content. Publication of both books coincided with the sudden announcement of Posner's retirement. This quirky and opinionated jurist went out with a bang, not a whimper, after serving nearly 36 years on the bench. He could have taken senior status; instead he withdrew completely, citing his court's handling of *pro se* appellants as the prime reason.

Posner has studied Holmes for decades. But is Posner nomocratic? To address this question, let's consider some of his recent work.

The Federal Judiciary presents "an unvarnished inside look"[64] at the federal court system, which, Posner insists, "is laboring under a number of handicaps,"[65] "habituated to formality, resistant to change, backward-look-ing, even stodgy."[66] Posner is a self-styled pragmatist who champions re-solving cases practically and efficiently through common-sense empiricism without resorting to abstractions or canons of construction. He adores Holmes, whose jurisprudence resembled the pragmatism of C. S. Peirce, William James, and John Dewey. His methodology relies on analyzing the facts and legal issues in a case and then predicting the reasonable outcome in light of experience and the probable consequences of his decision. Ac-cordingly, he follows his instincts unless some statute or constitutional pro-vision stands in the way. Most of the time, the operative rules remain malleable enough to bend toward his purposes.

This fluid approach to judging is not nomocratic. It stands in contradis-tinction to the approach of Justice Antonin Scalia, for whom Posner has little affection. In fact, Posner has established himself as Scalia's opposite. Where Scalia was formalistic and traditional, Posner is flexible and inno-vative. Where Scalia was doctrinaire, Posner is pragmatic. Where Scalia was orthodox, Posner boasts, "I am willing to go [...] deep into the realm of unorthodoxy."[67] Posner's criticisms of Scalia seem irresponsibly personal, involving not only Scalia's originalism and textualism (legitimate objects of concern) but also his religious views on Creationism (about which, Posner declares, Scalia was "wrong as usual").[68] He calls Scalia's belief in the devil "[c]hildish nonsense"[69] and denounces Scalia's unhealthy lifestyle. In a low moment, he calls Scalia "careless" for dying next to a sleep apnea machine that the ailing justice wasn't using.[70] This rebuke is irreverent, but is it con-structive or extraneous? Does it advance Posner's judicial methods while weakening the case for Scalia's?

Aspiring to be "relentlessly critical and overflowing with suggestions for reform,"[71] Posner attacks the "traditional legal culture" that, he says, "has to a significant degree outlived its usefulness."[72] Cataloging the targets of his iconoclastic ire would be exhausting. He jumps from subject to sub-ject, castigating "judicial pretense"[73] and treating with equal fervor such weighty topics as statutory interpretation and such trivial matters as the de-notation of "chambers" versus "office."[74] He confers delightfully disrespect-ful labels (slowpokes,[75] curmudgeons[76]) on his colleagues but can also seem petty (complaints about food in the U.S. Supreme Court cafeteria come to mind). Most of his critiques have merit. His persistent assault on the sanctimony and pomposity of federal judicial culture is acutely entertaining, signaling to some of his more arrogant colleagues that they're not as important or intelligent as they might think.

Posner likes to shock. What other judge would assert that the Constitution is "obsolete"[77] or ask when we'll "stop fussing over an 18th-century document"[78] that institutes the basic framework of governance for the country? A bedrock principle underlying the separation-of-powers doctrine holds that the judicial branch interprets law while the legislative branch makes it. Posner, however, announces that federal judges legislate even though they're unelected. Conservative commentators would offer this fact as condemnation, but Posner extols it as an indispensable prerogative. Although he alleges that judges are political actors, he's impatient with politicians. He ranks as the top weakness of the federal judiciary the fact that politicians nominate and confirm federal judges and justices. (The president nominates and the Senate confirms.) The basis of this objection is that politicians are mostly unqualified to evaluate legal résumés and experience.

A refrain Posner employs to advance his argument—"Moving on"— might serve as his motto for judges, who, in his mind, must break free from undue restraints of the past. "The 18th-century United States, the 19th-century United States, much of the 20th-century United States," he submits, "might as well be foreign countries so far as providing concrete guidance (as distinct from inspiration) to solving today's legal problems is concerned."[79] This isn't meant to be hyperbole. It shows, again, that Posner isn't as nomocratic as Holmes, who, although he criticized useless holdovers in the law—i.e., obsolete rules that remained on the books—was deeply historical in his research and his method, surveying the growth of the law over centuries and contextualizing American rules alongside the experience of the British peoples.

Posner's citations to Wikipedia and tweets—yes, tweets—enact the forward-looking attitude that he celebrates: he's not afraid of new media or of pushing boundaries. Consider the time he asked his law clerks to doff and don certain work clothing to test facts presented by litigants in a case before him. His advice to colleagues on the bench: Let clerks refer to you by your first name; do away with bench memos and write your own opinions; stop breaking for three-month recesses; stagger hiring periods for law clerks;

don't employ career clerks; don't procrastinate; don't get bogged down in procedure at the expense of substance; be concise; read more imaginative literature; avoid Latinisms; abolish standards of review. If you're an appellate judge, preside over district-court trials. And whatever you do, look to the foreseeable future, not backward, for direction.

Readers of his book *Divergent Paths* will recognize in these admonitions Posner's distinctive pet peeves. He believes that judges who don't author their opinions are weak or unable to write well. If judges were required to write their opinions, he supposes, fewer unqualified lawyers would sit on the bench: inexpert writers, not wanting to expose their deficiencies, would not accept the nomination to be a federal judge. Posner's love of good writing is so pronounced that he praises Scalia, his chosen nemesis, for his "excellent writing style."[80] He sprinkles references to Dante, Tennyson, Keats, Fitzgerald, Nietzsche, T. S. Eliot, Orwell, and Edmund Wilson and supplies epigrams by Auden, Yeats, and Alexander Pope. Those who didn't know it wouldn't be surprised to learn that Posner majored in English at Yale.

A former law professor, Posner concludes *The Federal Judiciary* by assigning grades to the federal judiciary in eight categories: selection of judges (B), judicial independence (A-), rule of law (A), finality of judgments (B), court structure (B), management (C), understanding and training (C), and compensation (B+). Total? Around a B average. For all the fuss, that's a decent score. Posner's characteristic arrogance is grandly exhibited. "I'm a pretty well-known judge," he assures us.[81] His preface includes a short bibliography for "readers interested in learning more about me."[82] He names "yours truly"[83] (i.e., himself) in his list of notables in the field of law-and-economics, an indisputable detail that a humbler person would have omitted. Posner's self-importance can be charming or off-putting, depending on your feelings toward him.

Yet he's honest. And forthright. Not just the federal judiciary but the entire legal profession thrives off mendacity, which is not the same as a lie or embellishment. It's a more extravagant, systemic mode of false narrative that lawyers and judges tell themselves about themselves to rationalize and enjoy what they do. Posner sees through this mendacity and derides it for what it is. His frank irritability is strangely charming, and charmingly strange. The federal judiciary has lost a maverick but gained a needed detractor.

William Domnarski recently authored a biography of Posner. He is probably right when he writes that Posner, like his hero Oliver Wendell Holmes Jr., "seemed destined for a literary life."[84] Holmes modeled himself on Emerson; he was the class poet at Harvard and earned his reputation as a thoughtful if controversial man of letters who could write with panache. Posner, who, as I mentioned, majored in English at Yale, modeled himself on Holmes. "Holmes," Posner declared in a missive, "is the greatest jurist, at least of modern times, because the sum of his ideas, metaphors, decisions, dissents, and other contributions exceeds the sum of contributions of any other jurist of modern times."[85] Posner's writing similarly stands out for its flair and confidence.

Both men extended their influence beyond their legal opinions and have contributed to philosophy, becoming provocative historical figures in their own right. Posner has correctly invoked Holmes as a pragmatist, even if Holmes avoided the designation and referred to William James's pragmatism as an "amusing humbug." A member of the short-lived Cambridge Metaphysical Club that birthed pragmatism in the 1870s—and which also included James and Peirce—Holmes at least imbibed the pragmatism that was, so to speak, in the Boston air. Posner's pragmatism, however, is only tangentially related to the thinking of Peirce and James, and so one hesitates to call it pragmatism at all. In a move that must irritate Susan Haack, a University of Miami professor, Peirce supporter, and Richard Rorty critic, Posner distinguishes his variety of pragmatism—what he calls "everyday pragmatism"—from philosophical pragmatism. His thesis is most pronounced in his book *Law, Pragmatism, and Democracy* (2005). The quotidian pragmatism that inheres in the law is, in his view, practical and forward-looking and based on "reasonableness." It's not always clear how this mode of pragmatism intersects with, or diverges from, the so-called traditional or classical pragmatism, though it differs markedly—and refreshingly—from what Haack labeled "vulgar Rortyism," that Frenchified variety of structuralism that dispensed with truth as a meaningful category of discourse.

One suspects, given his outsized ego, that Posner delights in having placed his stamp on legal pragmatism, thereby forcing perplexed students in philosophy departments to come to terms with his ideas and square them with not only Peirce and James but also John Dewey, George Herbert

Mead, and W. V. Quine. Posner's self-importance can be charming or off-putting. You might see him as an erudite, spirited dandy playing the part of flamboyant intellectual; or, more cruelly, as a bitter sophist bent on celebrating his own idiosyncratic views and maliciously dismissing his opponents with callous words and harsh indictments. Certainly, his gratuitous rhetorical attacks on the late Antonin Scalia warrant this latter take. And yet the man speaks with a high, soft voice; loves and spoils his cat; and spends most of his time reading and writing. It's hard to condemn such things.

Posner is on record as having fancied himself as not just equal to, but more intelligent than, Learned Hand and Henry Friendly—two giants of American law—because he considered himself more informed about economics. This is surprising, chiefly because his self-assessment occurred before he became a judge. As a judge, Domnarski tells us, "he could seek to persuade his new judicial colleagues to follow him, so as to further shape the law as he saw it—in his own image."[86] He continues to shape everything, it seems, in his own image, including, perhaps, Domnarski's biography, which he read both in draft form and as a final manuscript. One wonders how heavily he edited his own biography—how much latitude he enjoyed in fashioning his story. He sat for interviews and emailed with Domnarski, which wouldn't be unusual or improper had he not been a primary source of his own legend, as he certainly appears to have been. As a young man, Posner exercised his authority as president of *Harvard Law Review* to include certain content over the objections of his peers. Might he have done this with his biographer?

Posner, an only child, is used to promoting himself, and his acquaintances at different stages of his life often note his arrogance. As early as high school, he would declare that "the Poze knows,"[87] and called himself "the mighty one,"[88] scribbling in yearbooks that he "welcomes you as a High Priest of Posner Worship."[89] You can write this off as playful, but you can't write off the fact that he cites himself in cases more than any other judge—though not by name, Domnarski points out, as if to acquit him of unseemly motivations. An editor of a peer-reviewed journal once complained that Posner had cited himself too often in a paper, to which Posner rejoined that self-citation was necessary because he had produced most of the relevant literature on the subject. "The Poze knows," the footnotes might have read.

Another time an exasperated Posner wrote to editors at Cambridge University Press, "Don't you know who I am?"—the same remark that landed Henry Louis Gates Jr. in hot water under different circumstances.

Although Domnarski connected with over 200 people to piece together his biography of Posner, Posner's personal opinion of himself seems to control the narrative and crowd out contrary valuations that critics may have offered. It's not that Posner's accomplishments and reputation are unearned. He's worked hard to become perhaps the best-known and most prolific federal circuit judge in the history of the United States, and his talents and learning are unquestionable and impressive. The person who emerges in Domnarski's biography is exceptional at what he does, but difficult to like. He graduated first in his class at Harvard Law School but was not popular. He remains good with ideas—just not with people. He'd rather disseminate brilliant theories than keep them to himself, even when they're in bad taste or poor form. Whether that's a virtue or vice depends upon one's priority for manners and decorum.

Posner's most remarkable and admirable quality, it seems to me, is his ability—even willingness—to accept constructive criticism in stride. He doesn't take evaluations of his work personally, and he invites opposition to fine-tune and improve his ideas. He instructs his clerks to criticize his draft opinions line by line so that he can perfect his rationale. "[W]e should want" and "insist upon," he wrote to a colleague, "challenge and criticism; the rougher the better; for one of the great dangers of achieving eminence is that people are afraid to criticize you and then you end up inhabiting a fool's paradise."[90]

Posner has referred to himself as a "monster," a characterization he's also reserved for Wagner, Tolstoy, Nietzsche, Wittgenstein, Proust, Kafka, and Michelangelo. The term thus seems like an odd form of self-approbation rather than regret or self-loathing. It accords with his grand notion that he is "a Promethean intellectual hero,"[91] not just some federal judge who happens to be well read. Posner remains "a writer first and a lawyer second."[92] He's correct that, as he told one correspondent, "the modern practice of law does not offer a great deal of scope for the poetic imagination."[93] Law schools have divided faculty into fields and sub-fields, and specialists in different areas of practice are increasingly unable to speak to one another in a common idiom or with shared vocabularies. Posner studied at

Yale under Cleanth Brooks, who directed Posner's research on William Butler Yeats, so he knows a thing or two about the poetic imagination and memorable expression.

But maybe the law is not about poetic imagination. Maybe it requires a prosaic and mechanical mind that can dispassionately and without fanfare adjudge the soundness of legal arguments presented by the parties to a case. If so, Posner may have been better suited for a different profession, one he would have loved and within which he could have more appropriately flaunted his creativity. Being an English professor, though, would've been out of the question; he dismisses much of what English literature departments regard as scholarship as "bullshit."[94] He uses the same word to describe work in the legal professoriate, of which he was once a seminal figure. By age 30, in fact, he had achieved the rank of full professor at the University of Chicago Law School. He cultivated the image of an iconoclastic rabble-rouser willing to subject all human activity to cost-benefit analysis. He popularized the law-and-economics movement and eagerly imparted that economic efficiency supplied the right methodology for describing and delineating common-law judging, which involved practical resolutions to concrete problems. The doctrinaire Posner of this period drifted far from the Communist roots of his mother. More recently, though, he's alleged that capitalism is a failure and moved decidedly to the left on key issues.

Perhaps because of his haughtiness, the law can seem boring and routine without him. There's something to be said for the color and liveliness he brings to his office, and for his belief that "the law really is a very limited field for a person of literary bent."[95] Domnarski's treatment may seem deferential, but it doesn't cover up Posner's naked, sometimes brutal honesty. Posner is willing to say what others aren't, and able to say it more eloquently. If, as Domnarski avers, Posner considers the average lawyer to be like Bartleby or Ivan Ilych—fancifully tragic figures—then he must disdain or pity those lawyers who come before him in the courtroom and submit their briefs for his relentless scrutiny. The 1987 *Almanac of the Federal Judiciary* states that lawyers who argued before Posner found him to be "arrogant, impatient, dogmatic," and "opinionated," and that he "dominates arguments" and "cross-examines lawyers as if they were 1–Ls in a Socratic exchange with a professor."[96] The man is important, no doubt, but never learned how to play nicely. Ever the Darwinian, Posner has suggested that great books prove their merit over time in the competition of the marketplace; perhaps his reputation will too.

Posner is oddly and stunningly prolific. He has not only contributed to scholarly discourse but also written his own legal opinions. That places him in a small minority among federal judges. Posner is justifiably proud of his prolificacy and diligence, and he's neither apprehensive nor ashamed about castigating his peers—another quality that sets him apart.

Over the years, Posner has tried to, in his words, "pull back the curtain"[97] on his colleagues, our Oz-like federal judges, exposing their failures and inadequacies—what he calls, channeling Star Wars, the "dark side"[98]—lurking behind the glow and aura and imprimatur of state power. Posner suggests that federal judges are not adept at preventing "hunch" or "ideology" from influencing their decisions.[99] Because of their inadequate knowledge and limited training, he adds, federal judges too often resort to feeling and intuition—their "unconscious priors"[100]—to resolve difficult facts and issues. He believes the legal academy should curb this judicial inadequacy, insofar as scholars could, in their teaching and writing, guide judges with clarifying direction. Yet he sees a troubling gulf between law schools and the bench, one that, he insists, "has been growing."[101]

His book *Divergent Paths* seeks to "explain and document" this gulf, "identify the areas in which federal judicial performance is deficient, and explain what the law schools can do to remedy, or more realistically to ameliorate, these deficiencies."[102] Posner is as hard on the professoriate as he is on the federal judiciary, indicting the former for its dislocation from the bench and the latter for its "stale" culture.[103] To his credit, Posner criticizes only the federal judiciary and the elite law schools with which he is familiar. He does not purport to speak for, about, or against the state institutions and non-elite schools to which he has had little exposure, which lends his critique credibility.

Little else in the book, however, is modest. Posner is his typical boisterous (one might say arrogant) self, and his characteristic crankiness is on grand display. Whether it bothers or delights readers depends, I suspect, on the extent to which they agree with him. If you're in accord with Posner on this topic—the institutional and cultural barriers separating federal judges from legal scholars—you'll find his frank attitude and no-holds-barred criticism to be entertaining. In equal measure, someone else might find them off-putting. The same goes for the book: whether you enjoy it will depend on your affinity for Posner.

Like Holmes, his hero, Posner sees Darwinism—natural selection in particular—at work in all aspects of human experience. For example, the legal academy is "Darwinian" because "each species of professor must find an academic niche in which he can avoid destructive competition from other professors."[104] As a result, professors gather together in protective communities—an "academic ecology,"[105] in Posner's words—based on shared disciplinary interests. "Their need to communicate with persons outside their niche," Posner opines, "like the need of a squirrel to learn to eat dandelions as well as nuts, is minimized."[106] This metaphor supposedly illustrates that the academy has become divorced from the judiciary. Although amusing as figurative language, it's perhaps not borne out by facts or evidence, nor by the data Posner presents in tables in his introduction. At best, then, Posner's complaint is anecdotal, not empirical, and that's disappointing coming from this learned judge who earned his reputation as an empiricist.

"Increasingly law school faculties cultivate knowledge of fields outside of law but pertinent to it," Posner says, "including economics, psychology, statistics, computer science, history, philosophy, biology, and literature."[107] The gradual incorporation of disparate disciplines in law schools has, Posner believes, developed in tandem with the growing academic neglect of judicial activity. Put simply, law schools no longer primarily study the behavior and methodology of judges as they once did. Moreover, as law professors have proliferated and law schools have increased in size and number, legal academicians have found ample audiences among faculty and scholars and thus have not suffered from their dislocation from judicial institutions or from the flesh-and-blood judges who decide concrete cases.

Posner decries, with Trump-like enthusiasm, the "refugees"[108] from other, less lucrative disciplines who've sought asylum in law schools. He claims, with apparent disgust, that "many of these refugees have a natural inclination to base their legal teaching and writing on insights gleaned by them in the disciplines that were their first choice."[109] Yet he never adequately demonstrates that interdisciplinarity—and the concomitant diversification of perspectives and backgrounds among legal faculty—damages or thwarts legal education. In fact, what he seems to decry is the current curriculum of legal education, which, to his mind, should focus on judicial behavior and opinions rather than on other areas of the law. He stops short of proposing that administrators build a wall around law schools and make other departments pay for it, but he would, I sense, favor a moratorium on faculty immigration to law schools, and possibly mass deportations for the faculty he deems unworthy or unqualified.

But what Posner dubs "the Ph.Deification"[110] of law faculties is not necessarily bad. Posner himself reveals the disadvantages of being a generalist, which is what law schools prepare their students to be. His own understanding of pragmatism, or rather misunderstanding, is itself evidence that he would have benefited from deeper learning in that subject (say, more reading of Peirce and James and less of Dewey and Holmes) before adopting it as his personal methodology and proclaiming its virtues to the world. His literary criticism in Law and Literature betrays a sometimes-embarrassing unfamiliarity with the trends and history of that discipline, and his early forays into the economic analysis of law have failed to influence the economics profession or to contribute anything of lasting value to professional economists. Indeed, it is perhaps because he knew more than untutored lawyers about economics—though substantially less than actual economists—that his "economic analysis of the law" for which he became famous was as influential as it was.

The legal community, and legal scholarship in particular, would benefit from welcoming qualified specialists and, in so doing, broaden the parameters of legal study and force lawyers out of their insularity. Professors of legal writing ought to be equipped with academic training in writing and the English language. Isn't the systemic problem of bad legal writing self-perpetuating when legal writing professors are drawn, not from professional writers and teachers, but from lawyers? Moreover, professors of corporate law or finance ought to have academic training in those subjects—training that goes beyond the rudimentary glosses that find their way into judicial opinions written by non-expert judges. To read judicial opinions on a particular subject is not a fruitful way of learning that subject. A judge may have no experience in the insurance industry, for instance, when a difficult subrogation case arrives on his docket, yet he or she must handle the case and likely write an opinion on the facts and issues involved. The judge must rely on the evidence and briefing proffered by the parties to the case, not on personal expertise, which he or she lacks. Accordingly, the resulting opinion—inherently and intentionally limited to what it can accomplish—will not likely be sufficiently edifying or insightful to have staying power, that is, to teach future students and practitioners about the fundamentals of insurance.

Yet Posner is right to grumble about how the legal academy is populated by professors with little practical experience in law. In fact, law is the one discipline in which, counterintuitively, the more practical experience you have, the less marketable you are as a professor. He's probably right, too, that there are too many law schools and too many law professors—and, hence, too many lawyers for the saturated legal market. Targets of Posner's ire include jargon, esoterica, obscurantism, and wordiness ("the fetishism of words"[111]); the so-called Bluebook, which is a standard reference tool for lawyers concerning forms of citation to authorities (which is "maddening,"[112] "superfluous,"[113] "cancerous,"[114] and "time-consuming"[115]); student editing of law reviews (for which "neophytes"[116] rather than peer reviewers make the critical editorial decisions); excessive, obtrusive, and needless footnoting in legal scholarship (due in part to the aforementioned neophytes); the culture of secrecy and mystery among federal judges; the decline in legal treatises; hyper specialization among professors; the political nature of judicial appointments and confirmations (including an emphasis on biological diversity rather than diversity of backgrounds and experience); lifetime tenure for federal judges; legal formalism; the unintelligibility of legal opinions to non-lawyers—the list goes on. If you're familiar with Posner and follow his writings, you've probably heard these grievances already. But they're worth repeating if, in book form, they can reach larger audiences. Still, it's either dishonest or imperceptive for this one-time opponent of same-sex marriage to now claim that bigotry alone explains the conservative and Christian position on that issue.

Posner is willing to depart from judicial norms and conventions. He believes that case precedent should not govern causes of action that entail novel issues and circumstances. Controversially, he encourages judges to look beyond the briefing and the record to ferret out the truth and context of matters inadequately illuminated by the parties to the case. Some of his suggestions will seem remote to the average reader and aimed at an elite (if not aloof) audience of politicians and federal judges. Whether federal judicial salaries account for regional cost-of-living differentials, for instance, matters little to most Americans. Nor do we care, frankly, whether judges lack collegiality; we just want them to rule the right way. One would hope personality conflicts wouldn't influence the operative rules that shape human experience, but it turns out that judges can be petty.

Posner fittingly includes a question mark in the title to the final section of *Divergent Paths*: "The Academy to the Rescue?" That punctuation mark reveals how skeptical—or at least tentative—Posner remains about the likelihood that his subjects will institute proper and constructive change. Most of his proposed solutions are sensibly plain: if student editing of law reviews is bad, do away with student editing of law reviews; if the law school curriculum is bad, change it; if judges write poorly, offer them training in writing through continuing legal education courses; if litigants and lawyers travel too far and at too great expense, allow them to videoconference.

Divergent Paths succeeds in demonstrating the need to refocus the legal curriculum on judicial behavior, if only by exposing judges' decision-making to scrutiny (and ridicule) and demystifying the glorified processes of judicial deliberation. "Most judges evaluate cases in a holistic, intuitive manner," Posner submits, "reaching a tentative conclusion that they then subject to technical legal analysis."[117] Their goal is to arrive at decisions that comport with prevailing notions of morality, justice, and common sense. Statutory idiosyncrasies or awkward case precedents will not, in Posner's view, prevent these judges from reaching the result that people untrained in the law would likewise reach because of their ethical predispositions and basic sense of right and wrong. Judges are people too, and for the most part, they want to do what's reasonable.

Humility has few friends among judges and law professors, so it is fun, one must admit, to watch Posner serve these cognoscenti a still-steaming pan of humble pie. But even sympathetic readers will grow weary of the relentless complaining after hundreds of pages of it. Perhaps Posner should have minded his own dictum: "If you want a flawless institution go visit a beehive or an anthill."[118] Then again, if Posner—who inhabits both the judiciary and the academy—doesn't speak up, who will?

Posner is an important figure, but he does not exhibit nomocratic jurisprudence. His admiration for Holmes, and his scholarship on Holmes, should not be taken as evidence of his nomocracy. Nor is he teleocratic, however. Justice Stephen Breyer is an example of a teleocratic jurisprudent. His top-down, expansive mode of judging is the opposite of Holmes's restrained, bottom-up mode that reflected the historical experience of the common-law system as it was inherited from England.

Justice Stephen Breyer, the Anti-Nomocratic Judge

It is an unfortunate truism that the longer one remains in the legal profession, the less educated he becomes. The law, as the saying goes, is a jealous mistress: She does not permit solicitors to invest time in rival passions—e.g., philosophy, history, and literature—let alone cultivate the niceties and nuances of expression that distinguish the lettered from the unlettered. It is tough to read Dickens and Henry James when you have got billable hours to meet, and slogging through appellate cases rewards only a rudimentary, distilled understanding of the principles that great minds have reworked for centuries. There is simply not enough time for punctual judges and practicing attorneys to master biblical hermeneutics or study Shakespeare, and developing the whole person—learning to live well and wisely—falls far beyond the scope of legal practice and proficiency.

Justice Stephen Breyer was off to a promising start to an educated life when he studied philosophy at Stanford University and then attended Oxford University as a Marshall Scholar. He graduated from Harvard Law School in 1964 and began his legal career as a clerk to Justice Arthur J. Goldberg of the United States Supreme Court. In 1967 Breyer entered the academy—first Harvard Law School and later Harvard's Kennedy School of Government—where he focused on administrative law. His scholarship was neither groundbreaking nor exceptional, but it was sufficient to secure him a full professorship and to demonstrate a superior understanding of an unpopular subject. Breyer was, at this time, becoming the welcome exception: a literate lawyer.

Then things went wrong, gradually and by slow degrees. Breyer took the bench on the United States Court of Appeals for the First Circuit in 1980 and, thereafter, became less interesting and bookish and more programmatic and expedient. Perhaps he was overworked or overtired, inundated with cases and bogged down by the mostly mundane tasks of judging. Perhaps, as should be expected, he paid more attention to his docket than to the philosophers who had enriched his thinking during his youth. Perhaps he never wanted the life of a scholar and previously had spilled his ink to game the ranks of the professoriate, an arduous scheming no longer necessary once he had achieved a position with life tenure and nearly unparalleled retirement benefits. Perhaps a want of constructive idleness and leisured meditation hardened his contemplative faculties. Whatever the reason, Breyer's scholarship fell off, his writing suffered, and the lamp of his imagination went out. He poured his soul into cases.

Breyer did manage to exhibit flashes of his former acumen in *Active Liberty*, but his book *The Court and the World*, notwithstanding the cheering pother it elicited, is a snoozer and not particularly edifying. The introduction consists of the kind of tedious mapping and framing that only the student editors of law reviews would tolerate. Breyer separates the book into four parts. Two animating themes underlie each of the four parts of this book: the meaning and import of the rule of law in a globalized world and the incorporation of foreign trends and norms into the legal system of the United States. The latter theme involves principles of comity, or the idea that one jurisdiction will give weight, deference, and authority to the acts, orders, or rulings of another jurisdiction. Breyer's thesis is that "the best way to preserve American constitutional values (a major objective that I hold in common with those who fear the influence of foreign law) is to meet the challenges that the world, as reflected in concrete cases on our docket, actually presents. Doing so necessarily requires greater, not less, awareness of what is happening around us."[119] Standing alone, this declaration seems benign and uncontroversial, hardly worth sustained critique or impassioned defense. Yet something is rotten in the state of Denmark, and arguments that seem nonthreatening are not always as they seem.

Breyer's attempts to realize his thesis in *The Court and the World* and raise questions regarding whether he has, in the way he celebrates the transnational turn in judging, betrayed his own provinciality and proven his own misunderstanding of foreign developments as he puts paternalistic presuppositions on display. Rather than modeling a greater awareness of "what is happening around us"[120]—his stated goal—Breyer demonstrates a profound unawareness of international trends and norms, not to mention a paternalistic view of the role of American courts in relation to the cultures and values of peoples beyond the borders of the United States.

Breyer advocates, as well, approaches to judging that, if widely followed and accepted, could fundamentally undermine his notions of comity and international interdependence; thus, his jural prescriptions, such as they are, ought to be approached with extreme caution if not rejected outright, at least until a better case can be made for them.[121] Although Breyer purports that he "does not pretend to offer any ultimate or even provisional solutions" to the challenges presented by globalization, or that he "merely surveys what is for many an unfamiliar and still-changing legal landscape,"[122] he champions certain methods and viewpoints that lead inexorably to predictable and definite outcomes.[123]

My chief criticisms of Breyer are threefold: (1) he affirms the obvious and, thus, contributes nothing meaningful or constructive to our ongoing conversation about the role of foreign law in domestic courts; (2) he defends a transnational turn in jurisprudence at the expense of the liberal, democratic principles he purports to value; and (3) his lack of historical and philosophical understanding, or his refusal or inability to employ that understanding in the service of rational argument, undermines his reliability and undercuts any lasting merit his arguments for transnational adjudication and jurisprudence might enjoy.

The gravamen of Breyer's argument is that because of communications technology, ease of travel, and globalization, the influence of foreign law on United States courts is on the rise. That is indisputable and self-evident. No reasonable person doubts that we live in "an ever more interdependent world—a world of instant communications and commerce, and shared problems of (for example) security, the environment, health, and trade, all of which ever more pervasively link individuals without regard to national boundaries."[124] It does not follow from this obvious given, however, that a knowledge of foreign laws and legal institutions should be accompanied by their binding application in the courts of the United States, or that any hesitance to embrace unprecedented levels of extraterritorial-based experimentation with the domestic legal system constitutes, in Breyer's words, "stand[ing] on the sidelines" or a "withdraw from the international efforts to resolve the commercial, environmental, and security problems of an increasingly interdependent world."[125] Such language borders on bad faith and casts doubt on Breyer's credibility, integrity, and motivation. After all, he does not attempt to explain or even address the potential arguments of his opponents, who are never named in the text (unless they are his colleagues on the bench), nor does he concede when his opponents' points are valid. Instead, he militates against straw men and caricatured positions that, in his telling, stand in the way of necessary progress and experimentation. Lest I surrender to the same dishonest tactics here, I turn now to key examples from *The Court and the World* to substantiate my three presiding criticisms—and to reveal Breyer as an anti-nomocratic judge.

It is helpful at the outset to note a structural dichotomy that frames Breyer's argument. "[T]he important divisions in the world," Breyer opines, "are not geographical, racial, or religious but between those who believe in a rule of law and those who do not."[126] With this tidy summation Breyer presses into two sides all the world's religious varieties and cultural multiplicities, each with their own normative codes and modes of participation in government and politics. The risk of Breyer's oppositional pairing is plain: inattention to nuanced realities, simplification of complex systems and beliefs, reduction of complicated theories, neglect of rivaling perspectives, and so forth. That is not to say such casual coupling has nothing to recommend it; sometimes easy heuristics and graspable models are helpful. Consider, for instance, Aristotle's ten predicates or the hypothetical State of Nature. Yet a justice on the United States Supreme Court who urges American judges "to understand and to appropriately apply international and foreign law"[127] should avoid the type of essentializing that subsumes important, distinguishing characteristics of diverse legal systems under two broad categories, one good and one bad. This simplistic dichotomy does manifest injustice to those cultures and communities—many of them more traditionalist, religious, localist, and conservative than their European and American neighbors—which consider themselves to be governed by the rule of law, however different that version of the rule of law may seem from the standards and structures figured in Breyer's operative paradigm.

To his credit, Breyer is upfront about his assumption that "the United States will remain a preeminent world power due to its military and economic strength and the prestige of certain features of American life, including our experience in creating, maintaining, and developing a fairly stable constitutional system of government."[128] And he is likely right on that score as a matter of factual probability. He also exhibits an endearing pride when he intones that the American legal system has "allowed a large multiracial, multiethnic, and multireligious population to govern itself democratically while protecting basic human rights and resolving disputes under a rule of law."[129] Yet inherent in his commendation of the American legal system is the unexamined presumption that the legal norms of other, more traditionalist places and cultures are inferior to those of the United States or else poor foundations for the rule of law in practice. "When, therefore, I use the frequently heard term interdependence," Breyer avers, "it is with these assumptions"—i.e., those assumptions which affirm the superiority and staying power of the American legal system—"firmly in mind."[130] These assumptions, however valid they may seem at first blush, signal a telling paradox, if that is the right word. To wit, Breyer admires the tolerance and accommodation made possible by liberalism and democratic constitutionalism, but in prioritizing tolerance and accommodation he would open the American legal system to their opposite. Developing in tandem with the proliferation of transnational norms and institutions is the equally rapid spread of radicalism and reaction, exemplified most notably in Islamic terrorism (and, in certain manifestations, Sharia Law) but evident to a lesser degree in the pseudo-nationalist movements and organizations percolating across Europe. Breyer's call for the adoption of foreign laws and legal norms could mean the eventual obliteration of the very flexibility and latitude that enable jurists like him to look abroad for instruction and guidance.

Breyer is right in one vital respect: Interdependence has a "particularly worrisome manifestation"[131] as a result of national-security threats, the judicial response to which has been to increase presidential powers at the expense of constitutional fidelity. Breyer's thesis regarding national security and presidential power is laudably direct and succinct:

> This Part will show the Court steadily more willing to intervene and review presidential decisions affecting national security, even to the point of finding a related presidential action unconstitutional. What is notable is that this progression toward assertiveness has occurred even as threats to national security have become more international, indefinite with respect to manner, and uncertain with respect to time. Indeed, threats today are less likely to arise out of a declaration of war by another sovereign power and more likely to be posed by stateless international

terrorist networks. They are also more likely to last for many years, perhaps indefinitely. The change in the Court's approach together with the change in circumstances is, I would argue, no mere coincidence.[132]

What follows is less direct and succinct as Breyer undertakes to supply an abbreviated history of the political-question doctrine and its implications for the scope of executive authority.

To prove the relevance and significance of the political-question doctrine to current affairs, Breyer discusses *Zivotofsky v. Clinton* (2012)[133] in which the United States Supreme Court (hereinafter sometimes referred to as "the Court") determined that issues pertaining to passport regulation were not purely political questions outside the province of the judiciary. The principal focus of this section, however, is historical, surveying with sweeping strokes everything from Abraham Lincoln's suspension of habeas corpus to Woodrow Wilson's prosecution of dissenters during wartime to Harry Truman's seizure of steel mills, which were private property. Accordingly, Breyer analyzes *United States v. Curtiss-Wright Export Corp.* (1936) (which held, *inter alia*, that the President of the United States is constitutionally vested with plenary executive authority over certain foreign or external affairs; that the powers of external sovereignty enjoyed by the United States federal government do not depend on affirmative grants of the United States Constitution; and that the United States Constitution, and the laws passed pursuant thereto, have no force in foreign territory);[134] *Korematsu v. United States* (1944) (which held that the executive exclusion orders providing for the detainment of Fred Korematsu, an American citizen of Japanese descent, were constitutional);[135] and *Ex parte Quirin* (1942) (which upheld as constitutional the jurisdiction of U.S. military tribunals—created by executive order—used to prosecute German saboteurs in the United States).[136] Under these cases, the president enjoys wide discretion and privilege in matters of national security and foreign affairs. If Breyer's summaries of these cases repay rereadings, it is because they are useful guides to landmark cases—but no more useful than any of the student briefs or encyclopedia entries that can be found online.

To his credit, Breyer rejects the guiding rationale in *Curtiss-Wright, Korematsu,* and *Quirin* and finds wisdom in *Youngstown Sheet & Tube Co. v.*

Sawyer (1952), which held that the president did not possess the inherent power, purportedly in the public interest, to order the Secretary of Commerce, during wartime, to seize the private property of steel companies that were wrangling over labor disputes. *Youngstown Sheet*, whatever else it stands for, represents a stark departure from the mode of absolute deference to executive power adopted and perpetuated by the Court in earlier eras.[137]

Why did the Court reverse course in *Youngstown Sheet*? According to Breyer, "Judges are inevitably creatures of their times, and the Steel Seizure justices had just seen totalitarian regimes destroy individual liberty in Europe. While they did not necessarily fear the rise of an American dictator, knowledge of what happened to other democratic societies must have been sobering."[138] This explanation would have us believe that a mere awareness of foreign affairs—not fidelity to the terms of the Constitution—motivated the decision in *Youngstown Sheet*. Although the events of World War One and World War Two and other 20th-century geopolitical struggles no doubt loomed large in American memory, Justice Black's opinion in *Youngstown Sheet*, as well as the concurrences with that opinion, grounded themselves in the text of the Constitution, not in extraconstitutional historical analysis or commentary on current events.

Breyer acknowledges that presidents will, as a matter of course, seek to exercise vast authority to resolve urgent conflicts, but he believes the Court's institutional duty is to ensure that executive power is prudently circumscribed. "We should," he says, "expect presidents to make broad assertions of presidential authority, especially during an emergency, when in the rush of immediate events they face immediate problems requiring immediate solutions. The Court, by contrast, playing a different institutional role, can and must take a longer view, looking back to the Founding, across the nation's history, and sometimes into the unforeseeable future. No matter how limited an opinion the justices try to write, their holdings will be taken as precedent, perhaps for a very long time."[139] Looking to history and tradition to demarcate executive power is, of course, good, but Breyer appears to disregard the fact that constitutional interpretation—the way in which judges and justices read and apply provisions of the constitution—is embedded in historical networks and processes. A judge or justice may not undertake historical inquiry that is divorced from the text of the Constitution, which must provide the framework and serve as the source for judicial decisions no matter the era or the sociopolitical exigencies. If history were to instruct judges and justices that certain provisions of the Constitution were unwise or improper, judges and justices would nevertheless be bound by those provisions and could not remake or ignore them based on their personal interpretations of historical events. Reworking or revising the text of the Constitution falls to the legislature, which is electorally accountable to the citizens, whose cultures and values, which are likewise historically informed, shape and guide the amendment process recognized in the Constitution.

Breyer suggests that the so-called "Guantanamo Bay Cases"—*Rasul v. Bush* (2004),[140] *Hamdi v. Rumsfeld* (2004),[141] *Hamdan v. Rumsfeld* (2006),[142] and *Boumediene v. Bush* (2008)[143]—represent a new trend, or "the culmination of an evolution that may continue."[144] Advocates for some Guantanamo Bay detainees had, during the presidency of George W. Bush, begun filing writs of habeas corpus and other, similar actions in the courts of the United States, challenging the detainees' imprisonment on foreign soil as well as the government's position that the detainees were not entitled to, and thus not denied, access to the legal system of the United States. Although these cases reaffirmed the longstanding authority of the executive branch in certain areas, they also pushed back against executive powers, vesting in the detainees the right to challenge their detention in the legal system of the United States. These cases collectively established that individuals detained as enemy combatants were entitled to due process of law, notwithstanding their citizenship or executive prerogative, and they effectively curbed the government abuse occasioned by special military commissions and the suspension of habeas corpus. The Court ensured that the rule of law, however strained, obtained in times of war as in times of peace. The days of *Curtiss-Wright* and *Korematsu* were, the Court proved, no longer with us. Breyer attributes this development to a growing awareness of other countries and cultures. "The intrusion of the world's realities into our national life," he says to this end, "no longer seemed, as it once had, such an anomalous thing, justifying anomalous results."[145]

Justice Breyer is correct that the "world's realities" have forced a rethinking of the judicial role and judicial authority, but, again, he closes his eyes to other realities, namely those demonstrating how constitutionally limited the judicial role and judicial authority are and must be. He characterizes the allegedly new approach as "engagement," as if, in this particular context, it were not already the prescribed role of the judicial power under the Constitution. "Rather than sit on the sidelines," Breyer says, "and declare that cases of this kind pose an unreviewable 'political question,' or take jurisdiction but ultimately find for the President or Congress as a matter of course, today's Court will be more engaged when security efforts clash with other constitutional guarantees. It will listen to the government and consider its arguments, but it will not rubber-stamp every decision."[146] The problem with this characterization is twofold: first, it suggests that the Court is doing something that the Constitution does not require the Court to do and ignores the possibility that the Court in earlier eras might have been acting unfaithfully to the text of the Constitution as the justices shirked their constitutional duties; second, it could operate as a basis for validating judicial "engagement"—one might say "activism"—in other areas such as the Fourteenth Amendment, under which the Court has forged a grotesque line of precedent, supposedly emanating from the substantive-due-process and equal-protection clauses, that has less textual basis in the Constitution than does the sort of judicial engagement manifest in the Guantanamo Bay Cases.

However appropriate Breyer's concerns about presidential power may be, they are undercut by his reticence to admit that our own Constitution has equipped us with adequate remedies for the problem. He preaches that, in the future, the Court must achieve a "greater willingness to understand and take account of both the world and of the law beyond our borders," as well as a "readiness to meet the various challenges of doing so,"[147] as though the Guantanamo Bay Cases had nothing to do with the laws within our borders and everything to do with the laws beyond our borders. Leaving aside the problematic jurisdictional and legal status of Guantanamo Bay, a military prison located within the borders of another nation—one that is not an ally of the United States—the fact of the matter is that the Guantanamo Bay Cases involved disputes over provisions in the United States Constitution and the laws of the United States. The Court did not divine its conclusions from, or predicate its rationale on, some greater understanding of the world and extraterritorial law. Thus, Breyer overstates the importance of interdependence in these cases.[148]

Although it is true that "[o]ther courts and legislatures have faced and are facing similar threats to their nations' peace and safety" and that those institutions "have engaged in similar projects to those before our Court of balancing security and liberty," nothing those courts or legislatures say or do is binding on the courts in the United States,[149] even if their solutions, which Breyer does not specify, "serve as constructive examples that our Court could put to good use."[150] Nothing in Part I of Breyer's book supports this conclusion. Instead, that portion of the book reveals how the laws of the United States have, over time and despite setbacks and mistakes, worked better than foreign laws to check power grabs and mediate conflicts as the Court gradually came to adopt rather than disregard certain principles enshrined in the Constitution. If anything, foreign law in this section of the book—as evidenced by the legal architecture of the 20th-century totalitarian regimes that loom in the background of Breyer's narrative—serves as an illustration of what not to mimic and incorporate into the American system.

I pretermit examination of Part II of *The Court and the World* because its thesis—that courts in determining the reach of domestic statutes must consider the effects of doing so on foreign laws and practices[151]—is straightforward and unremarkable. Moreover, its lengthy treatment of the Alien Tort Statute and other such legal texts is unlikely to interest those unfamiliar with or uninterested in that subject. This section of the book, in which the focus shifts from constitutional analysis to statutory construction, bears out what Breyer means by comity. Breyer urges the United States Supreme Court, and presumably other, inferior courts, "not simply to avoid conflict but also to harmonize analogous American and foreign law so that the systems, taken together, could work more effectively to achieve common aims."[152] This is an expansive interpretation of comity in that it encourages judges not only "to ensure that domestic and foreign laws d[o] not impose contradictory duties upon the same individual,"[153] the traditional view of comity, but also that judges "increasingly consider foreign and domestic law together, as if they constituted parts of a broadly interconnected legal web."[154] To achieve comity, so understood, judges must familiarize themselves with foreign laws and customs and can do so through academic journals, treatises, and articles.[155] This advice gestures towards Breyer's proposal that American judges consider themselves, and conduct themselves as, diplomats.

This proposal, which takes shape in Parts III and IV of the book, is not as brazen as it may initially seem because Breyer turns his eye on the role that treaties and other international agreements have played in the domestic legal system. A feature of international law with felt ramifications on the everyday lives and economies of domestic citizens, treaties force judges to contemplate international relationships. Presidents have, over several decades, exercised treaty powers more frequently and on subjects increasingly more domestic. They have created new agencies that promulgate and enforce rules and regulations, thus leading to new and bigger bureaucracies. "How has the Court's approach to the interpretation of international agreements adapted to these changes?" Breyer asks.[156] His answer, in part, is that "[i]t has become more important to find interpretative solutions that are workable, thereby showing that a rule of law itself can work."[157] "[I]t has," he adds, "become more important for the courts to understand the details of foreign and international rules, laws, and practices."[158] Breyer substantiates this claim with discussions of child custody, international arbitration, and the delegation of authority from domestic to international bodies created by treaty or other such mechanisms.

A certain smugness inheres in Breyer's remark that "judges who would hesitate to consider decisions of foreign courts when interpreting the American Constitution do not hesitate to consult such decisions when treaties are in question."[159] Surely, though, Breyer knows the difference between incorporating foreign legal principles into opinions when those principles have merely persuasive value (and no binding operation) in a case and deciphering the outcome-determinative rules in treaties that are at issue in the case as well as a valid source of law under the Constitution.[160] There is a palpable difference between judges in a death-penalty case considering data about how many countries recognize capital punishment[161] and judges in a child-abduction case interpreting the Hague Convention on the Civil Aspects of International Child Abduction, to which the United States is a party. The latter activity has caused the Court to venture "into uncharted legal territories, reckoning with (and at times applying) foreign laws concerning what once were almost exclusively local matters."[162] It stands to reason that the Court would consider how judges in other countries, bound by the same child-abduction treaty, would interpret the text of that treaty, but why should the Court therefore consider another country's capital-punishment laws to which the United States never submitted itself, by treaty or otherwise?

Breyer is on better footing in his discussion of the mandatory arbitration provided for in international treaties, which, as they multiply, will increasingly require interpretation by American judges.[163] For obvious reasons, this method of resolving transnational commercial disputes has become more common than court litigation. "[W]hen borders are crossed," Breyer explains, "arbitration offers the crucially important advantage of forum neutrality—parties can appear before a neutral decision maker without having to be hauled into the other's courts. The practice is therefore particularly popular among investors in developing countries, who are often skeptical of the local court systems."[164] It can be vexing to resolve complex disputes between private parties and nation states for numerous reasons, chief among them being the lack of a widely accepted forum for judicial review;[165] furthermore, the jurisdictional effects of economic globalization are not yet fully known, a fact Breyer acknowledges.[166] Thus, alternative dispute resolution, including and especially arbitration, seems like an area in which Breyer could have done more clarifying and elucidating. With perhaps his strongest points coming in his chapter on arbitration, it's a shame he spends so little time on the subject, which is rapidly evolving and becoming ever more important to the economic activities not just of governments and large corporations, but of private individuals and small businesses.

It is the matter of socioeconomic, cultural, and political evolution that betrays Breyer's provincial paternalism. Of course, times are changing. Yet when Breyer announces that "[c]hange is upon us,"[167] he seems blissfully unaware of the nature of the change. He is never recklessly explicit about it, but he appears to imply that the United States ought to follow liberal trends that he apparently sees in other countries.[168] If he is correct that "the Court will increasingly have to consider activities, both nonjudicial and judicial, that take place abroad,"[169] then, depending on what he means by "consider," we may need to prepare ourselves for, to name one possibility, radical Islamic jurisprudence or the spread of intransigent government and messianic statism. Or if Breyer finds unpalatable the form of Islamic law that ISIS, Boko Haram, al-Qaeda, al-Shabaab, or the al-Nusra Front seek to impose on their subjects, perhaps he would prefer China's surveillance and its restrictions on speech and the press; India's abolition of the jury trial; Singapore's criminalization of littering, chewing bubble-gum, and possessing pornography; or laws prohibiting homosexual activity—some of which carry the death penalty for their violation—in countries from Afghanistan and Saudi Arabia to Dominica and Malawi. I express no opinion here on the value or merit of any such laws outside the United States of America. I raise these examples only to demonstrate the implications and potential ramifications of Breyer's arguments, which are intended to promote a different vision.

In Breyer's paradigm, "foreign" and "international" appear to mean nothing more than "Western European," since he fails or refuses to consider the legal institutions of any Asian, South American, Middle Eastern (Israel excluded), Russian, or African nations. Nevertheless, Breyer seems unaware of the direction the political winds are blowing in the actual flesh-and-blood Europe. Breyer does not strike me as one who would welcome the construction of the chain-link, razor-wire fence—authorized by Hungarian President Viktor Orban—that stretches more than 100 miles along the border of Hungary. Nor do Breyer's views seem compatible with those of Marine Le Pen and the French National Front, or Laszlo Toroczkai, the youthful Hungarian mayor of Asotthalom, or Geert Wilders, the Dutch founder of the Party for Freedom. Breyer wants Americans to look to Europe to undermine nationalism, yet nationalism is on the rise in Europe.

The French have banned face-covering attire so that Islamic women may not wear a burqa or a niqab. The Swiss People's Party has become increasingly popular, the Swiss having restricted immigration under a quotas law established by a 2014 referendum. The effectiveness and long-term viability of treaties such as the Schengen Agreement among European nations has been called into question. Secessionist movements have sprung up in Scotland, Catalonia, Flanders, and Venetia, and the United Kingdom has exited the European Union, whose future is in jeopardy, as pointedly demonstrated by Jürgen Habermas's recent plea for European solidarity.[170] The unintended irony underpinning Breyer's love affair with Western Europe is that, in urging the gradual adoption and enduring "consideration" of foreign laws by American judges, he has laid the groundwork for measures at odds with his liberal, democratic principles.

A vital sense of the interconnectedness of nations has impressed itself deeply in the imagination of certain elites in the United States. It is liable to the type of paternalism exhibited in *The Court and the World*. In some circles the mere mention of foreign norms or institutions confers upon opinions a prestige too quickly confounded with profundity and intelligence. Even so, the discriminating reader will find few profundities in Breyer's book. Of his two chief shortcomings, that of stating the obvious (globalization has caused foreign law to play new roles in domestic controversies) and that of opening domestic courts to the incorporation of foreign law notwithstanding the relevant terms of domestic law or the restraints on such incorporation established by statute or the Constitution, the latter is more damaging. Domestic law has mechanisms for dealing with foreign laws. Those mechanisms resolved most of the cases and controversies Breyer discusses in the book. Thus, Breyer hardly replenishes the field of transnational adjudication with fresh insight or makes a compelling case for the embrace of foreign law.

Even regarding the death penalty, Breyer's advice to look to foreign law for guidance could backfire. According to Amnesty International, executions worldwide were up 28% in 2014.[171] A quick appraisal of Amnesty International's country profiles on the death penalty reveals that those countries which have abolished the death penalty are experiencing population decline.[172] The death penalty remains popular and prevalent in emerging countries.

Despite his grand vision of judges as diplomats who divine from foreign principles the right and proper course for social action within their jurisdiction,[173] Breyer gently insists on merely humble objectives, muting the vast implications of his argument with careful qualifications such as this one:

> This book is based upon my experience as a judge. It does not survey the whole of international law or even of foreign law as it affects Americans. Nor does it comprehensively describe the instances in which courts must deal with questions involving that law. It illustrates and explains what I have seen and why I believe there is an ever-growing need for American courts to develop an understanding of, and working relationships with, foreign courts and legal institutions.[174]

Breyer's description here of what his book does not do is also an adumbration of what his book cannot do: no single book could survey the whole of international law or foreign law as it affects Americans; no single book could, comprehensively, describe the interaction of international or foreign law with American courts. Nor could Breyer speak from the perspective of someone not himself. Few people, I suspect, object to gaining a greater understanding of foreign courts and legal institutions. Yet the phrase "working relationship with foreign courts and legal institutions" remains problematic. What does it mean? Breyer's book provides no shortage of possible answers, but the inquisitive reader will come away dissatisfied at the want of clarity.

Breyer's arguments, finally, are as nothing without the sonorous prose of a Justice Holmes or a Justice Cardozo. Anyone could have written this book, which should have been set apart by the fact that its author is a sitting justice. Breyer tells us nothing any close observer of the Court or the legal system could not have said and likely would have said with superior skill and rhetoric. He teases us with passing mention of interactions that are "typically invisible to the general public,"[175] but those interactions remain equally invisible in the book; there are no details about backroom deliberations, about how or why judges and justices compromise their hermeneutics or jurisprudence in the face of international pressure or as a result of some "global" perspective. We're not told about our Supreme Court justices' private discussions, research methodologies, philosophical influences, reading habits, or reliance (or non-reliance, as the case may be) on law clerks, amicus briefs, historical documents, or foreign scholarship. One wonders whether the young, more philosophical Breyer would have developed a more striking argument for his views on transnationalism, or whether he would have inhabited these views at all. His anti-nomocratic viewpoint is precisely the opposite of what I advocate here. Rather than expanding an already expansive government, judges and justices should restrain themselves to textual limitations and local scale and avoid centralizing, nationalist jurisprudence.

Against Centralizing, Nationalist Jurisprudence

One might infer from his subjects—George Washington, Alexander Hamilton, and Abraham Lincoln—that Richard Brookhiser, a longtime editor at *The National Review*, favors a particular form of government: large, centralized, powerful, nationalistic, and anti-Jeffersonian. His biography *John*

Marshall: The Man Who Made the Supreme Court supports that impression, celebrating Marshall while glossing his many flaws. "John Marshall is the greatest judge in American history,"[176] Brookhiser declares in a grand opening line that sets the lionizing tone for the rest of the book. But by which and whose standards?

Those of the long-lost Federalist Party, apparently. Marshall favored the federal government over the states, defending the United States Constitution—the terms of which had been quietly orchestrated by a secret convention of elite men—from Antifederalist and, later, Republican attacks and saving the national bank from constitutional challenge. His policies were "those of Washington and his most trusted aide, Alexander Hamilton."[177] Washington was Marshall's "idol"[178] whose "example would inspire and guide him for the rest of his life."[179] Marshall's reverence for Washington was "personal, powerful, and enduring,"[180] in both war and peace. Washington convinced Marshall to run for U.S. Congress, a position he held before becoming U.S. Secretary of State and the fourth Chief Justice of the U.S. Supreme Court; Marshall, in turn, became Washington's first biographer.

The Supreme Court was Marshall's vehicle for instituting the Federalist vision of government even after the Federalist Party had perished. Marshall strengthened the Supreme Court, which previously had the appearance of triviality. He discouraged seriatim opinions—the practice of each justice offering his own opinion—prompting his colleagues to speak as one voice and authoring numerous opinions himself. He increased the number of cases that the Supreme Court considered per term and established the principle of judicial review in *Marbury v. Madison* (1803), holding that the judiciary may strike down legislation that contravenes the Constitution. He masterminded consensus among the justices even though the Supreme Court was populated by presidential appointees from rivaling political parties. His decisions in *Fletcher v. Peck* (1810), *Trustees of Dartmouth College v. Woodward* (1819), and *Gibbons v. Ogden* (1824) gave muscle to the growing federal government, weakening the position of the states.

"Washington died, Hamilton died, the Federalist Party died. But for thirty-four years," Brookhiser intones, "Marshall held his ground on the Supreme Court."[181] Were it not for Marshall, the Supreme Court would not enjoy its outsized influence and prestige today. We may, however, be entering into an era in which the Supreme Court loses some of the esteem that Marshall carefully cultivated for it. Conservative politicians have for decades objected to the powers exercised by the Supreme Court. In the wake of the confirmation hearings of Justice Brett Kavanaugh and the appointment and confirmation of Justice Amy Coney Barrett, however, partisans of the left have begun to fear the possibility that the Supreme Court will move in a different direction, one that effectively undermines the work of administrative agencies, restrains the courts, and restores power to the states. With few admirers on the Left or the Right, can the Supreme Court maintain its legitimacy as the arbiter of high-profile disputes with long-term ramifications on the lives and institutions that touch upon the everyday experiences of millions of Americans?

Brookhiser is a master storyteller with novelistic flair, deftly rendering the colorful personalities of such American giants as John Randolph of Roanoke, Aaron Burr, Luther Martin, Francis Scott Key, James Kent, George Wythe, John C. Calhoun, Patrick Henry, Samuel Chase, Aaron Burr, Roger B. Taney, and Andrew Jackson. Who would have thought the story of "the Simpleton Triumphant"[182]—Brookhiser's moniker for Marshall, who "never lost his country tastes and habits"[183]—could be so gripping? That each of these diverse characters figures prominently in Marshall's biography demonstrates the sheer longevity and importance of his storied career. Divided chronologically into four sections, each focusing on different periods of Marshall's life, *John Marshall* is also organized thematically, with formative cases determining the theme: The chapter titled "Bankrupts," for instance, is principally about two cases—*Sturges v. Crowninshield* (1819) and *Ogden v. Saunders* (1827)—while the chapter titled "Bankers and Embezzlers" examines *McCulloch v. Maryland* (1819).

Cringeworthy lines do, unfortunately, find their way into the book. "It is an almost universal human experience," Brookhiser states, "to seek surrogates to correct the errors or supply the lacks of one's parents."[184] Is that so? He claims that a letter "describing a ball in Williamsburg . . . might have been written by one of Jane Austen's young women."[185] "A good lawyer," he quips, "goes where the business is and makes the best case he can."[186] Such sweeping and superfluous assertions detract from the otherwise delightful prose.

Brookhiser seizes on the confusion and fluidity of the legal system in early America, adding needed clarity and context regarding the state of the common law—if that term applies—at that time and place. Too often lawyers, judges, and law professors parrot the phrase "at common law" before pronouncing some rule or principle. The phrase "at common law," however, should ring alarm bells: "at common law *when?*" should always be the resounding reply. The common law, after all, contained different rules in different eras and remains in flux; it is a deliberative process, not a fixed body of immutable rules. To say that *the* rule "at common law" was this or that is to betray an ahistorical understanding of the Anglo-American legal tradition. Brookhiser proves he's an historian by avoiding that error.

His conception of originalism, on the other hand, is crude. He claims that Marshall's opinion in *Dartmouth* "went beyond originalism to the text,"[187] implying a rejection of originalism, which, in his view, involves the recovery of the intent of the framers. "The framers had their intentions," he says, "but the words in which they expressed them might give rise to new, different intentions. The originalism of the Constitution's history and the originalism of its words could diverge."[188] But the "original intent" approach to originalism has long been discredited. Justice Antonin Scalia popularized an originalism that interpreted the *original public meaning* of the text itself, rejecting the fallacy that the framers or a legislature possessed a unified intent; the words as written in the Constitution or a statute are instead the result of political compromise and must be construed reasonably according to their ordinary meaning at the time of their adoption. This hermeneutic ensures that present legislators may pass laws without concern that the judiciary will later alter the meaning of those laws. Brookhiser is therefore wrong to treat "literalism" and "originalism" as mutually exclusive: "Marshall's opening flourish paid little heed to the intentions of the framers—it was literalism that he was expounding, not originalism."[189] On the contrary, literalism is fundamental to originalism.

Brookhiser's most serious omission is Marshall's odious attachment to slavery. Paul Finkelman recently took Marshall to task in his book *Supreme Injustice*, decrying the jurist's "considerable commitment to owning other human beings."[190] Finkelman targeted scholarship on Marshall that was, in Finkelman's words, "universally admiring."[191] Brookhiser, however, is another admirer, making no effort to rehabilitate Marshall on issues of race or human bondage—perhaps because he *can't*. Marshall was plainly racist and owned hundreds of slaves, a fact on which Brookhiser does not dwell.

Marshall "bought slaves to serve him in town and to work on the farms he would soon acquire,"[192] Brookhiser briefly acknowledges, adding elsewhere that Marshall "was a considerable slave owner, who owned about a dozen house slaves in Richmond, plus over 130 more slaves on plantations in Fauquier and Henrico Counties"[193]—numbers far shy of Finkelman's estimate. An ardent nationalist who dedicated his career to erecting and preserving the supremacy of the federal government, Marshall nevertheless compromised his principles when it came to slavery, deferring to state laws if doing so meant that slaves remained the property of their masters. He didn't free his slaves in his will, as had his hero, Washington. His extensive biography of Washington, moreover, didn't mention that Washington had freed his slaves.

"The morality of slavery did not concern [Marshall] in any practical way," Brookhiser submits without elaboration.[194] "Marshall let the institution live and thrive."[195] That is the extent of Brookhiser's criticism, which improperly suggests that Marshall passively observed the institution of slavery rather than actively participating in it. Brookhiser gives Marshall a pass, in other words, withholding analysis of Marshall's personal investment in human bondage.

Marshall "hated" the author of the Declaration of Independence, who had inherited slaves whereas Marshall had purchased them.[196] Finkelman notes that, as chief justice, Marshall "wrote almost every decision on slavery" for the Supreme Court, "shaping a jurisprudence that was hostile to free blacks and surprisingly lenient to people who violated the federal laws banning the African slave trade."[197] Marshall's rulings regarding indigenous tribes were problematic as well. He had not only "ruled that Indians could not make their own contracts with private persons,"[198] but also opined, notoriously, that Indians were "domestic dependent nations," thereby delimiting the scope of tribal sovereignty in relation to the federal government and the several states. Jefferson's thinking about slaves and natives has undergone generations of scrutiny that Marshall has somehow escaped.

Marshall does not come across as a loving or affectionate family man. Four of his children died; only six grew to adulthood. His wife Mary Polly suffered depression. Meanwhile, Marshall was out and about attending parties, working long hours, drinking liberally, and spending lavishly. He traveled to France shortly after the death of two of his children—abandoning

Mary Polly while she was pregnant with yet another child. He wrote Mary Polly from France, where, Brookhiser speculates, he may have developed romantic feelings for the Marquis de Villette, a recently widowed French noblewoman. His son John Jr. became a drunk who was "kicked out of Harvard for 'immoral and dissolute conduct.'"[199] Brookhiser suggests that John Jr. "imitated his father's conviviality too literally."[200] Justice Story lost a daughter to scarlet fever. He had no idea when he related this news to Marshall that Marshall, his friend and colleague, had lost four children. Marshall must not have spoken much about his family. When he sought to console Story, he couldn't remember in which order his children had died, nor the age of his daughter at the time of her death.

The line from Hamilton and Marshall to Story, Clay, and Lincoln that once enamored Progressives is embraced by the leading historian at conservatism's flagship magazine. Brookhiser takes up the mantle of Albert J. Beveridge, who glorified Marshall and Lincoln for their expansion of federal power (Beveridge authored multivolume biographies of Marshall and Lincoln). Perhaps there's a larger story to tell about this book if it represents the appropriation of a past figure for present purposes. Writing during the presidency of Donald Trump, Brookhiser perhaps felt the need to insist that "Marshall, Jefferson, and Lincoln were not only populists" because they also shared philosophical allegiances, namely the belief in "rights, grounded in nature."[201] One wonders, given his call to "look for other men to address" our "perplexities" and "challenges,"[202] what Brookhiser has in mind. Marshall has no clear parallel in current politics. Whether that's good or bad depends upon perspective, but Marshall must undergo more rigorous critique before he is presented as a model for improvement.

Finkelman's treatment of Marshall is much different. Finkelman himself is an anomaly: a historian with no law degree who's held chairs or fellowships at numerous law schools, testified as an expert witness in high-profile cases, and filed amicus briefs with several courts. He's now the president of a university. Federal appellate judges, including justices on the United States Supreme Court, have cited his work. Liberal arts professors anxious about the state and fate of their discipline might look to him to demonstrate the practical relevance of the humanities to everyday society.

Finkelman specializes in American legal history, slavery and the law, constitutional law, and race and the law. His book *Supreme Injustice* tells the story of three United States Supreme Court Justices—Marshall, Story, and Roger B. Taney—and their "slavery jurisprudence."[203] Each of these men, Finkelman argues, differed in background and methodology but shared the belief that antislavery agitation undermined the legal and political structures instituted by the Constitution. Had they aligned their operative principles with the ideals of liberty, equality, and justice enshrined in the Declaration of Independence, liberty rather than racism and oppression might have defined antebellum America.

Finkelman insists that the legacy of Marshall, Story, and Taney had enormous implications for the state of the nation, strengthening the institutions of slavery and embedding in the law a systemic hostility to fundamental freedom and basic justice. These are strong allegations, attributed to only three individuals. Yet the evidence adds up.

Start with Marshall, a perennially celebrated figure who, unlike many of his generation, in particular his occasional nemesis Jefferson, has escaped scrutiny on matters of race and slavery. Finkelman submits, as I've mentioned, that scholarship on Marshall is "universally admiring"—an overstatement perhaps, but one that underscores the prevalence of the mythology Finkelman hopes to dispel.[204] Finkelman emphasizes Marshall's "personal ties to slavery"[205] and "considerable commitment to owning other human beings."[206] He combs through numerous records and presents ample data to establish that Marshall, a life member of the American Colonization Society, "actively participated in slavery on a very personal level."[207] Finkelman then turns to Marshall's votes and opinions in cases, several of which challenged state laws and rulings that freed slaves. In fact, Marshall would go so far as to overturn the verdicts of white Southern jurors and the judgments of white Southern judges who, in freedom suits, sided with slaves and against masters.

Marshall could be an ardent nationalist attempting to effectuate the supremacy of federal law. One is therefore tempted to attribute his rulings against state laws in cases about slavery to his longstanding desire to centralize federal power. But that is only part of the story. Finkelman brings to light exceptions, including when Marshall selectively deferred to state law if doing so meant that slaves remained the property of their masters. Finkelman highlights these decisions to show that Marshall was hypocritical, compromising his otherwise plenary nationalism to ensure that contractual and property arrangements regarding slaves were protected by law.

Story was also a nationalist, having evolved from Jeffersonianism to anti-Jeffersonianism and eventually becoming Marshall's jurisprudential adjunct. Unlike Marshall, however, Story could sound "like a full-blown abolitionist."[208] His opinion in *United States v. La Jeune Eugenie* (1822) was "an antislavery tour de force,"[209] decrying slavery and the slave trade as "repugnant to the natural rights of man and the dictates of judges."[210] Yet he prioritized radical nationalism over the rights of humans in bondage. In *Prigg v. Pennsylvania* (1842), writing for the Court, he deemed unconstitutional a state ban on the extradition of blacks out of Pennsylvania for purposes of slavery. Story jumped at the chance to pronounce the primacy of federal law over state law even if it meant employing the Supremacy Clause to validate the Fugitive Slave Act of 1793. "A justice who had once thought slavery was deeply immoral," Finkelman bemoans,

> rewrote history, misstated precedents, and made up new constitutional doctrine to nationalize southern slave law and impose it on the entire nation. The decision jeopardized the liberty of every black in the North, whether free or fugitive. The injustice of this opinion was profound.[211]

Author of the notorious Dred Scott opinion, Taney is the most predictable of Finkelman's targets. By the end of the Civil War, he was vehemently denounced and widely despised. Progressives in the early 20th century, most notably Felix Frankfurter, rehabilitated his reputation in part because progressive economic policy during that era promoted Taney's approach to states' rights and political decentralization. The mood has changed; most historians now probably agree that Taney "aggressively protected slavery" and "made war on free blacks."[212] Few law professors would recall Taney's "early ambivalence about slavery and his defense of the Reverend Jacob Gruber,"[213] who was arrested for sermonizing against slavery at a Methodist camp meeting and subsequently charged with inciting slave rebellion. Finkelman's chapter on Taney thus runs with the grain, not against it.

At times Finkelman exaggerates or wishfully portrays the role of judges. He asserts that, prior to the Civil War, courts rather than Congress or the executive had "room for protecting the liberty of free blacks, liberating some slaves, providing due process for alleged fugitive slaves, enforcing the federal suppression of the African slave trade, or preventing slavery from being established in federal territories."[214] This claim may hold up in some of the cases Finkelman discusses (e.g., *LaGrange v. Choteau* [1830], in which Marshall declined the opportunity to enforce federal law that could have freed a slave who had traveled into free territory), but not in all of them. If a judge were faced with a problem of statutory construction, he (there were only male judges then) could have asked what the language of the statute meant, how it applied to the concrete facts and material rules before him, and whether it was constitutional, but anything more would have arguably exceeded the scope of his office.

The Constitution was silent about slavery until the Civil War Amendments, also known as the Reconstruction Amendments. Prior to them, any attempt to render slavery unconstitutional would have required appeals to natural law, natural rights, or other like doctrines that appear in the Constitution only in spirit, not in letter. The abolitionist William Lloyd Garrison believed the Constitution was affirmatively proslavery, calling it a "covenant with death" and "an agreement with Hell." If this is true, then when judges swore an oath to defend the Constitution (the basic framework of government with which all other laws in the United States must comport), they were also inadvertently vowing to defend the institution of slavery—unless the law is more than what statutes and the Constitution provide, in which case these judges could have reached beyond the positive law to principles pre-political and universal.

Finkelman suggests another alternative: that certain constitutional provisions supplied a basis in positive law for antislavery strategies and stratagem. He cites, among other things, the congressional powers exercised in the reenactment of the Northwest Ordinance and the enactment of the Missouri Compromise and Oregon Territory; the admission of new free states into the United States; the due process guarantees of the Fifth Amendment; the rights of criminal defendants protected by the Sixth Amendment; the Privileges and Immunities Clause; and the guarantees of the First Amendment. Each of these would have been problematic during the period Finkelman covers. There was not yet a 14th Amendment through which provisions of the Bill of Rights could have been incorporated to apply against the several states, although state constitutions contained protections of fundamental rights that federal judges recognized and affirmed. Moreover, the provisions Finkelman enumerates empowered Congress, not the courts, to pursue robust antislavery measures. Courts could have responded to and interpreted actions and directives of Congress, but they could not have initiated legislation or litigation. Had the Constitution enabled federal judges and the United States Supreme Court to strike down proslavery laws and regulations with ease, the Civil War Amendments might not have been necessary. But they were necessary to facilitate the demise of slavery.

Finkelman speculates about what the courts could have done to advance antislavery causes, but courts cannot do anything unless the right litigants bring the right cases with the right facts before the right tribunals while making the right arguments. Judges do not commence lawsuits but handle the ones brought before them. Finkelman could have examined some cases more closely to reveal how the facts, issues, reasoning, and holdings should have differed in rationale, not just in result. Too many cases receive only cursory treatment; lawsuits are more than picking winners and losers.

At one point, Finkelman accuses Marshall of reading a statute "in favor of slavery and not freedom,"[215] but the statute isn't quoted. Readers will have to look up the case to decide if Marshall's interpretation was reasonable or arbitrary—if, that is, his hermeneutics adequately reflected a common understanding of the statutory language or intolerably controverted congressional purpose and prerogative. Finkelman chides departures from precedent, but rarely analyzes the allegedly controlling cases to verify that they are, in fact, dispositive of the later controversy by analogy of received rules.

One is regularly left with the impression that the only issue in the cases Finkelman evaluates was whether a slave should be free or not. Many of the cases, however, involved procedural and jurisdictional complexities that had to be resolved before grand political holdings implicating the entire institution of slavery could be reached. We're still debating the ambiguities of federalism (e.g., how to square the Supremacy Clause with the 9th and 10th Amendments) that complicate any exposition of the interplay between state and federal law, so it can seem anachronistic and quixotic to condemn Marshall, Story, or Taney for not untangling state and federal law in a manner that in retrospect would appear to have occasioned more freedom and less bondage.

Then again, it's hard to fault Finkelman for subjecting these giants of the law to such high standards. That men like Marshall and Story have not been investigated as their contemporaries have in light of the horrors and effects of slavery speaks volumes about the willful blindness of the legal profession and the deficiencies of legal scholarship. Finkelman remains an important voice in legal education and has pushed scholarly conversations about slavery in new directions. Nomocratic constitutionalism must account for the badges and consequences of slavery without overlooking constructive teachings and examples from past eras. It must mine the past for what is good and useful and learn from the experiences of earlier generations without superciliously dismissing or celebrating historical figures according to contemporary standards and practices.

Nomocracy and the Rule of Law

"Donald Trump Could Threaten U.S. Rule of Law, Scholars Say."[216] So declared an ominous headline in the *New York Times*. MSNBC likewise ran a suggestive interview entitled, "Will the 'rule of law' survive under Trump?"[217]

Such alarming commentary presupposes the existence of the rule of law in the United States and appears designed to portray Donald Trump as a threat to that rule. *Reason*, however, republished and retitled a curious piece that first appeared in *The Week*: "The Immoral 'Rule of Law' Behind Trump's Deportation Regime."[218] The implication of this revised title (the original read, "How today's pro-immigrant activists are adopting the tactics of abolitionists"[219]) is that Trump is staunchly committed, rather than antagonistic, to the rule of law.

So which is it? Does Trump jeopardize or safeguard the rule of law?

The answer, if we assume the rule of law is in full force and effect in the United States, is probably situational: In some cases, President Trump undermines the rule of law while in others he reinforces it. But to know for sure, and to appreciate the difference, one must first understand what the rule of law is.

The rule of law encompasses multiple legal principles, chief among them is that the rules that govern society apply equally to all individuals within the prescribed jurisdiction. No person, not even the king or the president, is above the law. Law, not the arbitrary commands or categorical dictates of human rulers, is supreme.

Thus, the opposite of the "rule of law" is the "rule of man," or the idea that the formal, discretionary imperatives of a powerful sovereign necessarily bind his subjects and subordinates. The rule of law is a philosophical concept and a liberal ideal that gained ascendency during the Enlightenment (think Locke and Montesquieu) but that can be traced to antiquity (think Aristotle). The British jurist Albert Venn Dicey listed as its prime characteristics:

1. "the absolute supremacy or predominance of regular law as opposed to the influence of arbitrary power";[220]
2. "equality before the law, or the equal subjection of all classes to the ordinary law of the land administered by the ordinary Law Courts";[221] and
3. "a formula for expressing the fact that with us the law of the constitution, the rules which in foreign countries naturally form part of a constitutional code, are not the source but the consequence of the rights of individuals, as defined and enforced by the Courts."[222]

These suggest that the rule of law is a bottom-up rather than a top-down system of governmental ordering based on already enunciated and widely accepted precepts. The operative rules that regulate the normative order of human activity in a free society under the law are rooted in custom and tradition. A ruler or judge is, in such a happy jurisdiction, responsive to the controlling principles that are antecedent to his or her political election, appointment, or empowerment.

Hayek identified the rule of law as a defining attribute of the common-law system, which, in his view, stood in contradistinction to the civil-law system that instituted vast codes and complex administrative agencies to superintend the unvigilant populace. Legislatures, of course, are accountable to the people through elections; therefore, their enactments must reflect extant social practices and beliefs to satisfy voters. Administrative agencies, with their extensive rulemaking powers, are not so accountable. They are by design removed from legislative procedures and thus isolated from voters.

Hayek saw the common law as a decentralized form of social organization, and civil law as centralized planning and design. The rule of law, he thought, inhered in the former system but not in the latter. "The possession of even the most perfectly drawn-up legal code does not, of course, insure that certainty which the rule of law demands," he warned, "and it therefore provides no substitute for a deeply rooted tradition,"[223] which the common law embodied.

The rule of law encapsulates other seminal concepts as well: the predictability, consistency, reliability, neutrality, and clarity of working rules, for instance. These, however, are in some way derived from the principal teaching that, in Hayek's words, "all rules apply equally to all, including those who govern."[224] By any appreciable standard, the United States has not lived up to this high ideal in light of the growth of sovereign immunity and qualified immunity for government officials, the disparate treatment of individuals based on their political power and connections, and, among others, the rapid rise of the administrative state.

Lately the rule of law has become associated with a law-and-order mentality that emphasizes punishment, severity, and rigidity as touchstones of the legal system. The rule of law, on this view, is the instantiation of brute force or the execution of raw power, or perhaps an ideological construct meant to condition the populace into servile submission to government authority. This understanding of the rule of law has some merit: John Hasnas's article "The Myth of the Rule of Law" explains how rule-of-law rhetoric indoctrinates people into casual acceptance of the harmful government monopoly on the institutions of law. He decries the gradual acquiescence of ordinary people to, in his words, "the steady erosion of their fundamental freedoms" in the name of the rule of law.[225]

But the rule of law as an ideal, rather than a felt reality, aims to preserve rather than imperil fundamental freedoms. Perhaps there are those with ulterior motives who champion the rule of law to achieve concealed goals; perhaps government in its current form cannot actualize rule-of-law ideals. When rule-of-law discourse does serve the repressive function that Hasnas describes, it is unduly coercive and abusive. In its proper form, and as it was originally understood, however, the rule of law aspired to restrain government power.

In the minds of yesteryear patriots like Thomas Paine, the United States epitomized the rule of law. He averred that "in America the law is king," whereas "in absolute governments the king is law."[226] He said, as well, that "in free countries the law ought to be king; and there ought to be no other."[227]

If the law is no longer king in America, it's not because of President Trump. That he enjoyed immense and immeasurable power is evidence of the extent of the decline of the rule of law in this country. Having flouted and subverted the rule of law for decades, the radical elements of the progressive left in the United States now faced, during Trump's presidency, the inevitable consequence of their concerted activity—namely, that their coercive methods and institutions may be turned against them, and the authoritarian structures they created may service policies at odds with their own.

We can all learn a lesson from this revealing irony. Now that the Democrats hold the Oval Office, expect the cycle of central empowerment to continue to the detriment of human freedom.

How to Achieve Nomocracy?

Because nomocratic constitutionalism promotes bottom-up forms of spontaneous order that account for custom and tradition, seeking to minimize systemic coercion and conflict, it cannot spread by force or compulsion without violating its core tenets and teachings. Nomocracy and nomocratic constitutionalism must proliferate, then, through education and discourse. It must be learned, experienced, and accepted rather than imposed or coerced.

As improbable as it sounds, someone has written "a love letter to the teaching of law"[228] that can set us on the path toward nomocracy by framing the educational contexts in which nomocratic constitutionalism can be taught. Stephen B. Presser's *Law Professors* is less pedagogical than it is historical and biographical in approach. If not a love letter, it's at minimum a labor of love about the genealogy of American legal education, for which Presser is admirably passionate. Even more improbable is how a book about three centuries of law professors could be enjoyable. Yet it is. Every rising law student in the United States should read it as a primer; experienced legal educators should consult it to refresh their memory about the history and purpose of their profession.

Presser is the Raoul Berger Professor of Legal History Emeritus at Northwestern University's Prizker School of Law and the legal-affairs editor of *Chronicles*. He's a leading voice of what is sometimes referred to as paleoconservatism, and he maintains that our political dysfunction derives in part from the methods and jurisprudence of law professors. His book might be called a diagnosis of our social ailments, the cure being the repurposing of legal education. Beneath his silhouettes—two involve fictional figures (Lewis Eliot and Charles Kingsfield) while the other twenty deal with actual flesh-and-blood teachers—lies a structural dualism that enables him to classify his subjects under mutually exclusive heads: those who believe in higher law and divine order, and those who believe that laws are merely commands of some human sovereign. The former recognize natural law, whereby rules and norms are antecedent to human promulgation, whereas the latter promote positivism, or the concept of law as socially constructed, i.e., ordered and instituted by human rulers.

These binaries, Presser says, explain the difference between "common lawyers and codifiers," "advocates of Constitutional original understanding and a living Constitution," and "economic analysts of law and Critical Legal Studies."[229] Here the dualism collapses into itself. The common-law method is at odds with originalism in that it is evolutionary, reflecting the changing mores and values of local populations in a bottom-up rather than a top-down process of deciphering governing norms. Constitutionalism, especially the originalism practiced by Justice Scalia, treats the social contract created by a small group of founding framers as fixed and unamendable except on its own terms. The law-and-economics movement as represented by Judge Posner and Judge Easterbrook is difficult to square with natural law because it's predicated on cost-benefit analysis and utilitarianism. In short, it's a stretch to group the common law, originalism, and the law-and-economics movements together, just as it's strange to conflate legislative codification with critical legal studies. Distinctions between these schools and traditions are important, and with regard to certain law professors, the binaries Presser erects are permeable, not rigid or absolute.

Presser's narrative is one of decline, spanning from the late 18th century to the present day. It begins with Sir William Blackstone, "the first of the great modern law professors."[230] Presser may overstate the degree to which Blackstone propounded a common-law paradigm that was frozen or static and characterized by biblical principles. The influence of Christianity and moral principles is unmistakable in Blackstone's *Commentaries on the Law of England*, especially in its introductory and more general sections, but the vast majority of the treatise—which was intended for an audience of young aspiring lawyers, not scholars or jurists—describes basic, mundane elements of the British legal system and organizes judicial principles and decisions topically for ease of reference. Presser is right that, more than anyone else, Blackstone influenced early American lawyers and their conception that the common law conformed to universal, uniform Christian values, but Jefferson's more secular articulation of natural law as rooted in nature had its own adherents.

Other teachers included in Presser's book are James Wilson (after whom Hadley Arkes has named a fine institute), Joseph Story (whose commitment to natural law is offset by his federalist and nationalist leanings), Christopher Columbus Langdell (whose "original and continuing impact on American legal education is unparalleled"[231]), Oliver Wendell Holmes Jr. (whose career as a professor was short and undistinguished), John Henry Wigmore (whose "sometime idol"[232] was Holmes), Roscoe Pound ("a figure of extraordinary talent"[233]), Karl Llewellyn (the "avatar"[234] of the legal-realist movement), Felix Frankfurter ("no longer the God-like figure at Harvard"[235]), Herbert Wechsler ("the anti-Holmes"[236]), Ronald Dworkin (who reformulated the theories of John Rawls), Richard Posner (the subject of William Domnarski's recent biography), Antonin Scalia ("best known for his bold conservative jurisprudence"[237]), and several still-living contemporaries.

Presser is particularly hard on Holmes, relying on Albert Alschuler's harsh and often careless assessments of the Magnificent Yankee. He charges Holmes with embracing the view that judges were essentially legislators and suggests that Holmes was "policy-oriented."[238] Although this portrayal is popular, it is not entirely accurate. In fact, Holmes's jurisprudence was marked not by crude command theory (the Benthamite version of which he adamantly rejected) but by deference and restraint. Presser himself recalls Alschuler in claiming that Holmes "was prepared to approve of virtually anything any legislature did."[239]

So was Holmes a policy-oriented judge legislating from the bench, or did he defer to legislatures? Undoubtedly the latter. Only once during his

twenty years on the Massachusetts Supreme Judicial Court did he hold legislation to be unconstitutional. As a Supreme Court Justice, he almost pro-
grammatically deferred to state law. "[A] state legislature," he said, "can do
whatever it sees fit to do unless it is restrained by some express prohibition
in the Constitution of the United States," adding that courts "should be
careful not to extend such prohibitions beyond their obvious meaning by
reading into them conceptions of public policy that the particular Court
may happen to entertain."[240] Rather than imposing his personal policy preferences, Holmes believed that a judge's "first business is to see that the game
is played according to the rules whether [he] like[s] them or not."[241] If
Holmes's conception of judicial restraint and the Fourteenth Amendment
had carried the day, the holdings in *Roe v. Wade*, *Planned Parenthood v.
Casey*, *Lawrence v. Texas*, and *Obergefell v. Hodges*, among others, would not
have occurred.

Presser admittedly doesn't like Holmes, but he is polite about it. There's
a charming sense of collegiality in his assessments of his contemporaries as
well. He boasts of his own traditionalism without hesitating to call Duncan
Kennedy and Catharine MacKinnon "brilliant."[242] He disagrees with his
opponents without denigrating their intelligence and expresses gratitude
to faculty whose politics differ radically from his own. He describes a variety
of disciplinary schools, including critical race theory, which don't appeal to
him. And he gives some unjustly neglected thinkers (e.g., Mary Ann Glen-
don) the attention they rightly deserve while some overrated thinkers (e.g.,
Cass Sunstein) receive the attention they relish.

President Barack Obama is held up as the quintessential modern law
professor, the type of haughty pedagogue responsible for the demise of the
rule of law and the widespread disregard for constitutional mandates and
restrictions. Yet law professors as a class weren't always bad; in fact, they
once, according to Presser, contributed marvelously to the moral, spiritual,
and religious life of America. Presser hopes for a return to that era. He
wishes to restore a proper understanding of natural law and the common-
law tradition. His conclusion takes a tendentious turn that reveals his abiding conservatism. Those who agree with him will finish reading his book
on a high note. His political adversaries, however, may question whether
they missed some latent political message in earlier chapters.

But isn't that the nature of love letters—to mean more than they say

61

and say more than they mean? Presser's love letter to law teaching is enjoyable to read and draws attention to the far-reaching consequences of mundane classroom instruction. He's a trustworthy voice in these loud and rowdy times. And he's delightfully nomocratic.

Another friend and colleague, Bruce Frohnen, is demonstrably nomocratic. Conservatism lost a giant when George W. Carey passed away in 2013. Thanks to Frohnen, his longtime friend, we're able to hear anew Carey's prudent admonitions in these strange and interesting times. Before his death, Carey completed drafts of chapters on progressivism and progressive constitutional reform that later became substantial portions of two chapters in *Constitutional Morality and the Rise of Quasi-Law*, the book that Frohnen later completed. The final product is an impressively collaborative effort that substantiates the idea of constitutional morality, which Carey spent years developing. Nomocratic constitutionalism is similar in aim and content to Carey and Frohnen's constitutional morality.

The two men had planned to split the chapters in half. Having few disagreements between them, they reserved the right to approve and edit each other's contributions. Carey's untimely passing changed these plans. To honor his friend, Frohnen consulted Carey's work carefully, downplaying his own more "antifederalist" positions to accommodate Carey's more federalist leanings. If Jefferson and Hamilton would have agreed that the size and scope of the American government has become dangerous and unmanageable, then it's no surprise that Frohnen and Carey found common ground.

Constitutional morality denotes "the felt duty of government officials … to abide by the restrictions and imperatives imposed on them by a constitution."[243] It contemplates the "unwritten constitution," a concept central to Frohnen and Carey's argument that's drawn from Russell Kirk and Orestes Brownson, both of whom Frohnen in particular has interpreted thoughtfully and skillfully. Kirk defined the unwritten constitution as "the body of institutions, customs, manners, conventions, and voluntary associations which may not even be mentioned in the formal constitution, but which nevertheless form the fabric of social reality and sustain the formal constitution."[244] To maintain their authority and gain general acceptance in a community, written constitutions and positive laws must reflect the norms and values of the people they bind. Frohnen and Carey's narrative is about how quasi-law in the form of executive decree and the administrative state have become divorced from the people they govern. Quasi-law is anti-nomocratic. Nomocratic law, established by custom and long usage, is pre-political, i.e., always prior to the quasi-law of executive decree and administrative rules and regulations.

Frohnen and Carey's narrative runs something like this. Rule by executive command and administrative agencies has resulted in a decline of the rule of law in the United States. Odd, extratextual interpretations of the United States Constitution have dislocated its content from the common understandings of reasonably prudent Americans. The Progressive Era facilitated a shift in our approach to law that was qualitatively different from the teachings of checks-and-balances, decentralization, separation-of-powers, and other such nomocratic doctrines alive in the minds of our Founders, even those like Hamilton and the young Madison (as against the later Madison) who favored a strong national government. Consequently, we have found ourselves in a crisis of constitutional morality, there being little institutional and systemic accountability to curb the broad powers of bureaucracy, reckless and unelected federal judges, a delegating congress beholden to lobbyists and corporations, and the expansion of executive privilege, prerogative, and patronage.

Political rhetoric of limited government, common among Republican leaders, does not square with the manifest reality of the ever-growing managerial state. Heated discourse alone won't suffice to roll back federal programs and agencies. "What is required," say Frohnen and Carey, "is a retrenchment of the federal government into a much smaller but more detailed and legalistic form that allows more actions to be taken by other institutions, be they states, localities, or associations within civil society."[245] In short, these men call for devolution and subsidiarity. They make the case for localized control based on clear rules that are consistent with common norms and expressed in a shared idiom.

Championing the rule of law involves the recognition that, although morality does or should underpin laws, "we cannot use the tool of law to achieve perfect virtue, or freedom, or any other moral good."[246] Without denying the importance or reality of natural law, which is antecedent to human promulgation, Frohnen and Carey approach it cautiously, stating that it "is not a rigid code demanding that human law force all human beings into a straightjacket of specific individual conduct."[247] Seemingly skeptical of grand schemes for the magnificent systematization and organization of natural-law principles, they humbly submit that humans "can only do our best to develop practical lawmaking and interpreting virtues such that the laws we make will be efficacious in spelling out and enforcing duties in such a way as perhaps to encourage people to pursue virtue."[248] This nomocratic mode of thinking recalls Hume, Burke, Oakeshott, Kirk, and Hayek (all nomocratic thinkers) with its awareness of the limitations of human knowledge and its attention to the historical, institutional, and cultural embeddedness of standards and values.

If there is one take-home point from Frohnen and Carey's book, it's that government is not the instrument through which to facilitate the good, the true, or the beautiful. We should avoid the "new dispensation" that consists in "a government ruled not by formal structures and procedures but by the pursuit of putatively good policy through broad statements of programmatic goals and the exercise of broad discretionary power."[249] Disempowering the central government may be the obvious counter to this new dispensation, but we've been advocating that for decades. In fact, Frohnen and Carey believe that "there can be no simple return to the original dispensation," which involved "the Framers' constitutional morality, emphasizing procedure, caution, and restrained defense of one's institutional prerogatives."[250]

With no quick and easy remedy at the ready, Frohnen and Carey encourage something less magnificent and extraordinary: civic participation in local associations and mediating institutions such as families, clubs, schools, and religious groups, the kinds of little platoons that struck Alexis de Tocqueville, during his tour of America, as bulwarks against tyranny. "More important than any particular policy," Frohnen and Carey aver, "is the attitude toward law and policy making that must be recaptured."[251] Although they suggest that some form of separation or secession may become inevitable, the corrective they envision is rhetorical and discursive. We must, in their view, shape the political discourse through private associations, which, in the aggregate, engender the bottom-up processes of rulemaking that reflect the normative orders of local communities rather than the top-down commands of a faraway, massive, impersonal sovereign.

Adam MacLeod, my sometime colleague, likewise advocates for the role of mediating institutions in securing the moral foundations of property rights. His book *Property and Practical Reason* frames normative claims and pleas within the common law context. He gives his thesis in the book's crisp opening sentence: "This book makes a moral case for private property."[252] And he adds that "institutions of private ownership are justified."[253]

That institutions of private ownership are now jeopardized is upsetting. Before the 18th century, it was simply taken for granted in most Western societies that private property rights incentivized both work and custodianship and served moral ends. Leaders of advanced nations understood that the opportunity to own land or goods motivated people to work; that work, in turn, contributed to the aggregate health of the community; and that once ownership was attained, owners preserved the fruits of their labor and likewise respected the fruits of others' labor as having been dutifully earned. There were, of course, violations of these principles in Western societies, which is why the law protected and promoted private ownership.

Even absolute monarchs across Europe centuries ago understood the instinctual drive for personal ownership and, consequently, allowed their subjects to obtain at least qualified possession of land and real property. During the Enlightenment, however, philosophers such as John Locke awakened the Western intellect to the stark reality that private property rights were routinely violated or compromised by monarchs and sovereigns at the expense of morality and at odds with the natural law. Because humans own their bodies, Locke maintained, any object or land they removed or procured from nature, which God had provided humanity in common, was joined to those people, who, so long as no one else had a legitimate claim to such object or land, could freely enjoy a right of possession exclusive of the common rights of others.

It's surprising that MacLeod, defending private property, doesn't mention Locke, since Locke more than any other figure in the Western tradition—let alone the British tradition in which the common law emerged—made the reason-based case for the morality of private property ownership. "God," Locke said, "who hath given the world to men in common, hath also given them reason to make use of it to the best advantage of life and convenience."[254] On this score MacLeod echoes Locke without giving him attention.

MacLeod advocates the type of mediated dominion of private ownership that, he says, existed at common law. Under the common law, he argues, dominion was mediated because it was restrained by the normative guides of practical reasonableness. He does not fully delineate what unmediated dominion looks like. But presumably it has something to do with "many contemporary accounts" that, he claims, "view property as an individual right" and facilitate an "atomization of private property" that's "unnecessary and unhelpful."[255] An example might have polished off this point, since in the opening chapters it's not always obvious to which property arrangement mediated dominion is allegedly superior. He does, however, supply helpful examples of mediating private institutions under the common law: families and family businesses, religious associations such as churches or synagogues, civic associations, and other such cooperative forms that exercise modest control or otherwise influence a person's claim to outright ownership. For instance, one's community may reasonably insist that my absolute ownership of a weapon does not permit one's use of that weapon to threaten or injure another except in self-defense. It may likewise restrict the profligate use of scarce resources, or the reckless use of intrinsically dangerous resources to the manifest detriment of one's immediate neighbors.

Under the common law, which illustrates constructive administration of property rights, private ownership is never total or unqualified but always subject to reasonable restraint as prescribed by custom and community. MacLeod intimates that one thing that makes private ownership reasonable is its promotion of reasonable behavior; the very reasonableness of private property is self-perpetuating. The owner of property who's confident his ownership is legally honored and enforced will pursue future gain; as the number of such owners multiplies, the corporate prosperity of society increases. MacLeod rejects consequentialist arguments for private property and seeks to justify private ownership on the basis of morality. He shows that private ownership is not just optimal by utilitarian standards but is practically reasonable and morally good. In so arguing, he navigates around two anticipated criticisms: first that his defense of private property and promotion of common law standards and conditions are remedies in search of an illness, and second that beneath his proposed remedy is the sickness he wants to cure.

By discussing the work of Pierre-Joseph Proudhon, Jeremy Waldron, J. E. Penner, and Larissa Katz, among others, MacLeod proves he's not remonstrating against straw men but engaging actual thinkers with real influence on our working perceptions of property rights. The problems he confronts are palpable: regulatory takings, trespass, taxation, riparian-right disputes, adverse possession, and waste, among others. In depicting mediated dominion as a form of voluntary plural ownership that excludes state coercion, moreover, he reassures readers that a common law property regime does not contravene private ordering, despite the fact that the common law dates back to periods when English monarchs retained total and ultimate control of the land within their jurisdiction under the Doctrine of the Crown; forced owners to hold property rights in socage; confiscated property from rivals and dissidents; redistributed property in exchange for loyalty and political favors; and permitted and at times approved of slavery and villainy. These unreasonable elements of the common law tradition do not square with the case that MacLeod makes for practical reasonableness; yet the common law tradition he invokes is sufficiently flexible and adaptive to modify or eradicate rules that perpetuate unreasonable practices and behaviors. He reminds us, too, that "slavery was for a long time unknown at common law, and its rise in positive law derogated common law rights and duties."[256] In other words, the rise of the English slave trade "is a story of lawmakers first departing from, then returning to, common law norms."[257]

Following if not synthesizing John Finnis and Joseph Raz, MacLeod recommends in the property-law context something akin to perfectionist liberalism and value pluralism. The pluralism championed by MacLeod involves multiplying the options for deliberating agents: the more room there is for rational choice, the more diverse and numerous are the opportunities to exercise human reason. These opportunities may be circumscribed by the morality of the community that is inherent in the rules that reflect basic values. The law is by nature coercive, but it is good to the extent it enables practical reason and restricts bad behavior, as determined by the net, collaborative efforts of non-state actors. MacLeod calls these combined actors members of "intermediary communities."[258]

The trope of individualism and community is for MacLeod a framing device for advocating mediated dominion as an incentivizing force for moral action. He skillfully and meticulously affirms that private ownership, which is conditional on the reasonable limitations established by collective norms, is reasonable not only for instrumental purposes (because it works well and facilitates constructive social relations) but also because it is good in itself. Summoning the commentary of Thomas Aquinas, William Blackstone, James Madison, Alexis de Tocqueville, Joseph Story, Georg Friedrich Hegel, F. A. Hayek, Neil MacCormick, Ronald Dworkin, Richard Epstein, and Robert P. George, MacLeod also manages to work in unexpected references to writers who do not immediately spring to mind as jurisprudents: Richard Weaver, Wendell Berry, Charles Murray, John Tomasi, and Milton Friedman. This range demonstrates the importance of property law across disciplines and in broad contexts. The emphasis on mediating institutions and the common law manifests nomocratic elements in MacLeod's thinking and writing, but nomocratic constitutionalists are, like Oakeshott, deeply historical in their thinking, and natural-law theory is sometimes dangerously ahistorical and abstract in its tendencies. MacLeod's treatment of the common law can be ahistorical.

Let us consider what historical accounts of one celebrated feature of the common law, the writ of habeas corpus, might look like. The writ of habeas corpus—Latin for "you have the body"—is known as "the Great Writ." It generally is a procedural remedy commanding a custodian, such as a sheriff, to bring a detained party, such as a prisoner, before the court to show cause for the detainment and to prove whether the detainment is lawful or justified. If the detainment is not lawful or justified, the detained party may be released.

Sir William Blackstone, whose jurisprudence so influenced the American founders and the course of American history that his four-volume book, *Commentaries on the Laws of England*, continues to sell more copies in the United States than in England, once called the Great Writ "the most celebrated writ in the English law."[259] The American colonists who studied and praised Blackstone believed that, as Englishmen, they were entitled to the protection of certain fundamental rights, which the British government, under King George III, had selectively recognized and in some cases disregarded in the colonies.

The right not to be detained against one's will without a hearing or notice of the accusations against him had been recognized for centuries and formed the basis for the writ of habeas corpus. In 1215, King John signed the Magna Carta, which expressly prohibited him and his royal successors from imprisoning, disseizing, committing, or banishing freemen who had not received a judgment of their peers pursuant to the laws of the land. This principle received renewed expression in the Petition of Right during the reign of Charles I and, later, in the Habeas Corpus Act, which called for speedy recourse in the event of an unlawful detainment. The habeas remedy then passed from England to America by way of the common law, and none other than Thomas Jefferson declared, "Habeas Corpus secures every man here, alien or citizen, against everything which is not law, whatever shape it may assume."[260]

Nevertheless, Anthony Gregory ably demonstrates in *The Power of Habeas Corpus in America* that the Great Writ has a spotted and inconsistent history as well as a reputation for hope and freedom that does not align with stark expectations or reality. "Questions have reverberated from England to the United States," Gregory submits, "over who has the authority to suspend the writ's privilege and the very meaning of suspension itself. In our own time, no less than in past generations, jurists and scholars have labored to determine who enjoys the writ's protection, which executive officials must answer to which courts or judges, what defines habeas jurisdiction, and whether its boundaries should shift during emergency."[261] These vexing questions have become more urgent and complex in a shrinking world burdened with threats of terrorism.

Gregory's scope is wide. He maps more than 400 years of legal history in roughly 400 pages and reminds us that the origin of the habeas remedy was not libertarian: "The king's courts developed habeas corpus to centralize judicial authority and collect revenue."[262] His impressive sweep of history recognizes that "it took centuries before the writ was genuinely turned against the king's oppression."[263] Ever since the Norman Conquest, if not earlier, the writ of habeas corpus has been tied to royal or governmental prerogative. In the 17th century, in fact, the writ served as a procedural mechanism for ensuring that prisoners remained in prison rather than being released from prison; in our present era, the government has been able to circumvent the writ to indefinitely detain prisoners captured in the war on terror.

Michel Foucault made a career out of analyzing the paradoxical nature of power—that is to say, the ways in which the State enables forms of liberty in order to demonstrate its ostensibly unrivaled authority to suppress that liberty. Gregory adopts a similar approach, describing how prisoners petition for the writ and how courts and custodians respond. "For every vindication of a custodian's power," Gregory explains, "the authority to detain is upheld. For every undermining of a custodian's power, there is the affirmation of another official's power—a judge's power, to say nothing of the state's general power to decide whom to detain."[264]

This Foucaultian line of reasoning surfaces elsewhere in the book and provides a profound challenge to libertarians who would dismiss Foucault's thinking out of hand. In an astute and potentially groundbreaking moment, Gregory briefly discusses Foucault vis-à-vis the theories of Robert Higgs, Murray Rothbard, and Franz Oppenheimer; the connection between these men might surprise those unaware of the fact that Foucault himself, late in his career, advised his students to read Mises and Hayek.

At once a tool of liberation and authority, the writ of habeas corpus undermines State authority even as it validates and solidifies that authority. In other words, it enables the very power that it subverts. Because it destabilizes institutionalized power ultimately to sustain that power, the writ is, in Gregory's words, "mythical"[265] and retains an "idealistic mystique." That makes it all the more important not just to trace the history of this storied remedy, but to "demystify" it and expose it for what it is: a "tool of usurpation and centralization."[266] In this regard, Gregory's book is not merely a history but a call for awareness.

If Gregory's Foucaultian method is successful, as I believe it is, then it should cause productive irritation among libertarian jurists and jurisprudents who appear to be moving toward stodgy consensus on a number of pressing legal issues. It might be that other pet favorites of these legal libertarians—say, incorporation of the Bill of Rights against the states—are really short-term techniques serving as vehicles to long-term, centralized power. That is not to accuse any particular libertarian of having bad intentions, only to suggest that good intentions can be bound to discursive systems that we do not fully understand. Power is dangerous not because it's obvious, but because it develops gradually out of good intentions and seemingly innocuous actions. All students of spontaneous order ought to know better than to design or embrace abstract legal theories that endow the instrumentalities of a centralized judiciary with more nationalized powers, even if those powers seem, at first blush, favorable to liberty.

Sometimes it takes a non-lawyer like Gregory to remind lawyers of the philosophical implications of the practical and everyday functions of the law. Although focused on a single issue—the writ of habeas corpus—Gregory's book has potentially vast ramifications. It is a timely corrective and an impassioned warning to lawyers, think tanks, and policy analysts who have lost their way and in the name of liberty brought us deeper into statism.

Yet the question remains: What is a better alternative to the Great Writ that could protect individual rights against unwarranted detention and at the same time avoid the production of power? Gregory doesn't answer this question, but he does suggest that the writ secures freedom only in societies that value liberty. In other words, the writ is worthless in a society that does not treasure and promote freedom; it is a tool that can lead to oppression or liberty, depending on the prevailing ethos of the time and place. This point underscores the importance of culture, custom, and tradition to the instrumentalities and procedural technicalities and mechanisms of the law. Institutions follow culture, custom, and tradition. Laws and the way in which they are enforced reflect culture, custom, and tradition. Constitutionalism flourishes in disciplined and moral societies that, absent government coercion, self-regulate according to received wisdom and established practices while cherishing the freedom and worth of every human being. I believe that constitutionalism so conceived dovetails nicely with the jurisprudence espoused by Russell Kirk.

Remember Russell Kirk

Most remember Kirk, if at all, as the Dean of Conservative Letters, an erudite, bespectacled man with an aw-shucks grin and Anglophile tastes. Few remember Kirk as a jurisprudent or constitutional commentator. But Kirk's *Rights and Duties*, first published in 1990 as *The Conservative Constitution*, is a sweeping, Burkean survey of the American legal order. Portions of the book draw from Kirk's previous essays in, among others, *The Notre Dame Law Review*, *The Journal of Christian Jurisprudence*, *Law and Contemporary Problems*, *The World & I*, *Modern Age*, *The Intercollegiate Studies Review*, and *The Presidential Studies Quarterly*.

Some on the left and right may be alarmed by Kirk's mission to "understand the Constitution of the United States as a framework for a conservative political order."[267] After all, any call to enlist the U.S. Constitution in the ranks of conservatives or liberals seems self-defeating. Yet Kirk's notion of conservatism and liberalism is nothing like the infantile movement politics of the current Republican and Democratic parties. His notion is cultivated and historically informed, drawing parallels to the sobersided, Old Whig statesmen on the one hand, and to Lockean, Enlightenment philosophers on the other. A conservative, for Kirk, is the former, one who appreciates the rootedness of institutions and who rejects ideology of any stripe. Kirk's objective, then, is to show that the U.S. Constitution does not have as its telos the emancipation of the individual from historical and social convention. To that end, he contrasts the U.S. Constitution and the French Declaration of the Rights of Man and of the Citizen, which was more or less a vehicle for radical and often militant change. (It bears asking why Kirk compares this French document with the U.S. Constitution while downplaying the Declaration of Independence, which gushes with abstractions and revolutionary ferment.) Jefferson and Jacobins notwithstanding, Kirk's argument is that the virtues of the U.S. Constitution are, above all, its permanence and continuity, which would not exist without the ongoing consent and reverence of the citizenry.

Kirk's definition of constitution—"a system of fundamental institutions and principles, a body of basic laws, for governing the commonwealth"[268]— may sound strange to some conservatives because it implies that a constitution is not merely the written text on which originalism predicates its hermeneutics; rather, a constitution is a set of values and mores that transcends written words. A constitution is "made up of old customs, conventions, charters, statutes, and habits of thought,"[269] including religious customs, conventions, and so on. A constitution is by nature conservative because its purpose is to endure for generations, although in practice it is as mutable as its adherents. The problem is that not all constitutions are meant to endure—some are merely placemarkers, temporary solutions to be supplanted later, when the populace has had more time to deliberate about various provisions. To address this tangle, Kirk distinguishes successful and unsuccessful constitutions. Some constitutions, though conservative, have not endured as has the U.S. Constitution, which allows for changing opinions but resists spur-of-the-moment trends. "The Constitution of the United States," Kirk proclaims, "has endured for two centuries because it arose from the healthy roots of a century and a half of colonial experience and of several centuries of British experience."[270] Kirk mentions the constitutions of other nations only in passing. His is not a comparative treatise but a dissertation on the order and tradition of an Anglo-influenced American document, which embodies an Anglo-American ethos.

There are two forms of constitutions: (1) the written document that establishes the basic framework of government and (2) the mores, cultures, and manners that bind people who adhere to that written document. The aim of these twin structures is political harmony. Without political harmony, a constitution cannot last. The fact that the U.S. Constitution has survived so long testifies to the general content and accord among the American people throughout history. A populace will not continue to follow a constitution that is too rigid; nor will a constitution that is too flexible restrain the exercise of arbitrary power, either of tyrants or of elites. Thus, a good constitution must be organic, not evolving. The difference between these adjectives, though slight, is essential: the former abides by tradition whereas the latter serves, or has the potential to serve, fashionable ideologies.

Kirk argues for the necessity of original intent, coupled with a careful study of history, as a hermeneutic methodology. He acknowledges, however, the difficulties of ascertaining such intent. A "reasonable attachment" to the written text of the Constitution, not a "blinkered literalism," is his standard of interpretation.[271] Any significant departure from this standard could lead judges down the road towards archonacracy, a "national domination of judges,"[272] because it would give judges an infinite "power to do mischief."[273] Kirk's conservatism has little to do with legal positivism in that Kirk, according to Russell Hittinger, "subscribed to the dicta of Roman and English-speaking jurisprudents, who held that the natural law enters into the organic laws of a people through customs and usages, and eventually through the many judgments which go into the making of statutory law."[274] Recognizing the vagaries that trouble most notions of natural law—evidenced by public objections, during Senate nomination hearings, to Bork's positive law convictions and shortly thereafter to Clarence Thomas's natural law convictions—Kirk suggests that law is not absolutely natural or absolutely positive but that natural law authorizes positive law. Accordingly, positive law is not divorced from but married to natural law; it derives its lexicon of intelligibility from a discourse of higher principles. In this respect, Kirk subscribes to a long and venerable tradition: that of classical and Catholic natural law, an "old tradition of natural law [that] comes down from Christian divines."[275] Implementation and continuation of this tradition involves "moral law" that "should not be taken for graven tables of governance, to be followed to jot and tittle," but for guiding precepts that must "be appealed to in different circumstances, and applied with prudence."[276] It does not follow that judges may substitute their views of natural law for the law of the land, but views of natural law that are in keeping with history, tradition, and the sacred may—indeed should—inform judges' application of written law.

Although Kirk believed that "law necessarily is rooted in ethical assumptions or norms," which derive "from religious convictions," he did not pretend that the U.S. Constitution was or is a religious document.[277] He is not after hagiographic renderings of the Founders. The delegates to the Constitutional Convention neither aspired to establish "some civil religion as an alternative to Judaism and Christianity" nor set out to create a "work of politico-religious dogmata."[278] Instead, these delegates sought a "practical instrument of government."[279] They were not gods, but men. They were, of course, religious, and their "religious and moral convictions .... had something to do with [their] probity in prudential decisions."[280]

Kirk cites M. E. Bradford's suggestion that "with no more than five exceptions (and perhaps no more than three)," the Founding Fathers "were orthodox members of one of the established Christian communions: approximately twenty-nine Anglicans, sixteen to eighteen Calvinists (of various churches), two Methodists, two Lutherans, two Roman Catholics, one lapsed Quaker and sometime-Anglican, and one open Deist—Dr. Franklin, who attended every kind of Christian worship, called for public prayer, and contributed to all denominations." Tired debates over whether the Founders meant to establish a Christian nation are beside the point. More relevant is the fact that American government arose out of the common experience of a Christian people devoted, for the most part, to a republican order anchored by religious faith.

The Founders clearly did not intend to level Christian institutions— with the possible exception of Thomas Paine, whose antireligious fervor turned Americans against him—and the U.S. Constitution was not about preserving Christian institutions, so it cannot be said that our written Constitution is either an anti-religious or a pro-religious text. Our *unwritten* Constitution, however, is indisputably religious, shaped by a transcendent moral order based principally on Biblical teachings. Accordingly, judicial activism may not be as pressing an issue as cultural activism: the latter, after all, is a departure from a far more ancient constitution. Kirk believed that ideology fills vacuums left by the decay of religion. As more Americans profess themselves nonbelievers, we will see whether Kirk's predictions come true.

Although the U.S. Constitution is not sacred, the corpus of Anglo-American law "cannot endure forever unless it is animated by the spirit that moved it in the beginning: that is, by religion, and specifically by the Christian people."[281] Kirk lamented attempts to sweep away religious beliefs from our courts of law. He endeavored, therefore, to demarcate boundaries between a system completely separating church and state, on one extreme, and a system conflating all laws with Christian doctrine, on the other. We deceive ourselves if we downplay the influence of Christianity on American law; yet we vulgarize Christianity by equating everyday administrative procedures with divine justice or command.

The line of demarcation divides law from sources of law. Kirk explains the difference in this way: "The law that judges mete out is the product of statute, convention, and precedent. Yet behind statute, convention, and precedent may be discerned, if mistily, the forms of Christian doctrines, by which statute and convention and precedent are much influenced—or once were so influenced."[282] Put another way, the underlying principles of the American legal order, constituted by Christian thought and practice, ineluctably shape how legislators promulgate laws and judges interpret laws. Rules and regulations emerge and exist within a field of Christian discourse dating to the English common law and perhaps even to antiquity. Operative laws in the United States derive their intelligibility from a vast network of Christian interpretation and experience. Unless legislators and judges dispense with those laws altogether—an act Kirk would be loath to endorse—the Christian element persists even if only in broad categories or classifications.

There can be no pure Christian polity on earth in part because humanity is imperfect and imperfectible, and in part because the Church, historically, has been either hesitant or wrong to dictate state policies. Kirk does not believe humanity will ever achieve a worldly paradise. That, however, does not stop him from championing right law and moral order. His support for religious schools and his invectives against pornography stand as two examples of his Christian "activism," a label at which he would wince, he being a disinterested man of letters in the Arnoldian sense. Something of an armchair philosopher, albeit with ties to political organizations, Kirk did not wish to revolutionize the legal profession, which should, he said, "repair to Burke."[283] He declared that "in an age of virulent ideology, an age of immensely quick, unthinking communication, old institutions everywhere require intelligent defense."[284] He was, thus, a guardian of ancestral wisdom and of the moral imagination, duty-bound to teach and transmit an intellectual and spiritual inheritance that too many Americans have neglected. Christianity remains the bedrock of our society and government. Try as we might, we cannot break from that foundation—not without toppling the very order that holds us in place and protects us from ourselves.

"Christian belief," Kirk claimed, "works upon the political order in three principal ways: faith's influence upon statesmen; faith's influence upon the mass of mankind; and faith's shaping of the norms of the social order."[285] In an age of secularism, we must, I think, remember these three workings lest we forget who we are—and why our constitution is important. For a written constitution is nothing without a nomocratic constitution and nomocratic constitutionalism. A written constitution is only as good as the cultural and normative orders that precede it.

PART TWO: LITERATURE

I once called Paul Cantor, the Austrian economist and eminent English professor at the University of Virginia, "the incomparable Cantor."[1] Another apt, alliterative sobriquet would have been "model mentor." When others weren't, Paul was there for me. He helped me, taught me, guided me. He's an astute critic whose teaching and observations have influenced me.

I first met Paul at an Austrian Scholars Conference at the Mises Institute in Auburn, Alabama. He and I had been corresponding for a few years and had spoken over the phone—I was supposed to study under him for my doctorate in English until complicating factors disrupted that grand plan—but we'd never met in person. Quite by accident, I bumped into someone in a tweed jacket shortly after I delivered a Rothbardian paper on the rise of the state in Geoffrey of Monmouth's *The History of the Kings of Britain*. As the man turned around, I could see his nametag—Paul Cantor—and before I could apologize for running into him I had taken his right hand into mine and was pumping it up and down with great enthusiasm.

Meeting your hero is generally inadvisable; reality usually doesn't live up to expectations. Paul was the exception: his charm and humor, I was happy to discover, weren't limited to the written word. He was a great conversationalist, and I could have listened to him speak for hours. Since then, our friendship has grown, and just months ago I had the good fortune of participating with him in a Liberty Fund colloquium on Greek tragedy. A gentleman, he paid for our taxi ride to the airport and refused to accept any money from me in return.

Paul was educated at Harvard University, where he earned his B.A. in English in 1966 and his Ph.D. in English in 1971. His studies in Austrian economics began while he was a senior in high school in 1961 and 1962, when he attended Ludwig von Mises's seminars at New York University, an experience that shaped how he viewed the world and its beautiful, spontaneous complexity. He began teaching at Harvard in 1971 before moving to the University of Virginia in 1977, where he has remained ever since. He is now the Clifton Waller Barrett Professor of English at UVA and recently taught as a Visiting Professor of Government at Harvard.

Paul's career as a professor and literary critic has been divided between traditional areas of literary study such as Shakespeare's plays and English Romanticism, and more innovative areas such as popular culture, media studies, and Austrian economics and literature. His books in the former area include *Shakespeare's Rome* (1976), *Creature and Creator* (1985), *Shakespeare: Hamlet* (1989), *Macbeth und die Evangelisierung von Schottland* (1993), and *Shakespeare's Roman Trilogy* (2017), *Shakespeare's Rome* (2017), and his books in the latter area include *Gilligan Unbound* (2001), *Literature and the Economics of Liberty* (2009) (co-edited with Stephen Cox), *The Invisible Hand in Popular Culture* (2012), and *Pop Culture and the Dark Side of the American Dream* (2020). *Literature and the Economics of Liberty* was the first book-length work to integrate the methodologies and principles of Austrian economics with critical analyses of literary texts; it ushered in a new school of literary theory and expanded the reach and influence of Austrian economics to the humanities.

Literature and the Economics of Liberty is also the first work of its kind to not only acknowledge the import of non-Marxist economics to literary criticism but also to adopt free-market principles in its approach to literary texts. Paul and his coauthors demonstrated that Austrian economics, which, in Paul's words, "focuses on the freedom of the individual actor and the subjectivity of values, is more suited to the study of literature and artistic creativity than a materialist, determinist, and collectivist doctrine such as Marxism."[2] To fully understand the distinction between free-market and Marxist techniques on which Paul draws, one must understand the intellectual climate within literature departments and the history of literary theory and criticism in the 20th century. If you were to visit the nearest university library and to scan the tables of contents of any recent anthology of literary theory and criticism, you would find there no schools of economic theory besides Marxism. It isn't that other economic methods of literary theory haven't been tried. They have. But when they've been tried, they've either betrayed an elementary understanding of economics, incorporated Marxist offshoots, or merely dabbled in economic concepts without developing sustained economic analyses. Paul's book, therefore, is ground-breaking.

The Invisible Hand in Popular Culture extended and modified the idea that Paul calls, in *Literature and the Economics of Liberty*, the "poetics of spontaneous order."[3] Examining television and film rather than novels, plays, and poetry, Paul took to task the governmental entities that have regulated television and film. He showed that artistic innovation and creativity emerge through experimentation and the complex interactions between producers and consumers. In both *The Invisible Hand in Popular Culture* and *Literature and the Economics of Liberty*, he complicated the Romantic trope of the isolated artist whose singular genius, supposedly divorced from the networks of ordinary consumers, allowed him or her to create masterpieces that exceed common tastes and standards. Paul proposes that, in fact, commercialism and competition generate creativity and genius rather than stifle it—and that common tastes and standards are important signals to artists.

Paul is a funny man. When asked why he dedicated his book *Gilligan Unbound* to his old VCR, he remarked, "Well, some things are not easy to speak about in public. Let's just say that I spent a lot of nights with that VCR, and one thing led to another—some rewinds, a lot of fast forwards, every now and then a pause or two—and let's face it—eventually it just wore out. The VCR, I mean." There are no better ambassadors for liberty than those who, like Paul, are both lettered and humorous, kind and learned. Even enemies of freedom could not dislike Paul Cantor.

Paul explained in an interview in *The Austrian Economics Newsletter* in 2001 that his "project of looking at literature with capitalist eyes began when I prepared a paper for a 1992 Mises Institute conference, and won the prize for the best paper."[4] He added that he had been considering the relationship between literature and capitalism much earlier than 1992.

If it weren't for Paul, there would be no school of Austrian economics and literature. We need more entrepreneurial minds to reveal the value and insights of the Austrian school beyond its typical associations and predictable applications. Not everyone can be a professional economist, but everyone is affected by economics. Paul uses literary texts to articulate the humane aspects of Austrian economics and the enlightening force of free markets. He inspires an interest in Austrian economics among those who ordinarily would not see the necessity for free markets, who might not recognize or appreciate freedom, or who have been conditioned by professors to distrust capitalism. Literary theory and criticism have been the province of the left and the statists. Paul offers something different, something sounder, something more concerned with the absolute value and dignity of every human person. He is a man to celebrate. To him I dedicate this section of the book with the hope that it reflects his influence.

This deliberately meandering section of the book is, in many respects, personal. It opens with Harper Lee, who grew up with my grandfather, Julius "Jay" Farish, and then works its way through reflections about my beloved South during her most devastating period, the Civil War. It then detours through Ezra Pound and Ernest Hemingway and the eminent literary critic Harold Bloom before, alas, considering representative books by my former teachers James Seaton and Gilbert Allen, who, like Cantor, have shaped who I am as a reader of great literature.

Influence with or without Anxiety

"When I was a child, I spake as a child, I felt as a child, I thought as a child: but when I became a man, I put away childish things."[5]

"Lawyers, I suppose, were children once."[6]

Harper Lee's second novel *Go Set a Watchman* caused a ruckus among literary journalists and sent professional critics into a tizzy from which they haven't recovered. *Watchman* has been called a "weird book" that represents a "sharp departure from the original narrative arc,"[7] featuring characters who "certainly aren't the same as we remember."[8] Is this true?

I say no. The notion that *Watchman* is a stunning reversal or a prolonged retraction is predicated on ahistorical assumptions and a willful misreading of Atticus Finch and the ominous, violent, and dangerous world of the fictional, yet eminently recognizable, Maycomb, Alabama. Maycomb may have been the tired old town where people moved slowly and there was nothing to buy and no money to buy it with,[9] but it was also the brutal, highly irrational town where Atticus's first two clients could be hanged in the county jail,[10] where two children could be attacked by an angry drunk,[11] where the angry drunk could (most likely) beat and sexually abuse his daughter with apparent impunity,[12] where a lynch mob could materialize on the steps of the jailhouse,[13] where the Ku Klux Klan could descend upon the home of a Jewish man named Sam Levy,[14] where accusations of rape covered for perceived affronts to codes of female honor,[15] where women could not sit on a jury,[16] where an ostensibly mentally challenged social misfit could be hidden away in his home,[17] where a black man could not pity a white woman because of the position of privilege that pity entails,[18] where blacks could be segregated from whites and subjected to an entrenched caste system,[19] and, might as well say it, where the sheriff could close his eyes to the death of a man who was killed, however reasonably and justifiably, by the social misfit.[20] Maycomb wasn't a utopia in miniature; it was a lawless town where mistakes were fatal and fearsome social conventions were final.

The noisiest complaints about *Watchman* involve not Maycomb but the revered Atticus Finch. We should blame ourselves, not "inconsistencies in plot,"[21] for adopting Atticus as what one critic calls "the moral conscience of 20th century America"[22] and what another dubs our "moral conscience," which is to say as a refined Southern gentleman who was "kind, wise, honorable," an "avatar of integrity . . . who used his gifts as a lawyer to defend a black man falsely accused of raping a white woman," and who, even more gloriously, was the "perfect man—the ideal father and a principled idealist, an enlightened, almost saintly believer in justice and fairness."[23] This hopeful and hagiographic conception of Atticus, supported by the unforgettable, impressive images of a big and benevolent and bespectacled Gregory Peck, has always been belied by subtleties in the text. Atticus is assigned Tom Robinson's case, for instance, and does not voluntarily undertake Robinson's defense.[24] His treatment of Calpurnia can be condescending. He refers to certain white folks as "trash,"[25] suggesting an off-putting classism that readers may find excusable because it's directed at the rampant racism among Maycomb's poor whites.[26]

Despite these apparent blots on his character, Atticus can and probably should remain a hero, though not without qualification. He can no longer represent the impossible standard of perfection that no actual person or compelling fictional character could meet. If it wasn't clear before, it is now: Atticus is a flawed man who despite his natural depravity found the courage and wisdom to do the right thing under perilous circumstances. Consider what Uncle Jack says to Jean Louise Finch in the final pages of *Watchman*: "As you grew up, when you were grown, totally unknown to yourself, you confused your father with God. You never saw him as a man with a man's heart, and a man's failings—I'll grant you it may have been hard to see, he makes so few mistakes, but he makes 'em like all of us."[27] These words are aimed at adoring readers as much as at Jean Louise. They're not just about the Atticus of *To Kill a Mockingbird*. They are about any Atticuses we might have known and loved in our lives: our fathers, grandfathers, teachers, coaches, and mentors. Lee may have had her own father, A. C. Lee, in mind. After all, he was, according to Lee's biographer Charles Shields, "no saint, no prophet crying in the wilderness with regard to racial matters. In many ways, he was typical of his generation, especially about issues involving integration. Like most of his generation, he believed that the current social order, segregation, was natural and created harmony between the races."[28] Yet A. C. Lee defended two black men charged with murder, just as Atticus defended Tom Robinson.[29]

It simply isn't true that *Watchman* establishes an "abrupt redefinition of a famed fictional character."[30] For one thing, nuanced fictional characters like Atticus defy ready definition and simple categorization. It's foolish to try reconciling the two Atticuses because there's nothing to reconcile: Although there are two accounts of Atticus and questions remain as to whether we should read *Mockingbird* and *Watchman* as mutually exclusive stories or *in pari materia*, so to speak, there's only one Atticus, an open-ended personality without fixed traits and determined behaviors.[31] Of course, in a work of fiction, Lee could have given us two Atticuses—a young Atticus and an old Atticus, the Atticus of *Mockingbird* and the Atticus of *Watchman*—but even the text of *Watchman* undermines that theory. Jean Louise herself believes that Atticus was a different man when she and he were younger,[32] a notion that parallels common reactions to the portrait of Atticus in *Watchman*. Readers appear to be as outraged as Jean Louise is to discover that their understanding of Atticus was limited, sentimentalized, anachronistic, and glamorized. We now see the same Atticus under different social and political circumstances. Our reading of *Watchman* informs our reading of *Mockingbird*, and vice versa. In *Watchman* we have a more complete (and, arguably, more historically accurate) picture of Atticus that, in fact, does not contradict the portrayal of Atticus in *Mockingbird*.

Most of us who were raised in the South knew or still know people of a certain generation who might have represented a Tom Robinson against manifestly false charges while also supporting the segregationist order of the day. We've also known liberal-minded people who worked toward racial justice and equality but became disenchanted when the federal government and political organizers from other regions, who were not familiar with local needs and concerns, replaced them, condescended to them, or ignored their questions and tactics. A racist, it must be added, can hate injustice just as he can soften or alter his racism in light of unsettling facts.[33] People can be ensnared by conflicting emotions and attitudes, uncertain about themselves and their competing drives and influences. They can even do good things at odds with their bad ideas. In light of these hard and troubling realities, the Atticus of *Watchman* does not have to be different from the Atticus in *Mockingbird*. Indeed it would be a stretch to suggest that this same character, from this same town, was probably intended to be a different character with entirely different traits and an entirely different personality in the two novels.

We should not unconditionally condemn Atticus for being a man of his time, a product of the culture in which he lived and breathed, any more than we should disregard the complicated aspects of actual figures like, say, Abraham Lincoln, the Great Emancipator who nevertheless appears to have decried interracial relationships,[34] pronounced a belief in the inferiority of blacks,[35] and campaigned on a promise never to end slavery.[36] Such apparent contradictions should not mystify us because American history is full of them. Abolitionists such as the philosopher John Fiske, for instance, championed antislavery while adhering to forms of Darwinian evolution that exalted the supposed superiority of whites.[37] Ralph Waldo Emerson remains my hero in part because he advocated emancipation and the abolition of slavery, but he would be considered an ardent racist today, believing as he did in the innate superiority of white men.[38] This makes him a figure to be studied and understood: someone whose flaws can reveal blind spots in our own limited perspectives. Emerson, like Atticus, has something to teach us if we are willing to take him on his own terms, in light of his own moment in time and sensitive to the pressures and struggles that confounded him and his generation. Seeking the endearing or agreeable qualities of people who espouse views we despise enables us to ascertain why such people appeal to others and build followings, why they are not universally denounced or disparaged even if the ideas they embrace have been discredited. If we cannot learn to step into *their* skin and look around, we can expect deep-rooted social problems to persist.

Nor should we let people or characters like Atticus off the hook for adhering to the widely held racial attitudes of their time and place. The claim that "Atticus's views are not, in themselves, alarming for their time"[39] betrays a needlessly harsh perspective: alarming to whom? Certainly his views would have alarmed the Tom Robinsons and Calpurnias of the period. Yet I understand the commentator's point: Atticus should not be used as a pretext for abstracting into grand, systematic theories or generalizations replete with simplistic labels and closed categories that are ascertainable to us but would have baffled our predecessors.

This business about being on the right or wrong side of history is antiintellectual and misguided. History has no sides; it's not a finite shape with tangible boundaries; it's not a rudimentary dialectic or a rational teleology. It's rarely if ever a Manichean struggle between obviously good and evil forces. History just is. Sometimes the people who (by general consensus) are considered "good" have irredeemable flaws; sometimes the people who (by general consensus) are considered "bad" have redeeming traits. We do a disservice to ourselves and our posterity by mining the past for good guys and bad guys, repurposing people and events for dualistic, ideological narratives that our predecessors would not have recognized or understood. It's more promising and fruitful to look at history in its complex variety, appreciating the intricacy and multiplicity of human motivation, examining the confused network of shifting allegiances and divided opinions, and asking questions about evolved attitudes and changed conditions without sifting the historical record through present moral filters. Polishing or taking liberties with the past, while understandable and well-intentioned, can make us unwittingly complicit in the perpetuation of bad ideas by obscuring the root causes and true sources of our problems. Atticus should be treated as Atticus, the man he was, even in fiction, but not as an improbable demigod of our eager imagination.

Atticus was never a liberal hero or a racially progressive icon. He was never divorced from social and historical context, a lone and singular exception to the prevailing ethos of white rural society during an era burdened by poverty and racism. Nor was he, as Natasha Trethewey ironically labels him, "a kind of national hero, a progressive thinker who espoused the noble belief in equal rights."[40] Those labels were not intrinsic to Atticus; they were conferred upon him. Trethewey knows better. Alive to the stark multiplicity in Atticus's character, she recognizes fully the paradox underlying *Watchman*, a paradox that, she says,

> many white Americans still cannot or will not comprehend: that one can at once believe in the ideal of 'justice for all' – as Atticus once purported to – and yet maintain a deeply ingrained and unexamined notion of racial difference now based in culture as opposed to biology, a milder yet novel version of white supremacy manifest in, for example, racial profiling, unfair and predatory lending practices, disparate incarceration rates, residential and school segregation, discriminatory employment practices and medical racism.[41]

Paradox if not contradiction has always defined America to a large degree, especially with regard to race. We are a country founded as much on principles of freedom and liberty as on the atrocities of human bondage, slave labor, and racism. "How is it," quipped Dr. Samuel Johnson, "that we hear the loudest yelps for liberty among the drivers of negroes?"[42] Thomas Jefferson, author of the *Declaration of Independence* and champion of equality, nevertheless possessed slaves and speculated about racial inferiority in his *Notes on the State of Virginia*.[43] When Frederick Douglass escaped slavery and gained his freedom in the North, he grew disenchanted with the racism of Northerners, even abolitionists, and it wasn't until he visited England that he truly sensed freedom.[44] Supreme Court Justice Oliver Wendell Holmes Jr. fought for the Union Army as a soldier in the Twentieth Massachusetts, which included Southern sympathizers—Copperheads—and which returned fleeing slaves to Southern forces.[45] In the 20th century, while Woodrow Wilson was championing liberal reform and human rights, he was also screening *The Birth of the Nation* in the White House, a film that valorized the rise of the Ku Klux Klan.[46] The United States went to war with Nazi Germany and, in effect, ended German experimentation with the very forms of eugenics that Americans had first created and promoted.[47] We do not like to remember these fraught elements of American experience just as we prefer to remember Atticus in a purely positive way. In light of these troubling if extreme examples of American self-contradiction, Atticus appears not as an aberration or an outlier in his commitment to seemingly antithetical positions and conflicting moods and mindsets: He is American, through and through. That he is also Southern makes him a more complex case.

Watchman is not about "the toppling of idols," even if "its major theme is disillusion."[48] It's a non-didactic lesson about understanding people in good faith and with a clear head, attentive to their individual anxieties and motivations. This latest portrait of Atticus challenges us to consider him in the manner in which he considered Mr. Cunningham in *Mockingbird*, after young Scout has revealed the emotional power of childhood innocence on the steps of the jailhouse. "A mob's always made up of people," Atticus says, "no matter what. Mr. Cunningham was part of a mob last night, but he was still a man."[49] It turns out Atticus himself was involved with unsavory groups and causes, including white citizens' councils and the Ku Klux Klan, but he, too, was a man—one whose seeming contradictions should be analyzed to prevent our own failings and errors.

Michiko Kakutani has asked a series of rhetorical questions that reveal the kind of errant presuppositions and ahistorical idealism that underscore any indignation over Atticus's alleged transformation from the bigot in *Watchman* to the hero in *Mockingbird* (*Watchman* was purportedly written first):

> How did a lumpy tale about a young woman's grief over her discovery of her father's bigoted views evolve into a classic coming-of-age story about two children and their devoted widower father? How did a distressing narrative filled with characters spouting hate speech (from the casually patronizing to the disgustingly grotesque — and presumably meant to capture the extreme prejudice that could exist in small towns in the Deep South in the 1950s) mutate into a redemptive novel associated with the civil rights movement, hailed, in the words of the former civil rights activist and congressman Andrew Young, for giving us "a sense of emerging humanism and decency"?

How did a story about the discovery of evil views in a revered parent turn into a universal parable about the loss of innocence — both the inevitable loss of innocence that children experience in becoming aware of the complexities of grown-up life and a cruel world's destruction of innocence (symbolized by the mockingbird and represented by Tom Robinson and the reclusive outsider Boo Radley)?[50]

The answer to these questions is easy: there is no contradiction between the two stories save for the consistent inconsistency that reckless readers (including me) failed to see in *Mockingbird* but that is unmistakable in *Watchman*. Everyone is, like Atticus, characterized in some manner by inherent contradictions. Depending on who you are and what you do, your contradictions may manifest themselves in different ways. Who among us has not clung to competing views, prized incompatible ideals, accepted irreconcilable premises, advocated positions that undermined other positions we valued, changed our minds, updated our reasoning, revised our habits of thinking, doubted our most cherished beliefs, or insisted on courses of action that we knew were wrong or unstable?

The narratives of Jean Louise in *Mockingbird* and *Watchman* are as consistent as lived experience, which is marked by disruption and contingency, ambiguity and rupture, fragmentation and complexity. Only the careless would have accepted Jean Louise and Atticus as one-dimensional, self-contained figures unspoiled by the mores, customs, and vocabularies of their white discursive community. Such a sanitized view of Jean Louise and Atticus erases and rewrites rather than represents history in its variety and complexity. Jean Louise and Atticus are not stock character types; their thoughts and behaviors are irreducible and inexhaustible.

Watchman does us a great service by asking us, in Trethewey's words, "to see Atticus now not merely as a hero, a god, but as a flesh-and-blood man with shortcomings and moral failing, enabling us to see ourselves for all our complexities and contradictions."[51] *Watchman* admits us into the interior worlds of Jean Louise and Atticus with rare intensity and perhaps even horror and revulsion. It's perhaps more racially charged than some of today's Southern literature, and its tensions and resolutions are ambiguous and at times perplexing. For all her disgust at Atticus's racial views, for instance, Jean Louise seems to share them to no small degree. She was "furious" after learning about the U.S. Supreme Court's decision in *Brown v. Board of Education* (1954),[52] which caused her to stop "at the first bar she came to and [drink] down a straight bourbon."[53] She says "of course" she agrees with Atticus that "you can't have a set of backward people living among people advanced in one kind of civilization and have a social Arcadia."[54] She purports to agree with Atticus, although perhaps sarcastically, that African Americans are "backward, they're illiterate, that they're dirty and comical and shiftless and no good, they're infants and they're stupid, some of them."[55] And yet this young woman who holds such racist notions is vexed and outraged by her father's racism. If Atticus is a bundle of contradictions, so is Jean Louise.

I have written about how my grandfather grew up with Harper Lee and Truman Capote in Monroeville, Alabama. I was born into *Mockingbird* as others were born into money. For a decade I read *Mockingbird* every year as a sort of ritual. I admired Atticus and aspired to be an attorney like him. I named my dog after him. Were it not for Atticus I would have never attended law school. I share these biographical details to demonstrate that I take no delight in learning that Atticus truly is the man I always at some level suspected him to be: He could not transcend the evils of his time and place, but he gave himself over to principles of justice and law that were, in fact, timeless—that did, in fact, transcend the unavoidable limitations of his moment. The depiction of Atticus in *Watchman* teaches us that we as humans may and ought to disagree—sometimes passionately—but that it's worthwhile to contemplate why and whether there are any points on which we might agree, as well as to search out and understand the sources of hateful and hurtful ideologies. We might question whether the ideas we find abhorrent might be different if circumstances and conditions were different, if our surroundings and contexts could be altered.

The methodical and conscientious study of history explodes many agreed-upon terms and rhetorical niceties that have developed out of poor attempts to construct in our imagination a society free from racial conflict, to liberate ourselves from the burdens of a past that must be fully realized if any constructive momentum is to be achieved. One astute critic has observed that *Watchman* "is a much less likable and school-teachable book,"[56] which, in my view, is the highest praise the novel could receive. *Watchman* is not didactic or simplistic; it's not an easy script of moral instruction. In *Watchman* we've traveled from Songs of Innocence to Songs of Experience. Daniel D'Addario submits that "by striving to see [Atticus] with the eyes of an adult," Jean Louise "can come to understand what she stands for."[57] "*Mockingbird* was written through the eyes of a child," says another critic, adding that "*Watchman* is the voice of a clear-eyed adult."[58] I concur. We've grown up—all of us—and now, after *Watchman*, we can more judiciously and astutely read *Mockingbird*, like mature and sober adults, for the dark and unsettling portrait of society that it was, not for the idealistic bildungsroman that we wanted it to be.

Lee spent her final years on earth embroiled in lawsuits and making headlines for her alleged litigiousness. Marja Mills's *The Mockingbird Next Door*, published in 2014 while Lee was still alive, was a welcome and timely look at Nelle (as her friends and family call her) from another angle, one that offered a fuller and more complex portrait of the woman from Monroeville, Alabama, who gave the world arguably the most important if not the most read novel (*Mockingbird*) of the second half of the 20th century.

My grandfather, as I mentioned, grew up with Nelle and Truman Capote, who has also become the popular subject of films and biographies. I like many others staked an unofficial claim on Lee without her consent or permission. I'm jealous of those who write about her and concerned that she will be misrepresented or treated with that patronizing condescension that characterizes writing about the South by people who aren't from here.

Never mind that Nelle wouldn't have known me from Adam or that I never had an opportunity, through my grandfather, to meet her in person. I still asserted during her life a delusional right of possession, an undignified and defensive prerogative to write about her as if I understood her better than others, especially "outsiders." Transport me to Monroeville, however, and *I'm* the outsider, a young opportunist who wouldn't have been brave enough to knock on Nelle's door and probably wouldn't have been received there even if I had showed up bearing flowers and chocolates.

There's a certain territoriality that comes with Lee: If you have a connection to her, you feel that no one else should. A psychologist might diagnose this condition as neurosis. It's a Southern thing: Let's say you're a

Yankee who has moved down here—we might invite you into our homes and churches and to our cookouts and political rallies; we'll include you in our customs and traditions and celebrations; we'll compliment you and let you poke fun at our accents and strange fixations; but we will, some of us, to our own shame and in violation of our own standards of decency and decorum, eye you with suspicion and silently question your motives and place the burden of proof on *you* to demonstrate that you appreciate the South and all its colorful idiosyncrasies. We'll assume you think you're better than us, and we'll want you to prove that you don't.

So I was skeptical, I admit, when I heard that some journalist from Chicago had written a book about Lee. It's a bold move for someone who wasn't raised on grits—and who undoubtedly supposes the Big 12 or the Big 10 to be comparable to the SEC (we're talking football, of course, not academics)—to undertake to write about one of our most cherished penwielders. Nor was I surprised to see Lee disclaim Mills's book and more or less refer to Mills as a liar: someone from a faraway place who thought she could just swoop in and, within 18 months, gain Lee's good graces while writing a book that purports to render Lee's personality and character.

But then I started into Mills's book—and I enjoyed it. Well, some of it. It was, for the most part, agreeable. At least it sought to be respectful, honest, and genuine. I told myself I would approach it with an open mind, but deep down I didn't want to like it. I wanted it to offend me. I wanted to laugh at the stereotypes and caricatures. But I couldn't. Mills didn't give me the chance. She was careful and considerate, but in a way that highlighted her otherness: *she whudn't from around here.*

Despite my suspicion and her giddy ambition, I began to like and trust Mills as a narrator. She was no ordinary Yankee. Sure, she had considered Monroeville to be just another "unusual part of the country"[59] before she had visited there. And sure, she didn't even know that Monroeville was Lee's hometown until her editor had told her so, but she had made a concerted effort to write about Monroeville on its own terms, as a real place with real people, and to approach Alabama as one person should another person's grandmother: tactfully, and conscientious about how you'd want someone to behave.

That doesn't mean Mills does everything right in her book or that her prose is anything special. She supplies interesting details— for instance,

Alice Lee, Nelle's sister, may God rest her soul, lay flat on her back to read at night, holding the book directly over her face, and instead of counting sheep she ran through the names of Alabama counties or American vice presidents (in reverse order)—but the impression, at times, is that the reader is looking over a record of random details packaged in short and simple paragraphs. One gathers that Mills has converted a bullet-point inventory of memories into a list-like narrative. There's just enough storyline to overcome the warranted presumption that the book is but ornamented notetaking.

A writer can be forgiven for dispensing with manners in favor of verisimilitude; it's okay, for example, for Mills to refer to Alice as "ancient"[60] or to say her house smells "musty."[61] Mills constantly walks the fine line between accuracy and insult; she needs to tell the truth without offending the very people who were kind enough to admit her into their company—to trust her not to portray them in a bad light. Hence Nelle's preacher is "what used to be called a natty dresser,"[62] outfitted as he was in "Italian leather loafers, a crisp shirt and designer tie, [and a] navy blazer pressed just so,"[63] but he is also open and candid and charming and willing to share his private notebooks with Mills. Nelle herself is admired and glorified, but her seeming masculinity and decision not to marry do not escape the predictable insinuations.

A chapter about Julia Munnerlyn, "a tall black woman with wisps of graying hair" who was Nelle's "live-in help,"[64] makes an appearance so brief and contrived that it seems like an obligatory gesture to the cynical readers who will comb through the text for evidence of continuing racial injustices among backwards Alabamans, perhaps even among the Lee sisters themselves. The effect backfires, revealing an ironic form of racism common among those who pity people before relating to them: Julia looks like an afterthought, a caricature intended to alleviate the author's nagging sense that she's got to say something about African-Americans, this being, after all, a book about the author of a book that (arguably) did more than any other author to reverse the course of race relations in the United States.

Mills cultivates for herself a fawning persona that is both charming and hokey in its over-anxiousness to be awed. When she first meets Alice, she hears noises in another room and wonders, "Could that be Harper Lee in the kitchen? The possibility was electrifying. Was she listening to our conversation? Would she make an appearance?"[65] To say this suspense is manufactured would be an understatement. When Nelle finally does make contact with Mills, stating over the phone that "I wonder if we might meet," Mills purportedly feels as if "I had answered the phone and heard 'Hello. This is the Wizard of Oz.'"[66] The Wizard of Oz? Really? Mills had to collect herself after she hung up the phone. I had to collect myself after reading this passage, but not for reasons Mills would take kindly to.

If you can get beyond the distracting Mills—whose book is as much about her as it is about Lee—and focus on the *real* subjects, you'll find much in *The Mockingbird Next Door* worth discussing and pondering. Nelle and her sister Alice are so interesting and colorful that they can't be covered up by an imposing narrator. This won't be the last book about them. Nor, despite its claims, is it the first to receive Nelle's blessing. That's both a shame and a comfort.

Other authors—Casey Cep, for instance—are much more cautious, prudent, and self-aware than is Mills. Imagine my surprise when, out of the blue, in the winter of 2016, I received a message through my website from Cep. "I'm writing about your essay 'Harper Lee and Words Left Behind," she said. "It was a pleasure to read, and I'd love to talk with you about it. Any chance you have a direct email address or a telephone number at which I could reach you?"

The essay she referred to described my grandfather's childhood in Monroeville, Alabama, and his relationship with Harper Lee and Truman Capote.[67] I recognized Cep's name from an article she had written a few months earlier. I told her I'd be glad to talk. She replied that she was in the area that very day—in Lanett, in fact. For whatever reason, though, we didn't meet, but we did email back and forth.

How I regretted that missed opportunity as Cep's fame spread across the globe in 2019 and 2020, after the publication of *Furious Hours*, which involves the true-crime thriller that Lee allegedly wrote (in whole or in part) but never published. The presumed offender in the story is the Reverend Willie Maxwell, an African-American preacher in Coosa County, Alabama, who, in the 1970s, purportedly murdered two of his wives, his nephew, brother, neighbor, and, lastly, adopted daughter, Shirley Ann, and then collected death benefits on life-insurance policies that he secured and in which he was the beneficiary.

I lost that chance to meet Cep, but refused to miss *Furious Hours*. If Cep could render Maxwell with haunting sensitivity as Capote had deftly profiled Perry Smith, the convicted murderer from *In Cold Blood*, then I was, I knew, in for an exhilarating read.

Lee is just one of three key figures in *Furious Hours*, the other two being a colorful attorney named Tod Radney and, of course, Maxwell. Divided into three parts—"The Reverend" (Maxwell), "The Lawyer" (Radney), and "The Writer" (Lee)—the narrative shifts between these titular subjects but proceeds more or less chronologically. After all, Cep couldn't explain Radney's and Lee's involvement with Maxwell without first explaining what brought Maxwell into their lives.

These apparent murders left a target on Maxwell's back. Almost everyone in his community considered him a threat; reciprocally, he considered them to be threatening to him. In those days, the life-insurance industry, though thousands of years old, was still immature in the United States. "By the time the Reverend Willie Maxwell began buying life insurance," Cep explains, "the industry was wild the way the West had been: large, lawless, and lucrative for undertakers."[68] If you lived in Maxwell's town, you couldn't know for sure whether he had purchased a life insurance policy on *your* death. "[I]t was stunningly easy," Cep submits, "to take out insurance on other people without their knowledge, and somewhere along the line the Reverend Willie Maxwell started making a habit out of it."[69]

While those close to Maxwell died, one by one, under mysterious circumstances, as he steadily accumulated wealth from life-insurance payouts, people in Alex City grew uneasy. Everything about the situation was grotesque. Maxwell's neighbor Dorcas Anderson, for instance, was supposed to be a pivotal witness for the prosecution when Maxwell faced charges of murdering his first wife, Mary Lou, but Anderson changed her story at trial, baffling and angering "those law enforcement agents who had taken her original testimony."[70]

What was Dorcas thinking? What was her motive? The answer soon became clear: "In November of 1971, barely fifteen months after Mary Lou's body was found and only four months after he was acquitted of her murder, the Reverend Maxwell took another wife: his neighbor, and the state's would-be star witness, Dorcas Anderson."[71] Not long after that, poor Dorcas was dead, too.

Rumors circulated that Maxwell practiced voodoo; no one could explain how, by all appearances, he got away with murder. But *was* it murder? "[O]f all the deaths associated with the Reverend Willie Maxwell, only two," Cep points out, "had ever been declared homicides, and neither of those had resulted in convictions."[72]

Maxwell finally got what was coming to him. An army veteran named Robert Burns shot him three times in the head at Shirley Ann's funeral. Burns regarded himself as the heroic vigilante and wasn't alone in that opinion. Many locals were relieved to be rid of Maxwell.

As if these twists weren't curious enough, Radney—a liberal darling and sometime politician who had represented Maxwell in both civil and criminal matters connected to the murders—ended up defending Burns against the charge of murdering Maxwell. A representative of the New South with a national following, Radney was harassed and threatened because of his politics. He was a media sensation, the object of hate and adoration, and he acquired the moniker Big Tom.

Big Tom needed to stay in the limelight after his political career took a turn for the worst. What should he do but apply his legal skills to Maxwell's case, or cases. "All those years of representing Maxwell," Cep writes, "hadn't endeared Big Tom to anyone around Lake Martin, but it had helped him make his name as a lawyer who could handle any case."[73]

Any case, including that of Burns. Big Tom wound up on the other side of Maxwell this time. Fearful that Maxwell had a living accomplice who could exact revenge, folks in Alex City and around Lake Martin were reticent about Burns's trial, which was, by any measure, sensational. Then a jury found Burns not guilty by reason of insanity. "Like the dam on the Tallapoosa River," Cep intones, "the gates had closed on the Maxwell case, and ever so slowly the waters began rising."[74]

Cep never discovered whether Lee actually wrote a book about Maxwell. If Lee's manuscript exists, its title is *The Reverend.* Until her literary estate is unsealed, we probably won't discover whether she completed it, at what stage she abandoned it, or whether she undertook to compose it at all. In many respects, then, Cep wrote the book that Lee didn't write, or might not have written. Fans of Lee, or Nelle, will delight in the final section of *Furious Hours.* And lawyers will take special interest in Amasa Coleman Lee, Nelle's attorney father, and in Nelle's legal education, to say nothing of her research for Capote's *In Cold Blood*. One gets the idea that Cep was working on a biography of Lee when, over time and by slow degrees, the possibility of a different kind of book emerged.

Suspense and intrigue aren't the only commendable qualities of *Furious Hours*. Cep is a master stylist, her prose rhythmic and resonant and refined. Her opening passages about the Tallapoosa River and the Coosa River—too long to quote here—testify to her talent as a craftswoman. She presents, as well, extensive history about the South in general and Alabama in particular. George Wallace, Lurleen Wallace, Martin Luther King Jr., the Scottsboro boys, Booker T. Washington, Zora Neal Hurston, Mark Twain, Fred Gray, the victims of the Sixteenth Street Baptist Church bombing, Albert Brewer, Tammy Wynette, Jimmy Carter, Rosalynn Carter, F. Scott and Zelda Fitzgerald, Morris Dees—they're all here, if only in passing. Other figures who appear are ancillary to Maxwell's account, but significant to American history: John F. Kennedy, Ted Kennedy, Richard Nixon, Adlai Stevenson, Walter Kronkite, Dan Rather, Gregory Peck, and Lyndon Johnson, to name a few.

My story, I'm relieved to report, has a happy ending. Recently I was a panelist at the Mississippi Book Festival and noticed, on the program, that Cep was also a panelist. I sat in on her talk and marveled at the crowds that flocked to her as fans had flocked to Lee. Cep thanked me in her book, in light of our email correspondence and some leads I gave her, but the extent of "help" I provided did not merit the acknowledgment. I wanted, now, to return thanks for her kind gesture.

Eventually the crowds dispersed. There we were, two people who knew each other, in a manner of speaking, but didn't *really* know each other. A weird feeling sets in when a disembodied personality you've grown accustomed to in writing suddenly materializes as a flesh-and-blood human with whom, suddenly, you can speak.

We initiated conversation by shaking hands and exchanging pleasantries; soon the ice was broken and we hit it off. Her intelligence was profound; she was kind and thoughtful. When it came time to leave, we hugged like old friends, making sure to snap a photo of the saddle oxford shoes we both happened to be wearing. Before parting, she told me she wished she could've met my grandfather, who passed away in 2013. He would've enjoyed meeting her, too. What would Lee have thought of her, I wonder. We'll never know.

Although Lee is gone, she's ever present with me. She made my sweet home of Alabama a better place for me and my children.

Ernest Hemingway and Ezra pound made their mark on me when I read them as an eager college freshman planning to major in English. The story of their friendship is odd and interesting, and oddly interesting.

In 1921, freshly married to Hadley Richardson, his first wife, Hemingway arrived in Paris, a playground for writers and artists that offered respite from the radical politics spreading across Europe. Sherwood Anderson supplied Hemingway with a letter of introduction to Ezra Pound. The two litterateurs met at Sylvia Beach's bookshop and struck up a friendship that would shape the world of letters. They frolicked in the streets of Paris as bohemians, joined by rambunctious and disillusioned painters, aesthetes, druggies, and drinkers. They smoked opium, inhabited salons, and delighted in casual soirées, fine champagnes, expensive caviars, and robust conversations about art, literature, and the avant-garde. Pound was, through 1923, exuberant, having fallen for Olga Rudge, his soon-to-be mistress, a young concert violinist with firm breasts, shapely curves, midnight hair, and long eyebrows and eyelashes. She exuded a kind of mystical sensuality unique among eccentric highbrow musicians; Pound found her irresistible.

Pound was known for his loyalty to friends. Although he had many companions besides Hemingway—among them William Butler Yeats, James Joyce, T. S. Eliot, Marianne Moore, Robert McAlmon, Gertrude Stein, e.e. cummings, Pablo Picasso, Wyndham Lewis, T. E. Hulme, William Carlos Williams, Walter Morse Rummel, Ford Madox Ford, Jean Cocteau, and Malcolm Cowley—Hemingway arguably did more than the others to reciprocate Pound's favors, at least during the Paris years when he promoted Pound as Pound promoted others.

Pound was aware of Hemingway's talent for publicity: he and Hemingway had combined their genius to promote Eliot's *The Waste Land*. Hemingway introduced Pound to William Bird, an American reporter who arranged to publish an autobiographical piece about Pound's childhood. Bird was instrumental to the eventual publication of Pound's *A Draft of XVI Cantos*. Pound, for his part, secured for Hemingway a position as assistant editor of *The Transatlantic Review*. Their relationship matured into something symbiotic and mutually beneficial.

Pound edited Hemingway's work, stripping his prose of excessive adjectives. Hemingway remarked that Pound had taught him "to distrust adjectives as I would later learn to distrust certain people in certain situations."[75] Unlike, say, Conrad Aiken or Robert Frost, who resisted Pound's editing, Hemingway acquiesced to Pound's revisions. In exchange, Hemingway taught Pound how to box. He acknowledged that the scraggly Pound had "developed a terrific wallop" and had "come along to beat the hell wit the gloves."[76] Hemingway worried that "I will get careless and [Pound] will knock me for a row of latrines."[77] He even treated Pound to a night at the prizefights to brighten Pound's spirits as Pound battled various illnesses.

Pound, however, grew disillusioned with Paris, where his friends were gravitating toward socialism and communism. Paris, he decided, was not good for his waning health. Hemingway himself had been in and out of Paris, settling for a short time in Toronto. In 1923, accompanied by their wives, Pound and Hemingway undertook a walking tour of Italy. The fond memories of this rejuvenating getaway inspired Pound to return to Italy with his wife Dorothy Shakespear in 1924. They relocated, in 1925, to a picturesque hotel in Rapallo, a beautiful sea town in the province of Genoa, on the bright blue Tigullio Gulf.

Pound found the weather in Rapallo to be soothing and agreeable. It was Hemingway who had first recommended this scenic spot, having visited Sir Max Beerbohm there years before. Hemingway's tales of the sunshine, swimming, tennis, and other outdoor activity in Rapallo appealed to Pound, who fancied himself an athlete. The fact that his mistress Olga frequented Italy—where her father owned a house—made Rapallo all the more desirable, as did Dorothy's seeming willingness to share her husband with his lover.

The friendship remained intact as Pound settled into Rapallo. About to vacate Europe for Key West, Hemingway dashed off a missive to Pound that began "Dear Duce" and then boasted about how Papa, as people had begun to call Hemingway, was "going to know everything about fucking and fighting and eating and drinking and begging and stealing and living and dying."[78] Gradually, though, the Pound-Papa gulf widened.

The move to Italy also effectively terminated Pound's glory years in Paris, about which Hemingway wrote affectionately:

So far we have Pound the major poet devoting, say, one fifth of his time to poetry. With the rest of his time he tries to advance the fortunes, both material and artistic, of his friends. He defends them when they are attacked, he gets them into magazines and out of jail. He loans them money. He sells their pictures. He arranges concerts for them. He writes articles about them. He introduces them to wealthy women. He gets publishers to take their books. He sits up all night with them when they claim to be dying and he witnesses their wills. He advances them hospital expenses and persuades them from suicide. And in the end a few of them refrain from knifing him at the first opportunity.[79]

This last line is both teasing and fitting because there was, in fact, at least one assailant in Paris who didn't refrain: a man who attempted to stab Pound at a dinner party hosted by the surrealists.

Hemingway guessed that Pound might stay in Italy "sometime" even if he took "no interest in Italian politics."[80] Hemingway was right about Pound's love for Rapallo but wrong about his political affinities. More than anything else, Italian politics—and the rise of fascism—damaged Hemingway's regard for Pound, who became a zealous supporter of Mussolini and a reckless trafficker in conspiracy theories.

Hemingway grumbled that if Pound "actually and honest to God ... admire[d] and respect[ed] ... [Mussolini] and his works [then] all I can say is SHIT."[81] Hemingway, true to character, remained manfully playful, stating, "I will take practical steps by denouncing you here in Paris as a dangerous anti-fascist and we can amuse one another by counting the hours before you get beaten up in spite of your probity—which in such a fine country as it must be would undoubtedly save you."[82] Such slight criticisms may have been colored with a lighthearted tone, but the disapproval was plain.

When Hemingway and Guy Hickock visited Pound in northern Italy in 1927, Pound was living in self-imposed exile. Hemingway had recently converted to Catholicism and was enjoying renewed fame after the publication of *The Sun Also Rises*. He divorced and remarried that year, offering Hadley a portion of the profit from *The Sun Also Rises* as part of their divorce. Pound, meanwhile, was immersing himself in political theories that likely baffled Hemingway as much as they angered him.

Shortly after the stock-market crash in 1929 and the onset of a worldwide economic crisis, Pound took to writing in Italian. Mussolini's March on Rome had occurred seven years earlier, and since then he had assumed dictatorial control of Italy, suppressed opposition parties, and built a police state. Pound was enthralled. He met Mussolini in 1933, peddling strange monetary schemes to the fascist leader.

In 1933 Pound and Hemingway exchanged letters that highlighted their diverging attitudes toward Mussolini, fascism, and government. Pound, who'd embraced wild and polemical speculations about the economic theories of the American Founders—Jefferson in particular—began to decry capitalism and taxation while celebrating fiat currency and a convoluted system of state central planning. "Since when are you an economist, pal?" Hemingway mocked. "The last I knew you you were a fuckin' bassoon player."[83] Hemingway offered Pound some money, sensing that money was needed, but Pound declined it.

Pound was now enamored with Il Duce; Hemingway was furious. Hemingway hated government, he told Pound, and preferred organized anarchism and masculine sport to statist ideology. Hemingway saw through Pound's charlatanic flourishes and economic fallacies and accused Pound, quite rightly, of lacking clarity. Yet Pound's admiration for Hemingway's work did not diminish, and Pound, ever devoted, included Hemingway in an anthology that he was then editing.

Possibly the last time Pound and Hemingway saw each other, they were having dinner with Joyce on a warm summer night in Paris. Pound allegedly bloviated about economics and the decline of art and European civilization, and Hemingway and Joyce feared that Pound had gone mad. The date and details of the dinner are a matter of debate, as is the veracity of any account of that evening. But one thing is certain: Hemingway was frustrated with Pound's embrace of Italian fascism. By the time Pound voiced support for Franco in the Spanish Civil War, putting him once again at odds with Hemingway, their once thriving friendship had deteriorated beyond repair.

The falling out was no secret, and other writers took sides. William Carlos Williams wrote to Pound in 1938, saying, "It is you, not Hemingway, in this case who is playing directly into the hands of the International Bankers."[84] Hemingway conveyed his concerns about Pound to their friend Archibald MacLeish:

Thanks for sending the stats of Ezra's rantings. He is obviously crazy. I think you might prove he was crazy as far back as the latter Cantos. He deserves punishment and disgrace but what he really deserves most is ridicule. He should not be hanged and he should not be made a martyr of. He has a long history of generosity and unselfish aid to other artists and he is one of the greatest living poets. It is impossible to believe that anyone in his right mind could utter the vile, absolutely idiotic drivel he has broadcast. His friends who knew him and who watched the warpeing [sic] and twisting and decay of his mind and his judgement [sic] should defend him and explain him on that basis. It will be a completely unpopular but an absolutely necessary thing to do. I have had no correspondence with him for ten years and the last time I saw him was in 1933 when Joyce asked me to come to make it easier haveing [sic] Ezra at his house. Ezra was moderately whacky then. The broadcasts are absolutely balmy. I wish we could talk the whole damned thing over. But you can count on me for anything an honest man should do.[85]

Hemingway was referring to Pound's notoriety as a propagandist for radio and newspaper during the Second World War. Pound was a "crazy ... and harmless traitor,"[86] Hemingway concluded, and an "idiot"[87] who "ought to go to the loony bin."[88] And that's precisely where Pound ended up: He was admitted to St. Elizabeth's Hospital in Washington, DC, in 1945.

Pound's friends put their reputations at stake to help him. MacLeish, expressing both love and admonition, dashed off these words in a missive to Pound:

... your information is all second-hand and distorted. You saw nothing with your own eyes. And what you did see—Fascism and Nazism—you didn't understand: you thought Musso belonged in Jefferson's tradition and God knows where you thought Hitler belonged. I think your views of the history of our time are just about as wrong as views can be. But I won't sit by and see you held in confinement because of your views.

Which is what is really happening now. I am doing what I am doing partly because I revere you as a poet and partly because I love this Republic and can't be quiet when it violates its own convictions.[89]

MacLeish helped to orchestrate Pound's release from St. Elizabeth's, drafting a letter to the government on Pound's behalf that included Hemingway's signature, along with those of Robert Frost and T. S. Eliot. A year later Hemingway provided a statement of support for Pound to be used in a court hearing regarding the dismissal of an indictment against Pound.

Hemingway, who was now living in Cuba, did little else to help Pound. More for practical reasons than personal conviction, Hemingway, who was himself targeted by the American government, refused to sign a petition of amnesty for Pound. The petition had been Olga's idea, and Hemingway didn't believe the American people would rally behind the desperate pleas of an adulterous lover. Hemingway never visited Pound at St. Elizabeth's, but he did tell Pound, via Dorothy, that he had read and enjoyed *The Pisan Cantos*. And when he won the Nobel Prize in 1954, Hemingway announced that the year was good for releasing poets, a not-so-slight reference to his old friend.

Hemingway awoke on the morning of July 2, 1961, put a 12-gauge, double-barreled shotgun to his head, and, alone in the foyer of his home, blew his brains out. He was 61. Pound's friends and family didn't tell him about Hemingway's death, but a careless nurse did, and Pound reacted hysterically. The older of the two, Pound, at 72, was free from St. Elizabeth's, where he'd spent 12 solemn years. He had returned to his beloved Italy to finish out his long and full life. In the autumn of 1972, he died peacefully in his sleep in Venice, the day after his birthday, which he'd spent in the company of friends.

Of all writers, though, a literary critic remains my favorite to read: the late and great Harold Bloom.

What can be said about Bloom that hasn't been said already? The legendary Yale professor was a controversial visionary, a polarizing seer who, never tiresome or repetitive, recycled and reformulated parallel theories of creativity and influence with slightly different foci and inflections, for his entire career. He demonstrated what is manifestly true about the best literary critics: they are as much artists as the subjects they undertake.

Bloom's criticism is characterized by sonorous, cadenced, almost haunting prose, by an exacting judgment and expansive imagination, and by a painful, sagacious sensitivity to the complexities of human behavior and psychology. He was a discerning Romantic in an age of banality and distraction, in a culture of proud illiteracy and historical unawareness. Bloom reminded us that to be faithful to tradition is to rework it, to keep it alive, and that tradition and innovation are yoked pairs, necessarily dependent on one another.

Bloom cultivated the image and reputation of a prophet or mystic. His stalwart defense of the Western canon is well known but widely misunderstood. His descriptive account is that the canon is fluid, not fixed—open, not closed. It might be stable, but it's not unchangeable. The literary canon is the product of evolution, a collection of the fittest works that have been selectively retained, surviving the onslaught of relentless competition.

His prescriptive position is that, because human agency is a controllable factor in this agnostic filtering process, serious readers can and should ensure that masterpieces, those stirring products of original, even genius minds, are retained, and that the latest works are held to the highest aesthetic standards, which are themselves established and proven by revisionary struggle. The merit of a work is not found in the identity of its author—his or her race, gender, or sexuality—but in the text proper, in the forms and qualities of the work itself.

Bloom's book *The Daemon Knows* examined ambitious and representative American authors, its chapters organized by curious pairings: Whitman with Melville (the "Giant Forms" of American literature[90]), Emerson with Dickinson (the Sage of Concord is Dickinson's "closest imaginative father"[91]), Hawthorne with Henry James (a relation "of direct influence"[92]), Twain with Frost ("our only great masters with popular audiences"[93]), Stevens with Eliot ("an intricate interlocking" developed through antithetical competition[94]), and Faulkner with Crane ("each forces the American language to its limits"[95]). This mostly male cast, a dozen progenitors of the American sublime, is not meant to constitute a national canon. For that, Bloom avers in his introduction, he envisions alternative selections, including more women: Edith Wharton, Willa Cather, Marianne Moore, and Flannery

O'Connor. Bloom's chosen 12 represent, instead, "our incessant effort to transcend the human without forsaking humanism."[96] These writers have in common a "receptivity to daemonic influx."[97] "What lies beyond the human for nearly all of these writers," Bloom explains, "is the daemon."[98]

What is this daemon, you ask. As always, Bloom is short on definition, embracing the constructive obscurity—the aesthetic vagueness—that Richard Poirier celebrated in Emerson and William James and Robert Frost, Bloom's predecessors. Bloom implies that calling the "daemon" an idea is too limiting; the word defies ready explanation or summation.

The daemon, as I read it, is an amorphous and spiritual source of quasi-divine inspiration and influence, the spark of transitional creative powers; it's akin to shamanism and endeavors to transcend, move beyond, and surpass. Its opposite is stasis, repose. "Daemons divide up divine power and are in perpetual movement from their supernal heights to us," Bloom remarks in one of his more superlative moments.[99] "They bring down messages," he intones, "each day's news of the metamorphic meanings of the division between our mundane shell and the upper world."[100]

What, you might ask in follow-up, is the American sublime that it should stand in marked contrast to the European tradition, rupturing the great chain of influence, revealing troublesome textual discontinuities and making gaps of influence that even two poets can pass abreast? "Simplistically," Bloom submits, "the sublime in literature has been associated with peak experiences that render a secular version of a theophany: a sense of something interfused that transforms a natural moment, landscape, action, or countenance."[101] This isn't quite Edmund Burke's definition, but it does evoke the numinous, what Bloom calls, following Burke, "an excursion into the psychological origins of aesthetic magnificence."[102]

The Daemon Knows is part memoir, a recounting of a lifetime spent with books. There are accounts of Robert Penn Warren, Leslie Fiedler, and Cleanth Brooks. Bloom's former students and mentors also make brief appearances: Kenneth Burke, for instance, and Camille Paglia. And Bloom doesn't just analyze, say, *Moby Dick*—he narrates about his first encounter with that book back in the summer of 1940. He later asserts, "I began reading Hart Crane in the library on my tenth birthday."[103] That he remembers these experiences at all speaks volumes to Melville's and Crane's bewitching facility and to Bloom's remarkable receptivity.

Bloom has not shied away from his signature and grandiose ahistorical pronouncements, perhaps because they're right. Melville, for instance, is "the most Shakespearean of our authors,"[104] an "American High Romantic, a Shelleyan divided between head and heart, who held against Emerson the sage's supposed deficiency in the region of the heart."[105] Or, "Emersonian idealism was rejected by Whitman in favor of Lucretian materialism, itself not compatible with Indian speculations."[106] Or, "Stevens received from Whitman the Emersonian conviction that poetry imparts wisdom as well as pleasure."[107] These generalizations would seem to service hagiography, but even if they're overstatement, are they wrong?

My professors in graduate school, many of them anyway, chastised Bloom and dubbed him variously a reactionary, racist, misogynist, bigot, or simpleton; they discouraged his presence in my essays and papers, laughing him out of classroom conversation and dismissing his theories out-of-hand. Stubbornly refusing to assess his theories on their own terms, they judged these theories in the light of their results: the theories were bad because certain authors, the allegedly privileged ones, came out on top, as they always have. This left little room for newcomers, for egalitarian fads and fashions, and discredited (or at least undermined) the supposedly noble project of literary affirmative action.

They will be forgotten, these dismissive pedants of the academy, having contributed nothing of lasting value to the economy of letters, while Bloom will live on, continuing to shock and upset his readers, forcing them to second-guess their judgments and tastes, their criteria for aesthetic value, challenging their received assumptions and thumping them over the head with inconvenient facts and radical common sense. The school of resentment and amateurish cultural studies, appropriate targets of Bloom's learned animus, will die an inglorious death, as dogmatic political hermeneutics cannot withstand the test of time.

Bloom, on the other hand, like his subjects, taps his inner daemon, invokes it and rides it where it travels, struggles against the anxiety of influence and displays all of the rhetorical power and play of the strong poets he worships. Dr. Samuel Johnson and Northrop Frye reverberate throughout his capacious tome, and for that matter his entire oeuvre. Bloom's psychic brooding becomes our own, if we read him pensively, and we are better off for it.

Those who view literary study as a profession requiring specialized and technical training, who chase tenure and peer approval, publishing in academic journals and gaining no wider audience than groveling colleagues, do not possess the originality, foresight, or brute imagination necessary to achieve enduring appeal. Reading, done right, is a profoundly personal activity, an exercise in solitary contemplation and possible revelation; writing, done right, is transference: the redirection of complex states of consciousness and knowing from one person to another. A few sentences of Bloom's contemplative questioning, such as the following, are worth the weight of whole academic articles: "At eighty-four I wonder why poems in particular obsessed me from childhood onward. Because I had an overemotional sensibility, I tended to need more affection from my parents and sisters than even they could sustain. From the age of ten on, I sought from Moyshe-Leyb Halpern and Hart Crane, from Shakespeare and Shelley, the strong affect I seemed to need from answering voices."[108] Here Bloom invites Freudian investigation of himself, summoning the psychoanalytic models he uses on others.

Bloom's awesome and dedicated engagement with the best that has been thought and known in the world left him unafraid of the finish, of what comes next, as though literary intimacy and understanding had prepared him, equipped him, for the ultimate. It seems fitting to quote him on this score: "We are at least bequeathed to an earthly shore and seek memorial inscriptions, fragments heaped against our ruins: an interval and then we are gone. High literature endeavors to augment that span: My twelve authors center, for me, that proliferation of consciousness by which we go on living and finding our own sense of being."[109]

The heroic, boundless Bloom claims in *The Daemon Knows* to have one more book left in him. Yet the effusive then-octogenarian produced a handful more, including *Falstaff: Give Me Life*, which has been called an "extended essay" but reads more like 21 ponderous essay-fragments, as though Bloom compiled his notes and reflections over the years. The result is a solemn, exhilarating meditation on Sir John Falstaff, the cheerful, slovenly, degenerate knight whose unwavering and ultimately self-destructive loyalty to Henry of Monmouth, or Prince Hal, his companion in William Shakespeare's Henry trilogy ("the Henriad"), redeems his otherwise debauched character.

Except Bloom doesn't see the punning, name-calling Falstaff that way. He exalts this portly, subversive figure as the charming master of deception and rogue scheming, and more importantly as a courageous vitalist "unmatched in all of Western imaginative literature."[110] Bloom's astounding reverence for this clever, corrupting, calculating, mischievous Bacchanalian—whose life-affirming zest is as delightful as it is disconcerting—reveals he's capable of the same kind of strategic indulgence that animates his transgressive subject.

His opening lines to *Falstaff* establish an affectionate, worshipful tone: "I fell in love with Sir John Falstaff when I was a boy of twelve, almost seventy-five years ago. A rather plump and melancholy youth, I turned to him out of need, because I was lonely. Finding myself in him liberated me from a debilitating self-consciousness."[111]

This isn't academic prose. Bloom doesn't write scholarship in the sense in which English professors, who chase tenure and peer approval, understand that term. Could you imagine a graduate student in literature showing up at the Modern Language Association's annual convention and pronouncing from behind a podium that "Falstaff wants us to love him"?[112] Or that Falstaff "is the mortal god of our vitalism and of our capacity for joyous play of every kind"?[113] That would end a career before it began.

To hold Bloom to professional academic standards is fundamentally to misunderstand him. His criticism is art unto itself; it's genre-defying literature: part memoir, part fiction, part psychoanalysis. He's a character of his own creation, as imaginary as Falstaff, yet real and alive—though he has passed away. In his psyche, the mysteries of which he plumbed with Freudian apprehension, Falstaff, too, was alive—and, more than that, was a deified "embassy of life."[114] Bloom called him the "greatest wit in literature" whose vices "are perfectly open and cheerfully self-acknowledged."[115]

Immediately objections spring to mind: Didn't Falstaff take bribes from competent soldiers who wished to avoid battle, thereby dooming his innocent, rag-tag band of unready troops? Doesn't this bawdy gambler fake his own death to avoid injury and then seek credit for Hal's slaying of Hotspur? Isn't he a compulsive liar and self-serving fabricator? Rather than earn his keep, doesn't he mooch off borrowed and stolen money while fraternizing with lowly criminals in disreputable taverns? Doesn't he find stealing entertaining? Doesn't he fail miserably in his attempt to seduce married women? Doesn't he thrive in the seedy underbelly of impolite society?

No matter. The venerating and visionary Bloom sees Falstaff's flaws as part of his appeal. Falstaff, prefiguring Nietzsche and Sartre, stands outside ethical jurisdiction as the lovable *übermensch*, the seductive sum of his own deliberate actions and unbridled agency in a world without God. Falstaffianism can be reduced to an abrupt imperative: "*do not moralize*."[116] These are Bloom's italics, emphasizing, perhaps, the enthusiasm with which Falstaff rebuffs normative codes and basic standards of decency, vivaciously embracing the self—the subjective, knowing, self-aware "I" that wills a future into being—with laughter and existential rapture.

Kate Havard argued in *Commentary* that "Bloom must actually reckon with the sorts of things Falstaff does that would seem monstrous in real life."[117] I'm not sure about this mandate. Everyone is susceptible to wickedness. We're fallible. Yet the magnitude of our evil acts is proportionate only to our capacity and will for achieving them. Greater power over others has the potential to increase the enormity of our chosen wrongs. Two hearts, equally blameworthy, can enact varying degrees of harm. With our meanness and malevolence, depravity and double-dealing, we're all like Falstaff at some instant, even if we "cannot say that we *are* Falstaff"[118] (my italics this time) because Falstaff cannot be universal—he's too shrewd, raucous, and riotously convivial to be an archetype.

That we haven't occasioned rank violence or mass damage is only evidence of our own powerlessness to do so in our moment of darkness. Our minds have contemplated horrors that our bodies never brought to bear. Knowing this, one begins to appreciate Bloom's melancholy voice in such an adoring account. "Falstaff is no everyman," he intones, "[b]ut all of us, whatever our age or gender, participate in him."[119] This truth, if it is one, doesn't excuse Falstaff; rather, it makes his decisions disturbingly recognizable.

Falstaff stands for absolute freedom, challenging dogmatic pieties even as he uses them to his advantage. He signals human choice and authenticity, but he's elusive and multifaceted. "There is no single Falstaff," Bloom submits.[120] "In my youth and middle years I thought I knew Falstaff. That Falstaff has vanished from me. The better I know Sir John the less I know him. He has become one of the lost vehemences my midnights hold."[121]

This tragicomic Falstaff is so complex and ambiguous that he undermines expectations, avoids patterned behavior, and escapes simple explanation. "Falstaff is as bewildering as Hamlet, as infinitely varied as Cleopatra," says Bloom.[122] "He can be apprehended but never fully comprehended. There is no end to Falstaff. His matrix is freedom but he dies for love."[123]

Falstaff is a more cunning and charismatic version of Chaucer's drunkenly crass miller, whose hilarious tale of casual adultery lacks the stark intentionality that makes Falstaff so treacherously in control. He's like a flatulent Santa Claus, without the meekness or mildness of Christian self-denial. He is, in a word, exuberant, and as Bloom opined, "Exuberance in itself is a shadowy virtue and can be dangerous to the self and to others, but in Falstaff it generates more life."[124]

Bloom commendably acknowledged the charges leveled against him: "I am weary of being accused of sentimentalizing Falstaff."[125] He said he's "been chided for sentimentality when I observe Falstaff betrays and harms no one,"[126] and he pleaded with us to enjoy Shakespeare's rendering of the Fat Knight, adding, "Do not moralize."[127] The point is not to elicit agreement but to move you emotionally, although his expressive mode is less sentimental than it is spiritual or mystical. He had a jovial appetite for living, thinking, and loving that resembles Falstaff's in its sheer capaciousness—hence his aside that he's a "lifelong Falstaffian."[128]

The Book of Genesis asserts that God made man in his image. One wonders whether Bloom's ecstatic Bardolatry—he once called Shakespeare "a mortal god"[129]—leads to a different but related conclusion: that Shakespeare, as God, created Bloom in Falstaff's image. Although age thinned his once corpulent physique, Bloom was, at times during his final years, the boastful embodiment of the bombastic, iconoclastic genius (Sir John) whose chief weakness was his fondness and devotion. At other times, he was a prophetic seer haunted by the daemon, devoid of merry wit, laughter, or redemptive charm and enthused by ineffable forces to cry out with beautiful despair and angst. His gusto seems ever-present, as does his displayed interiority.

Yet there is no single Bloom. You may think you know him, but then he vanishes as a lost vehemence.

"He has never abandoned me for three-quarters of a century," Bloom muses of Falstaff, "and I trust will be with me until the end. The true and perfect image of life abides with him: robustly, unforgettably, forever. He exposes what is counterfeit in me and in all others."[130] Perhaps that's why Falstaff is so threatening: he lays bare that manipulative, liberated part of ourselves that we don't acknowledge or even fathom, that's alienated and estranged from other people, accessible only to the "I myself"—the only thing we know that we know.

Farewell, Harold Bloom.

Back when I was a pimple-faced graduate student in English and law, I ordered a book from Amazon titled *Cultural Conservatism, Political Liberalism: From Criticism to Cultural Studies*. The book had been out awhile, but I had only recently come across an intriguing piece written by its author, James Seaton, then a professor of English at Michigan State University. I read my purchase in earnest and then dashed off a complimentary email to Seaton days later. He responded, and we struck up a dialogue that continued for several years. I once visited him at the Russell Kirk Center for Cultural Renewal in Mecosta, Michigan, where he spoke to a small crowd about George Santayana. He had just edited two of Santayana's seminal essays for Yale University Press and had recruited Wilfred M. McClay, John Lachs, and Roger Kimball to contribute to the edition. He and I got along swimmingly. Annette Kirk ensured that he and I had time alone to discuss whether I should apply to a doctoral program in English or continue down the path of the law.

Seaton passed away suddenly in 2017. I'd heard he'd been ill, but was nevertheless surprised to receive that sad email from his son notifying me of the death. I was in my hotel room at a meeting of the Philadelphia Society when the email hit my inbox. I can't recall which city I was in, nor the subject of that meeting, but I could describe to you in vivid detail the way that hotel room looked—the desk against the window, the framed pictures on the wall—as I sat there contemplating the news. Seaton, or Jim, was a kind and thoughtful man who devoted considerable time and energy to my studies and career. To and for him, I will be forever grateful.

Literary Criticism from Plato to Postmodernism, his last book, has all the themes and qualities that first drew me to Seaton. It is a collection of Seaton's essays and reviews revised and synthesized into a comprehensive case for humanistic inquiry. Amplifying his arguments from *Cultural*

Conservatism, Political Liberalism and reformulating his principles about the value of literature to society, Seaton persisted in undercutting the discipline of cultural studies, which he decried for its "obligatory leftism."[131] His leading contribution—the subject about which he stood to forge new directions in the field of literary criticism—was to revitalize old contributions, namely, the humanistic tradition as defined by Irving Babbitt and as represented by Aristotle, Alexander Pope, Samuel Johnson, Matthew Arnold, Henry James, Edmund Wilson, Lionel Trilling, and Ralph Ellison. Chapters Two and Four of *Literary Criticism from Plato to Postmodernism* were profitable expressions of this project because they explained which critics (William Wordsworth and Samuel Taylor Coleridge) and which schools of criticism (Romanticism, Marxism, and the New Criticism) fall outside the humanistic tradition, in Seaton's opinion. These chapters, Four especially, are exciting, provocative, and significant. They supply the basis and much of the substance for the rest of the book and suggest that literature is not an agent of ideology, nor literary theory a master key that unlocks the door to grand solutions for political, scientific, and economic problems.

For those who are uninterested or unversed in literary criticism, however, reading Seaton will be like watching strategic athletic maneuvers—swing! parry! dive!—without a sense of what's at stake in a sporting match whose tactics and rules are unknown. From the start he frames his argument with Plato and Aristotle, but today's graduate students in English will be unclear what these men mean for the larger project of humanism or why they matter to contemporary audiences. With the exception of the Norton anthologies, most accounts of literary criticism in popular anthologies begin with Nietzsche in the late 19th century or with the New Critics in the early twentieth. The pinnacle of influence for these late critics roughly coincides with the development of English departments as institutions. To begin at the beginning—with the Greeks—will disorient those trained to look back at the literary canon through the prism of "contemporary" theories.

This remark is not a reproach of Seaton but of current literary studies; the chief merit of Seaton's methodology is to demystify literary studies and to affirm there's nothing new under the sun: the latest theories have definite antecedents (not necessarily good ones) and can be mapped by their continuity with other methodologies. Marxists of the Frankfurt School such as Herbert Marcuse, for example, follow in the wake of Plato: "Just as Plato had insisted on the necessity of censorship in his ideal Republic, Marcuse argued that suppression of free speech was required in the twentieth century for the establishment of what he considered true freedom."[132]

Seaton's knack for classification emerges forcefully in the opening chapter. Here he arranges under three heads the whole history of literary criticism: the Platonic, the Neoplatonic, and the Aristotelian. He defines literary criticism as "a continuing conversation" among these three traditions inspired by just two Greek men.[133] Adhering to the third category, the Aristotelian, which he calls humanistic, Seaton rejects the first because it questions the aesthetic value of literature, distrusts the sensory effects of literature, and treats great works as mere symptoms of ideological structures or institutions. "The philosophy of the Republic," Seaton explains, "leaves no room for judging poetry according to literary excellence; all that counts is its political and social impact."[134] Seaton rejects the second, the Neoplatonic, for defending literature and poetry on the narrow and quixotic "basis of the moral and spiritual elevation it made possible."[135]

By contrast, Seaton submits, the "humanistic view of literature" might be "a middle way between the Platonic condemnation of art and literature and the Neoplatonic elevation."[136] The humanistic view "remains Aristotelian" because it considers "literature as a source of insight about human life" and is willing "to judge grand theory by the norms of common sense."[137] While Plato would expel poetry and theater from his ideal Republic, segregate poetry from philosophy, and train his Guardians to submit their virtues to the service of the State, Aristotle calls for "individual judgment about the literary merit and relevance to human life of particular works from audiences and certainly from would-be critics."[138] Neoplatonist overstatement about the manner in which "poetry brings us closer to the divine"[139] also finds no place in Aristotelian humanism, which modestly maintains that literature "can tell us important things about human life but little about the universe."[140] Humanists write of the person as the person: they turn to literature to learn and to teach how to live well and wisely without fancying transcendental essences or utopian abstraction. The very crux of Aristotelian humanism is that "the importance of literature is linked to the significance of human life itself,"[141] not to the political, ideological, or religious convictions that a work of literature implicates.

The triadic paradigm (Aristotelian, Platonist, Neoplatonist) may seem reductive, and indeed it is, but such reduction establishes recognizable classifications that encompass a diversity of interests and approaches while shaping a vocabulary for arranging distinctive properties into taxonomies to set apart certain authors and texts. Despite his skill for categorizing and simplifying schools of literary criticism, Seaton is steadfast that literary criticism is distinct in function and form from science: the former is as much an art as the art it explicates, whereas the latter is an empirical discipline that ascertains the natural rules of the phenomenal world by gathering and testing concrete data, building consensus among experts, and denominating general propositions to describe observable events. The contrast is not as sharp or essentialist as I have portrayed it—the pragmatic tradition of Peirce, James, and Santayana falls somewhere between art and science—but the fact that literary criticism has splintered into innumerable, contradictory schools suggests that the disparate methods and judgments of literary critics are not derived from shared conditions or by recourse to the same techniques.

Criticism of the humanistic variety championed by Seaton is found today not in academic journals but in popular literary reviews and journals. It has the important civic function of educating and inspiring mass audiences. Humanism rejects the "implicit promise" of cultural studies "that adepts gain the ability to make authoritative pronouncements about all aspects of human life without going to the trouble of learning the rudiments of any particular discipline."[142] Humanism, instead, engages in public debate without resorting to naked polemics; its practitioners understand or at least appreciate the complexity of the cultural norms and standards of readers outside the ivory tower. Professors in the academy, on the other hand, disconnected from the lifestyles and manners and conventions of the general public, tend to write themselves into little corners, retreating from the potential scrutiny of educated laypeople and insisting that true scholarship "requires specialization on topics specific enough to allow for the production of new knowledge, not open-ended conversation about questions to which no definitive answer is possible."[143] Seaton's model of humanism advocates a different errand: "to make available to the larger culture the testimony of literature on human life ... by accurately assessing the literary merit of the witness."[144]

They waste it that do state it with no style. Seaton, accordingly, makes short work of the "dominant theorizing" that lacks "literary distinction,"[145] and he does so with his own unique style that remains as accessible to the educated layperson as it is to professional scholars of literature. His is not the delightfully repetitious, grandstanding prose of a Harold Bloom or Richard Poirier—the type of prose that, in its very makeup, shouts down the technical writing of hyper-professionalized humanities scholarship. Yet Seaton can turn a phrase with the best of them. Although it is a subsidiary point, the notion that a critic should write in a mode many people will enjoy is the literary equivalent to popular sovereignty: the common reader, not the expert, ought to determine which works continue to be read and therefore which become canonized. Like his guides Ralph Ellison and Dwight Macdonald, Seaton, mindful of his audience, takes pains to avoid jargon even as he discusses such theorists as Max Horkheimer and Theodor Adorno whose writing is riddled with esoterica.

Seaton ends *Literary Criticism from Plato to Postmodernism* with a hopeful note: "Although the task of addressing the arguments of the dominant contemporary theories is important, the decisive answer [to the question what to do now that the dominant theories dismiss the importance of literature to life and thought] will come from the literary criticism of the 21st century that conveys to the general public the pleasures and insights that poems, plays, and fiction continue to make available to all those willing to attend."[146] Let's hope the coming decades yield critics like Edmund Wilson and Lionel Trilling, who were "members of a humanistic tradition capacious enough to study the connections between literature and society while also insisting that poems, plays, and novels should be judged on their own merits as works of art."[147]

It isn't that the political and social sphere should be off-limits to critics, only that critics should, as Seaton does, subordinate their political and social presuppositions to aesthetic judgments, the most discerning of which account for the value of imaginative literature to plain living and high thinking. The best criticism helps us to understand how literature makes life better, more meaningful, and more fulfilling. Simple as it sounds, this proposition is tremendously complex because of the tremendous complexity of life itself. Held to his own high standards, Seaton succeeded: he forced his readers to consider what role literature has played in their development, and how that role played out in the lives of others. Good literature is more than a material object; it's a way of living, a crucial check on those who purport to know it all with utter certainty.

As a Southerner, I have a torn identity: at once proud and ashamed, innovative and preservationist, rebellious and deferential, opinionated and polite. When I travel the country, I act to dispel malicious presumptions and overcome misplaced stereotypes about why and how Southerners behave and who and how Southerners are. I am often greeted with the well-meaning phrase, "But you don't have a Southern accent." I'm not sure how I'm supposed to sound, what I'm supposed to sound like, or which expectation, precisely, I haven't met. For the most part, my interlocutors mean no harm. It's tough, however, constantly facing the burden of proof to demonstrate that, despite your background and upbringing, you are reasonable, benevolent, and intelligent after all.

What's frustrating is the sanctimonious presupposition among certain people from other parts of the country that their ancestors, and their home jurisdictions, stood on the right side of critical issues for purely correct and moral reasons. The truth, sadly, is that those reasons had little to do with rightness or morality and more to do with raw politics.

Nearly every Southerner was raised studying the Civil War, or, as some here still call it, the War Between the States. By the time I entered the public school system in Marietta, Georgia, in the 1980s, the War had long been a cornerstone of the curriculum, although Lost Cause mythology had dissipated and the Confederacy was hardly treated with tones of admiration. It became clear, however, that the War was more complicated than my teachers let on, that the events leading to and following this great conflict represented more than a morality play between competing forces of good and evil.

There was, for example, the case of the Roswell Mill, located a few minutes from the home where I grew up. More than a century ago, at this forsaken mill, the wives, mothers, sisters, daughters, and young sons of Confederate soldiers labored while the soldiers themselves (husbands, fathers, brothers, and sons) were off at war. One day Sherman's Army materialized at the mill and absconded with the women and children. When the Confederate soldiers returned to the mill town, their families were nowhere to be seen. No one knows exactly what happened to the women and children of the mill, which is why they are still, to this day, called "The Lost Women and Children of Roswell."

Recently trends in scholarship about the War have been uncritical in their assessments (or lack of assessments) of Union ideology as a contributing factor to the War. Gary Gallagher's recent book *The Union War*, a companion to his earlier *The Confederate War* (1997), corrects this trend. *The Union War* is restorative history and was timely at its publication in 2011, the year that marked the Sesquicentennial (the 150th anniversary) of the War. Gallagher submits that for the last four decades, as of his writing, scholarship on the War neglected to emphasize the ideology of Unionism, and he set out to improve the record.

Unionism is central to any understanding of the War. As Gallagher explains, "[T]he focus on emancipation and race sometimes suggests the War had scant meaning apart from these issues—and especially that Union victory had little or no value without emancipation."[148] Although Union soldiers may have understood that issues related to slavery precipitated fighting in 1861, for them that is not what the war was "about." Gallagher adds that a "portrait of the nation that is dominated by racism, exclusion, and oppression obscures more than it reveals,"[149] not least of all because it ignores the vast influx of immigrants and the relative receptivity toward different cultures that Americans championed to varying degrees, even at that time.

Gallagher's goal in this book is to disabuse readers of the notion that the War was, for the typical Union citizen-solder, "about slavery." The book asks three fundamental questions: "What did the war for Union mean in mid-nineteenth century America? How and why did emancipation come to be part of the war for Union? How did armies of citizen-soldiers figure in conceptions of the war, the process of emancipation, and the shaping of national sentiment?"[150] In answering these questions, Gallagher's focus is on "one part of the population in the United States—citizens in the free states and four loyal slaveholding states who opposed secession and supported a war to restore the Union."[151] Gallagher concludes that the War was, for the aforementioned citizens, one for Union, and that it only happened to bring about the emancipation of slaves. Emancipation was never the goal; it was a result.

"From the perspective of loyal Americans," Gallagher explains, "their republic stood as the only hope for democracy in a western world that had fallen more deeply into the stifling embrace of oligarchy since the failed European revolutions of the 1840s."[152] According to this reading, Southern slaveholders of the planter classes represented the aristocracy that was responsible for the creation of the Confederacy. The Southern elite seemed like a throwback to monarchy. Citizen-soldiers of the Union Army believed that by taking on the Confederacy, they were restoring democratic principles and preserving the "Union," a term that contemporary readers who lack historical perspective will have trouble understanding. Miseducated by Hollywood fantasies and adorations—consider the films *Glory* and *Gettysburg*—the average American today has lost all constructive sense of Unionism as it was understood to mid-19th-century Americans, especially in the North.

Gallagher repeatedly identifies problems in the recent historical record and then reworks and revises them. He criticizes the tunnel-vision of scholars who write about The Grand Review as an exercise in racial exclusion, for instance, and suggests that, instead, 19th-century descriptions of this procession indicate that "Unionism" meant something like "nation" and "America," signifiers antithetical to oligarchy that were only tangentially related to racial concerns.

By systematically picking apart various histories while summarizing and synthesizing a wealth of recent scholarship, Gallagher produced what could be called a prolonged bibliographical or historiographical essay with extended asides about what is wrong in his field. What is wrong, he suggests, is imposing contemporary preoccupations with race onto the mindsets of 19th-century Americans. Against this tendency, Gallagher reminds us of forgotten facts—for instance, that the passage of the Thirteenth Amendment concerned political unity before racial enlightenment, or that, over the course of the War, concerted military action by ordinary individuals (not the acts of rebel slaves, Abraham Lincoln, or congressmen) determined which black populations in the South became free. Gallagher interrogates the difference between Lincoln the "Savior of the Union" and Lincoln "The Great Emancipator." He supports the study of military history, which other academics have scorned. All of this plays into his claim that although "almost all white northerners would have responded in prejudiced terms if asked about African Americans, they were not consumed with race as much of the recent literature would suggest."[153]

The take-home point from *The Union War* is that devotion to Union had greater currency for most Americans than did any contemporary understanding of a commitment to race. "Recapturing how the concept of Union resonated and reverberated throughout the loyal states in the Civil War era," Gallagher submits, "is critical to grasping northern motivation."[154] This motivation was rooted in the belief that Union would preserve rather than jeopardize liberty, and had little to do with slavery except in that an important side result was liberty for all. Gallagher reminds us of the importance of Unionism to the War and to the psychology of the average Northerner at that time. He reminds us, as well, that race was hardly a chief concern to the typical Northern soldier, and that retrospective imposition of our concerns onto theirs is poor scholarship and bad history.

Compare Gallagher's account with that of Michael Kreyling, a professor of English at Vanderbilt University with an endowed chair and several books to his credit, who brings a literary touch to his brief history of the Civil War—not of its battles and heroes and victims and villains but of the manner in which Americans have recalled those things over time. A history about history, conceived as a series of lectures, *A Late Encounter With the Civil War* bears a title that seems to apply as aptly to Kreyling (he's had a long and distinguished career in literature but hasn't worked extensively in the field of Civil War studies) as it does to the current era's strained connection with its bloodiest conflict to date.

Kreyling focuses on "collective memory," a concept he purports to borrow from Maurice Halbwachs and Emile Durkheim and the premise of which is "that humans assemble or construct memory in the context of social life: we remember what our social groups require us to remember in order to maintain historical continuity over time and to claim our membership in them."[155] Collective memory is participatory rather than commanded, evolutionary rather than fixed, fluctuating rather than static; it emerges out of the conversations people within a given territory have regarding a particular event.

Kreyling is, of course, concerned with our "collective memory" of the Civil War. It is unclear which individuals enforce or control the regime of collective memory according to his paradigm, but presumably he means to suggest that all members of the community are at least partially complicit in the narrative perpetuation that becomes collective memory. He evokes collective memory to establish the "constructedness" of Southern narratives about the war and thereby to refute the assumption of Pierre Nova, who once claimed that "[d]ifferent versions of the Revolution or the Civil War do not threaten the American tradition because, in some sense, no such thing exists—or, if it does, it is not primarily a historical construction."[156] Kreyling submits, contra Nova, that historical memory is constructed because it involves both gradual initiation and exclusion: those who understand and promote the validated and official account are admitted into the group, members of which celebrate a shared past, whereas those who challenge the authorized narratives are marginalized or altogether excluded. What the approved story of the Civil War is at the moment of the sesquicentennial remained, he claimed, unknown because only years after such a landmark can we objectively evaluate its meaning and import.

Collective memory is not the same as personal memory. It is a "kind of complicated puppet theater" inasmuch as "we are the puller of strings" as well as "the figures pulled."[157] We not only "set dates for ceremonies of public memory and fill the ceremonies with choreographed activities,"[158] but also allow ourselves to be dragged along with such things; we resort to ritualistic commemoration to project the past onto our present, explains Kreyling, and to attempt to define ourselves both by and against our past.

Kreyling argues in his opening chapter that "the United States that formally remembered the Civil War at the semicentennial was different from the America of the centennial and sesquicentennial by one very powerful theme we can identify in retrospect: blood."[159] The subject of blood leads him into meandering discussions of *The Great Gatsby* and Bram Stoker's *Dracula*. This chapter becomes less about the memory of the Civil War and more about early 20th-century eugenicist fascinations with blood, an element of romanticized fiction that is "latent symbolic" or "cultural" because it "invades or pollutes the endangered citadel of whiteness."[160]

Theodore Roosevelt used the term "race suicide" to express a widely shared fear of racial degeneration, which was linked, Kreyling alleges, to a perceived collapse of civilization.[161] Kreyling ties "race suicide" to both the creation of and reaction to popular works by D. W. Griffith and Thomas Dixon Jr., implicating Woodrow Wilson in the rapid proliferation of racism—and not just by recalling Wilson's oft-discussed response to the screening of *The Birth of a Nation* in the White House.

Kreyling's second chapter maps the shift from memorialization to mass anxiety as race-relations in America forced the country to reconsider the meaning and purpose of the Civil War. Here Kreyling considers an array of figures—from Bruce Catton and Robert Penn Warren to Edmund Wilson and Flannery O'Connor—to substantiate the proposition that public interest in the Civil War was on the wane and overshadowed by the Civil Rights Movement and the Cold War. All of this is interesting, but we shouldn't be surprised that most of the population at that time was more interested in its present moment than in a war that had occurred a century earlier.

The third and final chapter speculates about "negotiations ... between what did happen" during the Civil War and "what we would prefer to remember."[162] I say "speculates" because Kreyling is careful not to seem rash or conclusory about our own moment. Rather than giving an answer, for instance, he says that "we need to ask" the question "[w]here is the South now?"[163] That we may ask that question at all shows how different our generation is from those which came before, as Kreyling demonstrates by surveying recent literary scholarship on the matter.

Wherever the South is now, it seems to have traveled far from "pure ancestor worship."[164] That doesn't mean our memory has become unproblematic. Kreyling sees in the historical fiction of Newt Gingrich and William R. Forstchen, for example, a disturbing turn to a counterfactual mode of ritual that distorts our understanding of past events. Kreyling rounds out his discussion of Gingrich and Forstchen (among other people and texts) with an upsetting observation: "we commemorate past wars with new ones."[165] Such a strong, ambiguous claim demands clarification, yet Kreyling doesn't provide it, perhaps because any long explication would detract from the lasting force and profundity of the closing remark.

As smoothly as this book reads, one wonders what its chief contribution is. It's certainly unique and innovative to, as Kreyling does, compare vampire fiction with the racist notion of thoroughbred whiteness that circulated at the semicentennial. On the other hand, there might be a good reason why this approach hasn't been tried, and it's not because no one has thought of it.

When a book doesn't move professional historiography in a direction that unearths obscure details, adds to the sum of knowledge on a precise topic, or sheds light on events by examining them from the unexplored perspective of cultural outsiders, it can rely too heavily on style and creativity and entertainment value. Kreyling's book isn't devoid of scholarship, but it does push the bounds of that genre. Perhaps its greatest achievement is its capacity to raise provocative questions about our present relationship to a conflict that in some ways seems so distant, but in others so familiar.

Making sense of the present requires full immersion in the past. Students today seem to avoid controversial or offensive material from previous eras rather than studying it on its own terms or in light of cultural changes. For this reason, few students are likely to know that the Confederacy had a literary culture and heritage, and fewer still would be bold enough to study or write about it.

Confederate literature and literary culture have not received the critical consideration that they warrant. Not only that, but they have been dismissed as scant and mediocre. Scholars of the South and of the Civil War— even those whose work has reached wide audiences—have paid more attention to other humanistic fields than to literature, particularly to Confederate literature and particularly during the so-called "fighting" years of 1861–1865. This neglect, argued Coleman Hutchison in *Apples and Ashes*, is regrettable because "the Confederacy gave rise to a robust literary culture."[166] In recent years Hutchison has fallen into disgrace after the media reported allegations of sexual misconduct against him. That sad situation has no bearing, of course, on the quality of his research into Confederate literature and literary culture.

Several factors account for the dearth of scholarship on Confederate literature, not least of which is the fact that the Confederacy existed for only a short time, during which Confederate writers had to overcome, among other things, ink and paper shortages; many of these men and women struggled to see their work reach print in cities occupied by Union troops. Accordingly, much of what might have become Confederate literature was lost or unpublished. Yet the relative shortage of Confederate literature was not due to lack of talent, but to printing paralysis.

Another reason Confederate literature has not become a common subject of study is the prevailing presumption that it is not worthwhile, largely because Confederate cultural values have been discredited. There is, today, a tendency to demonize or denounce any person who would take seriously the claims and writings of Confederate partisans, politicians, and highbrows. To take something seriously, however, is not to endorse it. Moreover, to proclaim certain intellectual matters off-limits—even if they are highly complex and provide instructive lessons for our own day—is dangerous and misguided. Hutchison is as aware of the importance of Confederate literature as he is of the importance of disclaiming it. "To write about the Confederate nation," he says, "is to risk being seen as endorsing its right to exist."[167] He adds, emphatically, that his book "is by no means an apology for the Confederacy or Confederate nationalism," and that he "finds almost nothing that is admirable in the politics and culture of the Civil War South."[168] That he feels so compelled to disassociate himself from Confederate ideology suggests how strangely anxious the impulsive and opportunistic readers can be in our current political climate.

Uninterested in matters of taste and judgment regarding the literary quality of his subjects, Hutchison submits that Confederate literature teaches not only about the nuances and cultures of nationalism, but also about 19th-century American (read: non-Confederate) letters more generally, since Confederate literature was in conversation with—and in contradistinction to—American literary nationalism. Among the distinguishing features of Confederate literature were its aspirational impulses and its focus upon an imagined and impossible future. In some respects, the South's *belles lettres* recognized the poignancy of a lost cause narrative before that cause was actually lost.

William Gilmore Simms, Edgar Allan Poe, Edward A. Pollard, Paul Hamilton Hayne—these and other writers figure prominently as the upper stratum of Southern literary society who sought cultural autonomy in their various rhetorical modes: novels, poems, plays, and so forth. Hutchison treats the *Southern Literary Messenger*, in which many of these authors published, as a key source of information regarding the "intense debate over the prospect of national literature."[169] This journal "offers an uncommon opportunity to read southern literary nationalist discourse both article by article and year to year."[170] Northern supporters of *The Southern Literary Messenger* included such luminaries as Washington Irving, James Fenimore Cooper, John Pendleton Kennedy, and John Quincy Adams.

The best way to categorize *Apples and Ashes* is as an interdisciplinary work about Confederate literary nationalism. With chapters addressing bookmaking, music, and memoir, *Apples and Ashes* is impressively researched and beautifully delivered. Hutchison has, in this relatively short book, pointed out what many of us already knew: that the Confederacy produced literature that is worthy of study for how and why it said what it said. Even more significant are Hutchison's observations about the role of literature in shaping Confederate expectations about its future. Confederate authors sought to cultivate a national literature that would endure. It hasn't. They failed. Because so few readers are familiar with this literature today, they see only the "ashes," not the "apples." That's a shame, but also the reality in which we live. Many protestors decrying the legacy of the Confederacy and dismantling Confederate monuments don't know what it is they are opposing. If they took a closer look at the relevant history, they might be surprised to learn how much they resemble the subjects they despise.

I've mentioned my mentors Paul Cantor and James Seaton. Gilbert Allen, a great poet and my former professor at Furman University, is another. He's authored or edited numerous collections of poetry and has taught thousands of students. His *The Final Days of Great American Shopping*, a collection of short stories, is intelligent, nuanced, poignant, and distressing—and hence not for everyone. If you've read more than one Nicholas Sparks novel this year, this book isn't for you. If you think Oprah is a guardian of culture, this book isn't for you. If you believe Fox News and CNN are edifying, this book isn't for you. If you think David Brooks, Charles Krauthammer, and Sidney Blumenthal are men of letters, this book isn't for you. If you prefer Dr. Phil to Jung and Freud, this book isn't for you. If Joel Osteen inspires you in a way that Augustine and Aquinas cannot, this book isn't for you. If, in fact, any of the aforesaid are true of your case, you might just be the unwitting target of Allen's biting satire.

Allen, I recall, loved cats, as well as his isolated, sylvan home in Traveler's Rest, South Carolina, far away from his native Long Island, both culturally and geographically. His spoken diction was always precise, as was the pencil-thin mustache that grayed above his lips. Tall and skinny, with belts so long they could've wrapped around him twice, he spoke softly and carried a big pen.

He committed poems to memory. I once heard him recite "Stopping by Woods on a Snowing Evening" to the tune of *La cumparsita*, a curious performance he allegedly repeats with other poems and tangos. Ancient or modern, free verse or rhyming, short or long, poetry is his lifework, calling, and passion. So, I suspect, he suffers, as honorable poets are wont to do. And his suffering only intensified when he had to mass-market this book—his first in prose—that criticizes mass-marketing.

The Final Days of Great American Shopping depicts a self-indulgent American suburbia starved for money and materialism, where people try to purchase happiness and other forms of fleeting satisfaction while fixated on their own or others' sexuality. These 16 stories, told in chronological order from the recent past to the immediate future—and, at last, to the year 2084—are not directly about sex. Yet sexual anxieties, appetites, and insecurities bear a subterranean, causative relationship to the acquisitive urge and cupidity that complicate many of the characters in Allen's dystopian community, Belladonna, a gated subdivision in South Carolina, probably near Greenville.

Allen's opening story is a complex portrait of loving and loathing, and the fine line between the two. A childless couple, Butler and Marjory Breedlove, still in their early 40s, struggle to remain compatible as they degenerate into a life of stultifying domesticity, having suffered through three miscarriages and the abortion of an anencephalic child. Butler is an insurance salesman and a beer-drinking baseball fan who pulls for an aging veteran against his own beloved Atlanta Braves. Marjory, the silent, brooding type, obsesses over her luxuriant, blooming flowers, the fecundity and fertility of which contrast with her own barrenness.

Butler, as if to compensate for the feeling of emasculation occasioned by his inability to sire offspring, sets out to install storm windows one Saturday morning while Marjory visits her mother. If Marjory cannot be gratified through sexual activity, he presumably reasons, then she'll derive pleasure from his dutiful, manly labor. A client has told him that storm windows are "easier than a second honeymoon" because they require just nine "screws,"[171] so there's little doubt that Butler's chore is substitutionary: it fulfills the need for virile exertion that, we may assume, is not met through copulation.

The problem is, Butler procrastinates and leaves the windows beside

Marjory's flowers for too long. Any boy who's used a magnifying glass to burn ants would've known not to do this, but not Butler. He doesn't consider what might happen to Marjory's flowers as he sets aside the windows to pursue booze and television. He does, however, manage to complete the window installation. When Marjory returns, he proudly reveals his handiwork, announcing, "I did it myself."[172] He's not fully aware of what it is until Marjory, ignoring the windows, gasps, "My flowers."[173] She stares at her garden as if peering into an "open grave."[174] The florae that were adjuncts for her lost children, that were little leafy lives she had created and sustained, are now dead. She can't bear the loss. Tragedy compels her to mourn on a closet floor in her nightgown. It's an intolerable image—her sitting there, grieved and defeated—that captures the sad inability of two people to live out their most primitive desires.

The seemingly banal agonies in this story of strained marriage are subtly and quizzically meaningful. What is the significance, for instance, of Marjory's decision to serve a scrumptious breakfast for Butler while she munches on blackened toast? Such a small gesture, but so gravely significant. With moments like these, impressively numerous in such a short, short story, Allen achieves, I think, the right amount of ambiguity: neither Butler nor Marjory is the "bad guy"; both seem thwarted from intimacy and happiness by forces beyond their control yet originating from their deliberate action. They mean well, mostly, but they're the same poles on a magnet, destined, it seems, to repel one another. Even their surname—Breedlove—raises interpretive puzzles, since breeding and loving are foreign to their relationship. Whether it's their childlessness or an accumulation of small disappointments that causes their desperation and despair remains unclear. Perhaps they recognize, as most of us do at some point, that they'll never become the people their younger selves wanted to be—and that this, whatever this may be, is all there is. Youthful aspiration is bound to become dashed hope, and once we've made ourselves what we are, there's no unmaking us.

John Beegle, a protagonist of another story who happens to have purchased health insurance from Butler Breedlove—each story is delicately linked—faces a different problem, or problems: a growing estrangement from his wife and the inability to connect with his teenaged daughters, one of whom has grown increasingly flirtatious in proportion to her budding breasts. John likes "to understand things, piece by piece," but he can't make sense of the females in his family. They move so fast, and he so slowly. This all changes when he discovers, in the garage of his new house, an "autogyro," or a small helicopter, circa 1961. This antique machine remains operational, and the more John works on it, the more his daughters take to him. He even revives his libido, surprising his wife with a "midday tryst."[175] The restoration of the helicopter refurbishes his own spirits, and he eventually takes the perilous contraption for a ride, rising high into the air until he can "see everything."[176] Like Frost's wistful narrator who imagines himself climbing a birch tree up toward heaven only to be set back down again, John, hovering in the sky, "begins to dream of his landing, of his own house."[177] He thinks of his family and of his return to the ground. Earth is, indeed, the right place for love.

Allen's book is full of characters like these: the widowed Priscilla Knobloch with her twelve-year-old, one-handed daughter; Ted Dickey, whose numerous speed-dating partners represent different social ailments from materialism to decadence; the unnamed hick hair stylist who likes to rear-end Porsches (just a "love tap"[178]) and talk about blow jobs; a thrift store worker and his wife, the menopausal Meredith, who start a non-profit corporation for religious "bedding"; Jorja Sorenson, a painter, and her husband, Houston, who collaborate on the sculpture of a fetus that draws the attention of none other than Marjorie Breedlove; and on and on. Through these hapless, heedless figures and their goods, interests, and acquisitions—television, cars, homes, designer shoes—certain symptoms of our national condition are projected: greed, consumerism, profligacy, extravagance, melancholy. It's not overstating to say that, with these stories, Allen has tapped into our national disorder. The quintessential American, restless and without a past, energetic and democratic, his works and beliefs at once enterprising and derivative—that iconic, preeminently rugged, relatable laborer—has, in our imagination, transitioned from self-reliant and industrious, always ready to "simply, simplify," to dark and pitiful, burdened by the wealth and joy that forever elude him.

Although Americans once envisioned a vast frontier of possibility, an unknown and ever-widening expanse of hope and promise, imbuing optimism and idealism wherever we went, we now, sketchy and insecure, stumble along looking for opportunities that don't exist, endeavoring to remain perpetually young and verdant, as if gray hair weren't a crown of glory and splendor. We want what we can't have and have what we don't want. Once we were Franklins and Jeffersons, Emersons and Whitmans; today we're Willy Lomans. Or Cher Horowitzes. Or Gordon Gekkos. Without guilt we can't identify with Reverend Dimmesdale or Hester Prynne. Without abstinence, we can't appreciate the allure of Rappacini's daughter. As coddled, perpetual children, we don't get Ishmael and Ahab, Frederick Douglass, or Jay Gatsby. We're so phony that we don't understand Holden Caulfield anymore.

So Allen has done us a great service. By mocking us and portraying our ominously recognizable and quotidian depravities, he's exposed the warring desires to which we've fallen prey: extravagance and simplicity, envy and indifference, aspiration and defeat, conformity and revolt. He's a spokesman for the disenchanted and disillusioned, for those who still possess the poetic vision about which Emerson intoned. He sees a double consciousness, a conflict of the mind, that drags us into woeful insipidity and angst. If reading his book isn't like looking reluctantly and masochistically into the mirror, or less figuratively into your own split psyche, then you're delusional or dishonest, or perhaps—just perhaps—the rare exception. These stories are harsh, biting, titillating, disparaging, and sarcastic, but they're also funny. Allen derides us, and perhaps himself, with humor. He's a sensitive man, and very quiet. Who knew that, beneath his silent façade, there was a hilarious personality?

I did. Because his poetry reveals that about him.

His first collection of poetry, *In Everything*, was spiritual and serious, a sort of Buddhist mystical meditation on Nature and Being. As time went on, he eased up and relaxed, moving from the intensity of numinous experience to the comic realities of everyday life. It's not that his writing became lighthearted, upbeat, or shallow. No, it remained pensive and complex and open to rigorous interpretation, sometimes even cosmic in scope. Yet there was something more playful and satirical about it. He came to enjoy social criticism as much as he enjoyed, say, the splendor of sentience and the complexities of the mind and soul.

This tendency towards the witty and quirky finds expression in *The Final Days of Great American Shopping*. It's evident in a pick-up line: "Would you like to go on a corporate retreat next month? As my tax deduction?"[179] It materializes in unsuspecting places such as the urinal, where a man talks on his cell phone as he urinates. It even surfaces in the epithet "Confederate Flaggots," which implies a phallic fascination with flag poles that's endemic among men "who dress up in nineteenth-century costumes to do unspeakable things to one another in public parks."[180] Not every attempt at humor, however, is successful: the narrator of the story "Friends with Porsches" speaks like a redneck, but not a real redneck—merely a forced caricature whose colloquialisms and ungrammatical syntax aren't quite believable as actual speech.

Allen's sardonic, unpretentious fiction renders a society that's abandoned the "errand into the wilderness"—as Perry Miller so aptly labeled the once powerful theme of American experience—for the errand into the shopping mall. Although some of the technology that appears in his stories is already dated—most of the stories were first published before iPhones and iPads made the Internet and email a ubiquitous, hand-held phenomenon—one senses in their representation a renewed and profane scrutiny that's both subversive and daring.

Are we in the final days of American shopping, as Allen suggests? If so, is that an apocryphal singularity, the secular equivalent to the eschaton? Maybe. Shopping, for Allen, is, after all, much more than evaluating retail merchandise with an eye toward a trivial purchase. It's systemic and magnificent, a fluid cultural sickness with no immediate cure. Alike in severity to those Old Testament, idolatrous practices that demand prophetic ministry, it signals a coming destruction and necessitates oracular warnings. Shopping has become the lord and king of us all. As for the other events of its reign, those which don't appear in Allen's book, are they not written in the records of the Internet, the annotations of our technology, and the annals of our digital media? Allen buries shopping with its ancestors. And he buries us, and our endless wants, with it.

PART THREE: CULTURE

My friend John Shelton Reed recently authored a book subtitled "A South-Watcher's Miscellany." What follows is my own miscellany regarding culture. The term "culture" has multiple origins, each bearing a relation to land and farming. Think *agri*culture or *cult*ivate. Culture, properly understood, requires time, effort, and labor. Accordingly, to become cultured, in the historical sense of that term, a person had to *work*, undertaking rigorous reading and learning and then discoursing with other learned people about matters of grave consequence. My hope is that the following essays and reviews rise to that level—that they both reflect and contribute to culture. Books are, in my view, at the heart of a rigorous culture; therefore, they're at the heart of this concluding section.

Phantoms of Terror

Born in America and raised in Britain, Adam Zamoyski is not a tenured university professor devoted to obscure subjects that appeal only to audiences of academic guilds. Nor does he write for a small readership. That's why his books sell and his prose excites; he can narrate a compelling account while carrying an insightful thesis. His book *Phantom Terror* bears a subtitle that might cause libertarian ears to perk up: "Political Paranoia and the Creation of the Modern State, 1789–1848."

Challenging the validity of modern states and their various arms and agencies is the daily diet of committed libertarians, but Zamoyski is not, to my knowledge, a libertarian of any stripe. Yet he challenges the modern State and its various arms and agencies, whatever his intentions or beliefs, and he refuses to shut his eyes to the predatory behavior of government. To appreciate the goals of his book, one must first understand how he came to his subject.

The story is simple: While researching, Zamoyski uncovered information suggesting that governments in the decades following the French Revolution deliberately incited panic among their citizens to validate increasingly restrictive policies. The more governments regulated and circumscribed individual freedoms, he found, the more they took on the shape of nation states: geopolitical entities that had their roots in 16th- and 17th-century Europe but had not yet fully centralized.

If there's a main character here, it's Napoleon Bonaparte. Zamoyski wrote about Napoleon in previous books, including *1812: Napoleon's Fatal March on Moscow* (2005) and *Rites of Peace: The Fall of Napoleon and the Congress of Vienna* (2008). Having escaped from exile in Elba in February 1815 and suffered defeat at the Battle of Waterloo later that year, Napoleon, once the Emperor of the French, had been reduced to the status of a prisoner, stripped of his dignity and rendered militarily ineffective, his health quickly declining. Tsar Alexander of Russia, seeing the great Napoleon neutralized, called for a holy covenant with Emperor Francis I of Austria and King Frederick William III of Prussia. For Alexander, who envisioned the State as the realization of divine conception, the three united rulers reflected the trinitarian Christian God from whom their autocratic, quasi-sacred powers derived. Alexander believed that the unsettling of tradition and order during the French Revolution could be counteracted or cured by the systematic institutionalization of despotic government. First, though, the masses needed to be instructed in the manifest nature of revolutionary threats lurking behind every corner, in every neighborhood, among friends and family, in unexpected places.

Then came the police, a new body of official agents vested with administrative powers and decorated with the symbols and insignias of authority. Until that point, the term "police," or its rough equivalent in other European languages, designated minor officials with localized duties over small public spaces. European states lacked the administrative machinery of a centralized enforcement network outside the military, whose function was to conquer foreign territory or defend the homeland, not to guard the comfort, health, and morals of communities in disparate towns and villages. The latter task was for parochial institutions, custom, churches, nobility, and other configurations of local leadership.

In the wake of the French Revolution, with its ritualistic brutality, mass hysteria, and spectacular regicide, sovereigns and subjects began to accept and support the power of centralized governments to deploy political agents, including spies and informers. According to Zamoyski, the growing police force—secret agents and all—was less interested in basic hygiene, sanitation, and safety and more interested in subverting the political clout and conspiratorial tendencies of local nobility. To maximize their power, emperors and government ministers gave color to grand falsehoods about their weakness. Only in their exaggerated vulnerability, catalyzed by true and imagined Jacobins, Freemasons, Illuminati, and other such bugaboos, could they exercise their strength. Seizing upon anxieties about civil unrest, rulers cultivated in their subjects a desire for police protection, supervision, and surveillance. Conspiracy theories worked in their favor. Francis ordered his police to be vigilant about the spread of Enlightenment ideas; he enacted censorship measures by which people disciplined themselves into obedience, leaving the police to serve, often, as mere symbols of control.

Zamoyski does not focus on any one state but moves from city to city, leader to leader, depicting how European governments staged rebellion for their own benefit. Several individuals figure prominently for their different roles during this turbulent time: Edmund Burke; Empress Catharine II of Russia; William Pitt; Klemens von Metternich; King Ferdinand VII of Spain; King Louis Philippe; Arthur Wellesley, the First Duke of Wellington; Charles Maurice de Talleyrand; Robert Steward, Viscount Castlereagh; Joseph Fouché, and marginal characters both stupid and intelligent, of high and low station.

Eventually repression and tyranny backfired. The State apparatus and its leaders across Europe adopted the very tactics and practices they feared in their opposition; they became the kind of terrorists they had attempted to crush. By transforming into their own worst nightmare, they brought about the revolutions (e.g., the Revolutions of 1848) that they meant to avoid and inspired the movements that they intended to eradicate.

Entrapment, espionage, propaganda, tyranny, sedition, secrecy, conspiracy, treachery, reaction, regime—it's all part of the story, and it reveals that the operations of power are counterintuitive and complex, even if they're logical. Hesitant to draw parallels with our present managerial nation states and their version of authoritarian rule, Zamoyski nevertheless marshals enough evidence and insinuation to make speculation about the current order inevitable. There's the shadow of Foucault in the background:

Zamoyski portrays power as dependent on its lack, exploring how those with authority allow certain freedoms to then suppress them. There's no power that's not power *over* something. Permitting only such personal autonomy and agency as can be later subdued enabled European governments to put their authority on display. States manufacture resistance to exercise—indeed show off—their muscle.

With their sprightliness Zamoyski's chapters win for themselves a certain charm. Zamoyski has not just recounted a sequence of events during a fascinating era but exposited an exciting theory about them. It's too soon to understand the logic behind the rumors, and the disinformation, we know that world powers—nation states—spread today. Zamoyski provides no direction to this end. He does, however, use history to awaken our imagination to the workings of global power, forcing us to ask questions and seek answers about the phantoms of terror that continue to haunt us.

Boswell Gets His Due

What is Enlightenment? The title of Immanuel Kant's most famous essay asks that question. Kant suggests that the historical Enlightenment was humanity's release from self-incurred tutelage, an intellectual awakening that opened up new freedoms by challenging implanted prejudices and ingrained presuppositions. "*Sapere aude!*" Kant declared. "Dare to be wise!"

Tradition maintains that the Enlightenment was an 18th-century social and cultural phenomenon emanating from Paris salons, an Age of Reason that championed the primacy of the individual, the individual's competence to pursue knowledge through rational and empirical methods, skepticism, and the scientific method. Discourse, debate, experimentation, and economic liberalism would liberate society from the shackles of superstition and dogma and enable unlimited progress and technological innovation, offering fresh insights into the universal laws that governed not only the natural world but also human relations. They would enable individuals to attain fresh insights into themselves and the natural world.

Robert Zaretsky, a history professor at the University of Houston and the author of *Boswell's Enlightenment,* spares us tiresome critiques or defenses of the Enlightenment by Foucault and Habermas and their progeny. He begins his biography of James Boswell, the great 18th-century biographer, with a historiographical essay on the trends and trajectories of the pertinent schol-arship. He points out that the Enlightenment may have begun earlier than people once believed, and in England rather than France. He mentions Jonathan Israel's suggestion that we look to Spinoza and company, not Voltaire and company, to understand the Enlightenment, and that too much work has focused on the influence of affluent thinkers, excluding lower-class proselytizers who spread the message of liberty with a fearsome frankness and fervor. He maintains, as well, that Scotland was the ideational epicenter of Enlightenment. Boswell was a Scot.

All of this is academic backdrop and illustrative posturing, a setting of the stage for Zaretsky's subject, Boswell, a lawyer and man of letters with an impressive pedigree and a nervous disposition, a garrulous charmer with Bacchanalian tendencies, and a fussy hypochondriac raised Calvinist and forever anxious, perhaps obsessive, about the uncertain state of his eternal soul. He marveled at public executions, which he attended regularly. He had daddy issues, always trying to please his unpleased father, Lord Auchin-leck, who instructed his son to pursue the law rather than the theater and thespians. When word arrived that his son had been sharing his private journals with the public, Lord Auchinleck threatened to disown the young James. Astounded by the beauty and splendor of Rome and entranced by Catholicism, Boswell was never able to untangle the disparate religious in-fluences (all of them Christian) that he picked up during his travels. He was equally unable to suppress *eros* and consequently caught sexual diseases as a frog catches flies.

Geography and culture shaped Boswell's ideas and personality and frame Zaretsky's narrative. "With the European continent to one side, Ed-inburgh to the other," Zaretsky intones, "James Boswell stood above what seemed the one and the same phenomenon: the Enlightenment."[1] This re-mark is both figurative and literal, concluding Zaretsky's account of Boswell's climbing of Arthur's Seat, a summit overlooking Edinburgh, and his triumphant shout, "Voltaire, Rousseau, immortal names!"[2]

Immortal names indeed. But would Boswell himself achieve immor-tality? He achieved fame, no doubt, for his biography of Samuel Johnson, the poet, critic, essayist, and wit — who except for one chapter is oddly ancillary to Zaretsky's narrative. Although the *Life of Johnson* is always con-sidered one of the most important books in the language, Boswell himself has been relegated to the second or third tier of the British literary canon and treated, poor chap, as a celebrity-seeking minor figure who specialized in the life of a major figure. If Dr. Johnson is Batman, Boswell is a hob-nobbing, flattering Robin. Boswell's friends have fared better — country-men and mentors such as Adam Smith and David Hume, for instance, and the continental luminaries Voltaire and Rousseau. But there are many in-teresting relationships to consider. To cite only one: Thérèse Levasseur, Rousseau's wife or mistress (a topic of debate), became Boswell's lover as he accompanied her from Paris to England. The unsuspecting Rousseau, exiled in England, waited eagerly for her arrival while a more astute Hume, who was Rousseau's host, recognized matters for what they were.

Zaretsky believes Boswell was an exceptional talent, notwithstanding his weaknesses, and certainly worthy of our attention. Glossing several pe-riods of Boswell's life but closely examining his grand tour of the Continent (1763–1765), Zaretsky elevates Boswell's station, repairs Boswell's literary reputation, and corrects a longstanding underestimation, calling attention to his complicated and curious relationship to the Enlightenment, a move-ment or milieu that engulfed him without necessarily defining him. Zaret-sky's large claims for his subject might seem belied by the author's professedly modest goal: "to place Boswell's tour of the Continent, and sit-uate the churn of his mind, against the intellectual and political backdrop of the Enlightenment."[3] To this end, Zaretsky remarks, "James Boswell and the Enlightenment are as complex as the coils of wynds and streets forming the old town of Edinburgh."[4] And so they are, as Zaretsky makes manifest in ten digestible chapters bristling with the animated, ambulatory prose of the old style of literary and historical criticism, the kind that English pro-fessors disdain but educated readers enjoy and appreciate.

Zaretsky marshals his evidence from Boswell's meticulously detailed missives and journals, piecing together a fluid tale of adventure (meetings with the exiled libertine John Wilkes, evenings with prostitutes, debauchery across Europe, and lots of drinking) and resultant misadventure (aimless-ness, dishonor, bouts of gonorrhea and depression, and religious angst). Zaretsky portrays Boswell as a habitual performer, a genteel, polite, and proud socialite who judged himself as he imagined others to have judged him. He suffered from melancholy and the clap, among other things, but he also cultivated a gentlemanly air and pursued knowledge for its own sake. The title of the book, *Boswell's Enlightenment*, assumes plural meaning: Boswell attained a self-enlightenment that reflected the ethos and ethic of his era.

Zaretsky's book matters because Boswell matters, and, in Zaretsky's words, "Boswell matters not because his mind was as original or creative as the men and women he pursued, but because his struggle to make sense of his life, to bend his person to certain philosophical ends, appeals to our own needs and sensibilities."[5] We see ourselves in Boswell, in his alternating states of faith and doubt, devotion and reason. He, like so many of us, sought to improve himself daily but could never live up to his own expectations. He's likeable because he's fallible, a pious sinner who did right in the name of wrong and wrong in the name of right, but without any ill intent. A neurotic, rotten mess, he couldn't control his libido and didn't learn from his mistakes. But he could write like the wind, and we're better off because he did. He knew all of us, strangely, without having known us. God help us, we're all like him in some way.

Donald Trump the Cowboy

Americans love film, a medium we've popularized across the globe. We're home to Hollywood; we pioneered cinema as an industry and an art form. Film has enabled cultural memory and iconography to survive in residual form from generation to generation. Since early motion pictures, images that flashed across our screens have become part of our communicative coding, manifesting themselves in political discourse in subtle, unexpected ways.

Perhaps the most foundational figure in American cinema is the nomadic cowboy, that romantic hero of the frontier whose moral ambiguity thrills and troubles us. Frederick Jackson Turner announced his frontier thesis in 1893, drawing attention to the rugged individualism and westward expansion that characterized American liberty and differentiated the New World from Europe.

The masculine figure of the cowboy embodies this thesis. He's an archetype. Garbed in buckskins and spurs, he conquers the wilderness and the Indians, exacting ruthless revenge on his foes and exercising his menacing skills to achieve justice, at least his notion of it. But he has a dark side. One is never certain whether he's a bad guy with good qualities or a good guy with bad qualities. He can be, like Wyatt Earp, both lawman and outlaw, and his very presence creates dysfunction, jeopardizing the harmony of the community and the stability of the nuclear family. Even Shane, the most impeccable of cowboys, endangers the affection between Joe Starrett and his wife and risks undermining the sense of corporate community he's fighting to uphold.

The cowboy is a paradox: heroic yet savage, mannered yet unruly, tamed yet wild, gentle yet violent. He's a beloved and mysterious loner, reckless in the pursuit of civilized life. There's dissonance in his desire to establish domestic settlement and close the frontier while exploring nature, roaming the open range, and maintaining noble independence. With his code of honor, he's the American version of the brave and chivalrous knight who rides off on quests and adventures.

Former presidents have sought to embed themselves in the Western genre, troping the image and lore of the cowboy. President Reagan, a friend of John Wayne, acted in Westerns and was known to clad himself in big shiny belt buckles and Stetson hats. George W. Bush played up his Texas swagger, wore boots and shot rifles, vacationed on his ranch and applied the pioneering spirit to foreign affairs.

Unlike his immediate predecessor, Donald Trump is a cowboy, or the semiotic mutation of one. That's why he appeals to so many Americans. This may come as a surprise. He might seem more like the cowboy's close cousin, the urban gangster. After all, he's a New York casino and real-estate magnate who wears dark suits and bright ties and displays his money and wealth. He's gaudy and flashy like Tony Montana, and a wealthy patriarch like Vito Corleone. He's charismatic and travels in groups, and there's a noirish quality to his messaging, which the media keeps calling "dark."

Yet his narrative arc is not one of dramatic rise and inevitable fall. Nor is he an immigrant figure with ties to drugs and organized crime. He is, instead, the brawling gunslinger, marked by vanity and bravado, irresponsible in his boastfulness. He speaks for a community not his own, glamorizing his triumphs and victories. His bombast and boisterousness have an inexplicably moral feel, as if he represents more than himself and speaks for others—the common man, the forgotten man, the ranchers and laborers. The cowboy stands up to cattle-baron cronies, just as Trump takes on leading news outlets and the so-called "establishment." He portrays himself as an outmatched Will Kane, ready to confront gangs of rivals against all odds—as he did in the 2016 election when he knocked off his primary opponents and then the presumptive Democratic president, proving an entire class of pollsters and the commentariat wrong.

Like Old Rough and Ready, Trump is vague on political positions and policy prescriptions. His supporters speak of the "Trump Train," a phrase suggestive of the 19th-century railroad, which dominated American industry. His derogatory comments about Mexicans and immigrants are alike in kind if not degree to those of Ethan Edwards regarding the Comanche. Think John Wayne in *The Searchers*.

Trump is married, but not domesticated. He blurs the lines between truth and embellishment, decrying and creating fake news in the same breath. He harnesses the power of the maxim from *The Man Who Shot Liberty Valence*: "When the legend becomes fact, print the legend." Trump's high-soaring rhetoric is reminiscent of an earlier moment in American history when there were, in the American psyche, clear winners and losers. The slightest insult can cause him to seek revenge that's both personal and heedless, having something of the showdown about it.

He's a tweet-dueler. The Internet being the new frontier, in an age when you can't get away with gratuitous killing, he trades characters, not bullets. And he's quick on the draw, able to unload rounds of tweets in mere seconds. Like William Munny, the aging anti-hero in Clint Eastwood's *Unforgiven*, Trump doesn't drink. His infatuation with Mexico and insistence on building a wall across the Southern border recall the boundary disputes of a bygone era. Imagine Santa Anna and the Republic of Texas as historical antecedents to current border anxieties.

Trump's carefully orchestrated press conferences, campaign rallies, and presidential addresses suggest that he demands a spectacle that's as visually magnificent as a John Ford film. He fancies the long-shot panorama with American flags in the background. He flies in and out of small towns, ever the roving myth, and doesn't have a single place to call home.

During a period of economic contraction, aging population, shifting demographics, and declining American power, ordinary Americans understandably look to a time of territorial growth, when heroes defeated "the Other," solved their problems, and overcame adversity. With the advent of

Google Maps and Street View, folks long for a past of exploration and geographic mystery—when there were borders between known and unknown lands. Trump talks about Greatness. Speaking in superlatives, he refers to things as Amazing, Huge, Tremendous, and Wonderful. His vision for America is as wide in scope as the Western landscape.

Trump is a construct of the mythic figure we've come to expect from viewing Western symbols, plots, and motifs. He reminds us of the William Faulkner line: "The past is never dead; it's not even past." The cowboy is indeed alive and well, even if he's a sign of the past. He comes in the improbable, astonishing form of Donald Trump. And he wants, or wanted, to win.

Teaching Humbly and without Malice

Russell Kirk has been dead now for over a quarter of a century, yet he remains the subject of student conferences across the United States and of the recent bestselling biography by Bradley J. Birzer. And, wonder of wonders, he's out with a new book.

Actually, it's a new edition of a 1957 book. *Russell Kirk's Concise Guide to Conservatism* was originally called *The Intelligent Woman's Guide to Conservatism*—a swipe at George Bernard Shaw's *Intelligent Woman's Guide to Socialism and Capitalism* (1928). This invigorating primer on the history and characteristics of American conservatism is of course suitable for female and male audiences alike, hence Regnery's revision of its title.

In 12 brisk chapters, Kirk addresses the following themes: the essence of conservatism, religious faith, conscience, individuality, family, community, just government, private property, power, education, permanence, and change. He concludes with the question: "What is the Republic?" His answer: "a commonwealth in which as many things as possible are left to private and local management; and in which the state, far from obliterating classes and voluntary associations and private rights, shelters and respects all these."[6]

Anyone familiar with Kirk will recognize in the opening chapter the "chief principles" of conservatism that in *The Portable Conservative Reader* (1982) and *The Conservative Mind* (1953) he condenses into six "canons." These involve a recognition of moral laws derived from God, a celebration of variety and diversity over coerced uniformity, the pursuit of justice, the protection of private property, a skepticism of power and centralization, a reverence for custom and tradition, and the rejection of utopianism or political programs predicated on a belief in the perfectibility of man.

At a time when conservatism stands in need of definition and direction, this book remains strikingly relevant. "[W]e need to undertake," Kirk admonishes his readers, "the conservative task of restoring in our generation an understanding of that freedom and that order which have expressed and encouraged our national genius."[7] Decades have passed since he penned these lines, yet the task remains.

Freedom and order aren't the only seemingly incompatible concepts that Kirk reconciles. He balances liberty with duty and charity and clarifies how conservatives can be both individualistic and communitarian at once. He explains why conservatives may embrace permanence and change without contradiction: Progress—"reasoned and temperate progress"[8]—develops "within the framework of tradition."[9] Moreover, "grand principles endure" while "their application . . . alters."[10] A conservative thus combines "a disposition to preserve" with "an ability to reform."[11]

Kirk targets, as well, the canard that conservatism is the greedy defense of capitalism, that the man or woman espousing conservative views is "a monster of selfishness" who is "morally impure, ruthless, and avaricious."[12] This caricature is still with us, though few thinking people would accept it as true anymore. After all, the Left dominates corporate America, Silicon Valley, Big Tech, Hollywood, higher education, and the mass media—with certain obvious exceptions. Commonsense conservatism, by contrast, flourishes in rural, agrarian America, in the heartland, in Southern states, in flyover territory, among blue-collar workers—not among the wealthy elites or rich CEOs. The idea that a small group of Randian, egomaniac "fat cats" controls American society is simply ridiculous. Were he alive today, Kirk wouldn't have needed to refute such silly stereotypes.

Kirk warns that "very powerful forces are at work to diminish the influence of the family among us, and even to destroy the family for all purposes except mere generation."[13] If he only knew. His treatment of the family seems dated by current standards—not because he embraced old-fashioned views but because the threats to the family that he predicted turned out to be greater than he could have imagined. He could not, for instance, foresee the redefinition of marriage that occurred through judicial opinions.

What, according to Kirk, is the purpose of formal education? Is it to equip students with the skills they need to excel in the workforce? To ensure that a democratic citizenry is sufficiently informed to refine and improve governing institutions? To bring about opportunities for historically marginalized or disenfranchised peoples? No. The purpose of education, he says, "is to develop the mental and moral faculties of the individual person, for the person's own sake."[14] One doesn't need to attend a university or earn a degree to fulfill this goal.

In our era of shouting pundits and social media sniping, Kirk's mild manner, Victorian prose, and relaxed tone are charming reminders that, even when the stakes are high, we can be civil and reasonable toward detractors. He eviscerates sacred cows—for example, the notion of equality that, if instantiated, would lead to a "boring" world "in which everyone was the same"[15]—cleverly yet with goodwill. The most egalitarian among us would entertain his controversial argument about equality because he does not provoke, incite, or inflame the passions. He teaches humbly and without malice.

Equality and diversity—ideals commonly associated with the Left—are, Kirk reminds us, incompatible to the extent that equality requires an eradication of the beautiful and remarkable distinctions that make each human being unique. The conservative is the true advocate of diversity, he points out, for it is the conservative who "desires to see the rich, invigorating, interesting variety of a society,"[16] not to "pull everyone down to a dead level of equality."[17] Our equality before God and the law admits of natural and inevitable inequalities between people. Any other form of equality is the *enemy* of diversity.

If you believe the chief end of inquiry is to cultivate "human dignity, human personality, and human happiness," and to understand and appreciate the "immortal contract between God and man,"[18] then you're a Kirkian conservative. All the weight of history, the entire strength of civilized society, depends on these for the preservation of freedom and order, which complement rather than oppose each other. In them, with God's grace and providence, we put our hope for the future.

Sex with the Dead

"Urge and urge and urge," Whitman intoned. "Always the procreant urge of the world." These words signal the life instinct, *eros*, that innate, libidinal drive for pleasure and survival.

Humans are compelled by life, attracted to it and aroused by it. The procreant urge motivates us to act, stimulates our choices and actions, shapes our personal identity. There's no subjectivity, no consciousness, absent coital awareness. The properties of life—what it means and how it appears to be alive—are conditions for their own perpetuation: to love life is to make it.

We are drawn to life, that inner bloom within the verdant body. We seek intimacy with the animated, energetic fertile parts, the warm, electric, pulsating body that's flowing with blood, propelled by agency and personality. The sensual qualities of living flesh stir up an intense and unconscious desire for the continuity of our kind.

We don't lust after death. We fear it. There's nothing sensual or stimulating about the deceased. Corpses seem gross, cold, repugnant, barren—material specimens for study and solemn contemplation, not potential sexual partners. A carcass or skeleton isn't a viable candidate for the type of emotional and psychic interaction that preludes reproductive exchange. The thought of desecrated corpses—let alone the erotic penetration of them—horrifies, disgusts, and disturbs us.

The body electric for which Whitman crooned and crazed, however, is enchanting and rapturous. It generates wild feelings and desires, which, when reciprocated, overtake reason and move the mind to fantasy. The mere sight, smell, taste, or touch of beautiful, excited flesh can occasion ardor and ecstasy: states of self-relinquishment. The possibility of sexual complementation, the radical equality of amorous transmission, the voluntary unification of eager bodies, the empowering sensation of penetration—these are the necessary, strange, wonderful stirrings that make life possible.

We hunger for the living body. Not a minute after it has been evacuated of life do we reject it, wince at it, withdraw desire from it, not because we have reached some deliberate, reasoned state of contemplation, but because of intuition and the primeval nature of our animal disposition. A deep, primitive, unconscious sense, not readily or immediately accessible to our subjective self, alerts our otherwise urging body to the fact that the inanimate object before us—the corpse—is not a thing to be desired, not a prospect for intercourse or sexual congress. The thing is reproductively useless; it's a copy of life, a leftover, a shell, a dummy, a facsimile; what was worthwhile and meaningful within and about it, what might have stimulated us moments before, is departed, gone, vacant, empty. We will not enter this thing, nor it us, with fertile organs and pleasure parts.

Yet people do. Herod, King of Judea, the story goes, preserved the remains of his second wife, Mariamne the Hasmonean, in honey so he could indulge himself with them for seven years. The Greek historian Herodutus claims in *The Histories* that wives of elite men were embalmed only after their carcasses began to rot to prevent embalmers from having a go at the still-beautiful bodies. This suggests there may be a class element to necrophilia—a sense of empowerment whereby the actor exercises authority over the dead body that he (it's almost always a he) lacks over the living. Camille Paglia agrees, saying, "Necrophilia was devised by the modern psyche to control and place sex after its sudden detachment from hierarchical systems."[19]

Grotesque tales of ancient necrophilia seem too remote in time and space to be verified or familiar. Paglia believes "necrophilia has gone out of fashion."[20] In the United States, however, in our own era, cases involving necrophilia exist, although they're rare, among the rarest of criminal matters. If necrophilia occurs, it's clandestine and, thus, probably more common than reports and the number of prosecutions suggest.

Two cases of necrophilia made national news in 2017. Joseph G. Martinez was arrested in Las Vegas and accused of penetrating the dead body of a 35-year-old homeless woman he purported to have met the night before. His arrest report indicates the woman had expired only two hours prior to his sexual contact with her.

Marcus D. Booker, a Georgia man, pleaded guilty to necrophilia, allegedly having initiated sexual contact, under the influence of crack-cocaine, with the corpse of a woman who had overdosed. Before she expired, the woman reportedly exchanged sexual favors for drugs; she and Booker were high and hallucinating. Her corpse was fresh when he inserted his penis into it.

Instances of sober sexual perpetrations against decaying victims of necrophilia are so uncommon that they're difficult to research.

Georgia criminalizes necrophilia specifically by statute.[21] In my home state of Alabama, and in most states, the code is silent as to this offense. Having sexual intercourse with a corpse is not expressly prohibited here. Criminal prosecution for such acts would likely occur under rape statutes on the logical ground that the inert and defiled victim—the dead person—did not consent to sexual intercourse. But *refusal* to consent generally is a necessary element of the crime of rape; therefore, a corpse cannot be raped, at least in theory, because it can't refuse consent. Rape is an offense against animated victims.

Rape is forever and inescapably reenacted in the mind of the victim, who, having to relive the violation, can never be restored fully to the emotional and psychic state he or she possessed before the rape occurred. A dead body suffers neither emotionally nor intellectually. It lacks awareness of its victimhood and has no memory of its injury. It feels no shame, remorse, anger, indignation, suffering—indeed, nothing at all. The true victims of necrophilia are those who knew the corpse before it was a corpse, when it was full of zest, personality, and spirit. The true victims are *alive.*

Whether the sexual penetration of a corpse constitutes rape, and whether it should be punished with the severity of rape, has never been settled perhaps because the states of mind affected by such illicit conduct belong to the living, not to the physical object targeted by the conduct. As inevitable corpses, we're all, in a sense, victims of necrophilia: we can imagine the sexual defilement of our eventual carcasses.

Proving the crime of necrophilia can be exceedingly difficult when allegations involve rape rather than, say, the violation of a body known for a sustained period to have been lifeless. How and from whom does law enforcement obtain express consent to examine a sexually desecrated corpse? Are only nearest relatives able to authorize the necessary forensic tests? What about the owners of property on which a dead body rests? Can they consent to an examination of the carcass on the grounds of property rights? How do prosecutors tell whether a ravished body was penetrated before or after death without the testimony of the deceased? Circumstantial or trace evidence of sexual intercourse doesn't tell us the exact moment of death. Therefore, postmortem forensic examinations and autopsies have minimal probative value for charges of necrophilia. Without witnesses, it's often impossible to say, in cases of rape-murder, which happened first, the rape or the murder.

So what happens in Alabama if one instantiates one's psychosexual fantasies on human remains?

The answer is unclear. Perhaps prosecution under the statute criminalizing abuse of a corpse. Another possibility would be to treat the human body as property and the offending act as trespass.

Libertarian philosopher Hans-Hermann Hoppe submits that humans have *a priori* property rights to their physical bodies.[22] It follows that one may dispose of one's body, or partition it, so long as the integrity of all property rights is respected.

But *is* one's body personal property? Locke predicates his theory of property on one's ownership of one's body. But to *possess* the body—to acquire ownership rights over it—one does not, in the Lockean sense, mix one's labor with it. The body is God-granted, the product of Nature. It's not severable in the sense of real property: you can only parcel so many pieces of it before you die. Sell your heart and lungs, and you're done. Forever. If you lose ownership in yourself, you've lost yourself (and your *self*).

A longstanding school of thought holds that the body of a child is the property of the child's parents, not of the child. On this view, property rights to the body aren't automatic or pre-political. How could they be if infants lack the requisite capacity to reason as an informed adult or to discern what acts are necessary for survival?

Another problem with treating one's body as personal property is that, when it expires, when death sets in, there's no consciousness remaining therein to exercise agency or mobilize the corporeal form; thus, whatever it was about the body that made it an asset is now a burden. Most of the physical features of the "property" are still there. What's missing is the resident life.

Although ownership rights to the body may in theory pass to heirs or issue, only trouble and pain, not worth or benefit, inhere in the transfer. If the body *is* property, it has little if any value upon death except in the service of scientific experiment or as food for the cannibal. Such value inures, not to the benefit of the person or spirit who inhabited the body, but to others necessarily alienated from the body, the nonresidents you might call them because they live elsewhere: within their own bodies.

Treating one's body as property thus raises perplexing concerns about ontology and metaphysics: Who am *I*? What am *I*? Where am *I*? What is my relationship to the muscular and skeletal frame that hosts me until I perish before it does?

The "Me Myself," as Whitman called it, cannot exist in a corpse, where there's no phenomenal, flesh-and-blood, post-mortem "me" or "you" remaining, at least not that we know of.

"Even the corpse has its own beauty," Emerson effused in a characteristically superlative moment. He may have been right, but his meaning doesn't seem sexual or erotic. That's not true of other writers. Paglia calls Emily Dickinson "a Decadent voyeur" whose "corpse poems are specimens of sexual objectification."[23] "She is that rarity," Paglia says, "a female necrophiliac and sexual fetishist."[24] Paglia also labels Keats's "Isabella, or the Pot of Basil" a "necrophiliac" poem.[25]

Necrophilia, however rare in the concrete world, has captivated writers of imaginative literature from Hrotsvitha of Gandersheim to Cormac McCarthy. It's the improbable source of aesthetic expression, inexplicably mythopoetic in its perverted powers, signaling archetypally the sexualized vampire, except in reverse: in place of the copulating cadaver, the living dead, is the depraved predator, ravenous for the lifeless.

Virginia Woolf and T. S. Eliot mention "nekrophily" or "necrophily." George Orwell said that necrophilia was Salvador Dalí's most notable characteristic, a statement with awkward resonance since a Spanish judge recently ordered the exhumation of Dalí's remains for a paternity test after a tarot-card reader claimed to be his illegitimate daughter. (The test proved otherwise.)

Whether Poe's "Annabel Lee" involved necrophilic fantasizing is open to debate. Poe is a curious case. Mark Winchell named him "the poet laureate of necrophilia."[26] Winchell examined him through the prism of Leslie Fiedler, who attributed "necrophiliac titillation" to Poe and Henry James on account of their identification of "the immaculate virgin with the girl dying or dead."[27] Fielder claimed that James was haunted by "the necrophilia that has always so oddly been an essential part of American romance."[28] He believed Poe inspired Vladimir Nabokov, whose *Lolita*, told as the mad confession of Humbert Humbert, renders not only necrophilia but pedophilia and child murder.

Humbert cites Poe as an aesthetic predecessor to excuse or justify his homicidal pathology. His first love, in fact, was named Annabel Leigh. His affection for her may have intensified *after* her untimely death. "In *Lolita*," submits Lucy B. Maddox, "Nabokov exploits the psychological implications of necrophilia, but without taking any of them literally."[29] She adds that "Humbert's version of necrophilia—that is, his need to verify a lover's death before he can speak without irony of his erotic desire for that lover—becomes a metaphor for a complex set of responses to the living, in which desire, guilt, and aesthetic sensibility become inextricably tangled."[30]

The female virgin is a literary type. Standards of beauty change from time to time and place to place, but evocations of beautiful young women—nymphs when they're deified—seem to be acknowledged and understood across traditions and cultures, at least if literary types are sufficient indication.

The elderly are nearer to death than youth; they betoken decay and deterioration. The female virgin, the literary type, besides being youthful and radiant *with* life, is also the potential bearer *of* life, the embodiment of fertility and potentiality. This figure isn't the fair maiden or the sensual temptress, which are more specific archetypes of courtly Romanticism and Christian convention, respectively. It's rather the portrait of the blooming female whose powers over men are deep and magical but not yet known to her. Think of the Naiads, not of Beatrice, the poisonous daughter of Rappaccini.

This stock character, reminiscent of nubile, sylvan goddesses, is so deeply embedded in literary and mythopoetic convention that we fail to recognize her as a standard against which deviancy is measured. Its opposite, in fact, is the rotting corpse, which the elderly are closer to becoming than she.

The prefix *necro* is Greek for "death" (*nekros*); the suffix *philia* means "love" in the sense of "friendship" or "affection" against other forms of love: *storge* (familial or instinctual love), *agape* (charitable or benevolent love, such as God feels toward humankind), and *eros* (romantic or passionate love). The *OED* states that the term *necrophilia* originated in psychology and is derived from the German *Nekrophilie*.

Such naming wouldn't exist if there weren't a thing to be named. The fact that necrophilia falls within a taxonomy suggests it has been around a long time, perhaps always.

But *how*? *How* could anyone become a necrophiliac? The mere thought of necrophilia induces nausea, fright, and loathing. One theory is that those who regularly handle corpses become so desensitized to death that they masturbate with corpses, not to gratify some decadent fetish but simply to climax with something not themselves, something remotely or formerly "human." Imagine a middle-aged loner who suffers from low self-esteem and is unable to attract a sexual partner. Say he finds work as an undertaker, gravedigger, or hospital orderly. He may, in time, aided by his spatial and social alienation, begin petting the feminine parts on dead bodies that, on living bodies, elude him. He thereby transitions from isolated misfit to moral monster.

Will his crime be discovered? Is there legal recourse or retribution to seek from him? Do the dead have rights to protect? It's hard to make an ethical case for ravaging a cadaver for organs or bones to be sold on market without the consent of the person, *the soul*, who once inhabited that body. But *why*? Is it only because prohibitions on such behavior protect and console the living?

Those of us who fear necrophilia do so because it involves what seem to us to be morbidly unnatural and deviant stimuli. We're appalled by its shocking power to facilitate arousal.

The horror of defying our nature, of rejecting those qualities that make us human, including life itself, always lurks, I think, somewhere in the inner recesses of reasonable minds. Those who're reflective enough rigorously to contemplate disturbing mental conditions dread the upsetting possibility that anyone is capable of degenerative pleasures absent the civilizing effects of societal norms. Disgust with necrophilia, moreover, has something to do with universal anxieties about death. Contemplating necrophilia is uncomfortable because it unites the life and death instincts that reason holds as mutually exclusive. Sexual stimulation and the drive for life are incompatible with the cessation of life. Yet the necrophiliac holds these tensions together, managing to act when conflicting impulses would, one presumes, inhibit action.

We cope with the exasperating irreversibility of a loved one's death by talking about afterlife and instituting rituals (funerals, eulogies, burials, and so on) to renew order and purpose to the disorienting reality that the deceased, or rather the personality which existed within the once-living body, is no longer concretely present. We alleviate fears of death by formalizing them into ceremony. Then we bury the dead and try to move on with life.

146

Most of us. Some, apparently, have sex with cadavers. Why? Answers to that question, whatever they are, must be perturbing. Necrophilia recalls not the abject submission or practiced humility of the infatuated lover elevating his beloved on a pedestal. There's nothing courtly or romantic about it. It could be that the necrophiliac is attracted, not to the corpse itself and whatever beauty it might retain, but to a grotesque ritual of domination and perversion. An unhealthy fetish for sexual empowerment and control are more widespread, surely, than necrophilia, but could the widespread cultural fetishizing of them lead to this troubling sexual abomination, namely sex with dead bodies?

Rituals of sexual conquest, encoded in discourse, understandable to the ancients who used them to exact punishments for "crimes of the flesh," are not readily explicable in current vocabularies; they're alien to our modern sensibilities, offensive to our progressive minds. Sure, there are Christian Greys, fictional and real, celebrating, in their own way, the obscene darkness of Marquis de Sade. Sadomasochism, for example, appears to have myriad champions and adherents.

Yet domination and its correlative inverse, subordination, are improbable as ideals. Nor do they feature order or ceremony to formalize and aestheticize their violent tendencies. The concept of absolute domination is neither titillating nor tempting but, to me, bothersome. Eroticism, on the other hand, requires consent and mutuality to be materially realized. It's not about intolerable coercion or control. It's a coming together, a unification that ardently perfects the mental and physical desires of two otherwise rationally autonomous agents. The beauty of it is the beauty of life itself, the reason we go on. It's the sprout that proves Whitman correct: all goes onward and outward. There really is no death.

The law ought to recognize that.

A law review article that, after 20 years, remains, in many respects, current, reduces criminal liability for necrophilia to three categories: (1) "judicial interpretation of rape and sodomy statutes to include intercourse with dead bodies"; (2) "judicial interpretation of abuse of corpse statutes to include intercourse with dead bodies"; and (3) "express statutory bans on intercourse with dead bodies."[31] The fact that the third category contains a *rare* form of liability raises questions about why most states fail or refuse to criminalize necrophilia by name. Nor does federal law prohibit necrophilia. Is necrophilia an unspeakable crime, *the* unspeakable crime, literally an offense that cannot be named or described in official, public discourse? Has the existence of necrophilia been collectively repressed and ignored, our aversion to it resulting in its omission from most penal codes?

Perhaps. And perhaps that's why descriptions or representations of necrophilia are seemingly more common in literary texts than in legal codes. There's something fantastic about necrophilia, something horrible and horrifying about the state of mind that enables it, maybe even something about the human psyche that relegates necrophilia to the imagined and imaginary, keeping it off the official records, as it were. The fear and terror evoked by necrophilia, the refusal of cultures to accept it as permissible, suggest that normativity governs sexual relations, that certain sex acts are out of bounds, obnoxious to sound minds and intolerable in decent society.

Lines must be drawn somewhere, but, in this context, the law isn't drawing them, at least not as often as you'd expect. If every state in the United States criminalized necrophilia by name, would it make a difference? Would there be more prosecutions for such offenders?

The answer is probably no. And that's *another* reason to fear.

Flourishing and Synthesis

That Edward W. Younkins is well and widely read is apparent in light of the diverse, mutually illuminating subjects he brings together in *Flourishing and Happiness in a Free Society*, a short but impressive book. These include Aristotle, Ayn Rand, and the Austrian economists Carl Menger, Ludwig von Mises, and Murray Rothbard. Such thinkers, and the schools they represent, are participatory, not wholly separate or distinct, in their celebration of capitalism. Each thinker has his or her own colorful methodologies and idiosyncrasies; but the differences among them are often overstated and under-analyzed, or treated with such closed-minded certainty that insistences on ideological purity preclude searches for significant commonalities.

The ideas championed by these thinkers are not only reconcilable, Younkins suggests, but complementary and profoundly, sometimes intimately, connected. "By combining and synthesizing elements found in Aristotle's writings, Austrian Economics, Ayn Rand's philosophy of Objectivism, and in the writings of neo-Aristotelian classical liberal philosophers of human flourishing," Younkins explains, "we have the potential to reframe the argument for a free society into a consistent reality-based whole whose integrated sum of knowledge and explanatory power is greater than the sum of its parts."[32] In an era of groupthink and infighting among those who profess individualism and liberty, reason and freethinking, the clarification of intersections between various lines of individualist thought is happy indeed. It's refreshing to read a book that aims to build rather than demolish, to coordinate rather than exclude. Differences of opinion are important, and there are certain issues on which reasonably and rationally minded people—Aristotelians, Objectivists, and Austrian economists included—will disagree. But differences of opinion are not all that matter.

Truth matters; knowledge matters; the future matters. To the extent that this book integrates the shared ideas and vocabularies of different thinkers, it, too, matters. It is, after all, through shared ideas and vocabularies, arrived at independently, over time, in disparate times and places, that individuals glean and confirm truth. Younkins seeks, to this end, nothing less than a reevaluation of existing paradigms in pursuit of perennial themes reflecting and describing truth. His is a work of synergy, fusion, and revivification.

Flourishing and Happiness in a Free Society opens with a "Preface" and an "Introduction" written by Younkins. These sections, while noteworthy, merely lay the foundation for what is to come. They contain no footnotes, but provide extensive recommended reading lists and summarize unifying premises among the book's principal foci: Aristotle, Rand, Menger, Mises, and Rothbard. In sweeping strokes, Younkins explains that later thinkers depended upon and revised earlier thinkers—that Rand, Menger, and Mises, for instance, borrowed from Aristotle even as they modified and reworked Aristotle. In conjunction with the "Conclusion," which recapitulates the most important theses and arguments of the book, these sections "bookend," as it were, the more substantive, detailed, and thorough chapters.

Each of these chapters transitions from a thesis to a summary of the schools of thought that Younkins shows are compatible and, finally, to the syntheses that describe this compatibility in detail. In the first two chapters, Younkins condenses his syntheses beneath the heading "Toward an Integrated Framework." These represent what Younkins calls "paradigms." Lest a reader misunderstand him, Younkins graphs these paradigms in flowcharts that will assist not only students struggling to reduce Younkins's arguments to digestible talking-points, but also experts who tend to over-scrutinize details and consequently fail to see the forest for the trees. I, for one, can see how a dedicated scholar, caught up in Younkins's attempt to reconcile the value theories of Menger, Mises, and Rand, might miss the importance of this reconciliation to the praxeological methods of Rothbard, which harmonize with Randian thinking to the extent that they concern "the nature of man and the world, natural law, natural rights, and a rational ethics based on human nature and discovered through reason";[33] that they agree "that the purpose of political philosophy and ethics is the promotion of productive human life on earth";[34] that they determine "the proper rules for a rational society by using reason to examine the nature of human life and the world and by employing logical deductions to ascertain what these natures suggest";[35] and that they agree "on the volitional nature of rational human consciousness."[36]

It's not possible in a short review to spell out each mark of solidarity or departure among Younkins's subjects, so let me cite an example from the "Introduction." Here Younkins lists elements of thought that his subjects have in common and that make up his synthesizing paradigm: "(1) an objective, realistic, natural-law oriented metaphysics; (2) a natural rights theory based on the nature of man and the world; (3) an objective epistemology which describes essences or concepts as epistemologically contextual and relational rather than as metaphysical; (4) a biocentric theory of value; (5) praxeology as a tool for understanding how people cooperate and compete and for deducing universal principles of economics; and (6) an ethic of human flourishing based on reason, free will, and individuality."[37]

My only complaint with a list like this—and like other such lists in the book—is that it is so general as to lose its force. Although the elements in the list signify an underlying pattern, they are so vague, broad, and fluctuant that they could include schools of thought that clearly do not comport with the values and theories of Aristotelians, Austrians, or Objectivists. For instance, neoconservatism would seem to rely on an "objective, realistic, natural-law-oriented metaphysics," just as it would seem to rely on a "natural rights theory based on the nature of man and the world."

It's crucial to note, then, that the elements Younkins lists cannot be taken in isolation but must be viewed in relation to the other elements. The elements, though different, work in concert; they are interactive, combining and cooperating. It bears noting, too, that they do not add up to a "master science" or "cure-all" for human organization. Rather, they provide the intellectual fodder necessary for ideas to take root and blossom. Younkins cultivates a consistent, ordered application of multiple strands of theory, but he does not champion a top-down, one-size-fits-all political program based on the ideas he brings together. As he himself says, in plainly "evangelical" terms,

> We must work in and through other people in order to get them excited about and dedicated to furthering the prospects of a free society. We have tremendous opportunities because each of us simultaneously participates in numerous associations with others. We can master and clearly present abstract systematic free-market theory in a readily accessible manner, advocate specific measures moving America in the right direction, discern ways in our daily lives in which we can practice the freedom philosophy, and create attention-creating devices such as slogans through which we can attract potential new believers. We must each use our rationality to select the actions that will consistently and constantly bring us toward the future free society in which we would want to live.[38]

When Objectivists are asked whom they admire among economists, they usually name Mises and reference *Human Action*. The objections and qualifications that follow this endorsement, however, specify that Mises's economic work is more appealing than his philosophy. Objectivists find Mises's philosophy to be too pragmatic and perhaps epistemologically deficient; they nevertheless endorse his economics—a tribute they would not extend to Hayek, whom Rand deplored. Despite that, Objectivists and Austrians have been longstanding supporters of capitalism, and the Austrian school has served as an economic surrogate (of sorts) for Objectivists, though never without qualification. *Flourishing and Happiness in a Free Society* touches upon but doesn't belabor major differences of opinion because Younkins seeks to "develop a powerful, reality-based argument for a free society in which individuals have the opportunity to flourish and to be happy."[39] He seeks, in short, to "outline the essentials of a worldview leaving it to philosophers and economists to fill in the details and to evaluate, critique, revise, refine, and extend [his] systematic understanding."[40]

I'm surprised, to some degree, that more people haven't meticulously and systematically expounded upon the correlations and congruities within and between the schools of thought that Younkins treats with vigor. I know several individuals who seem, at least in principle, to adhere to the teachings of Objectivism and Austrian economics simultaneously. These individuals, despite conflicts, still think of the schools as paired. These individuals, moreover, are not always able to convey why they think this way, but perhaps what they have in mind involves the interrelations that Younkins describes. Perhaps these individuals can support Objectivism and Austrian economics at once because on some sublimated level, they consider the two schools as joined in modus and method. If that's the case, then Younkins ought to be celebrated for expressing what scholars have already sensed: that the constituent parts of Aristotelianism, Austrian Economics, and Objectivism are generative and instructive when taken together.

Debunking the Demographers

Demography can be dull; to call it unimaginative would be to give it too much credit. But then there is Jonathan V. Last, who upends the demographic genre with *What to Expect When No One's Expecting*, a work of dark humor that undertakes social science with honesty, wit, and razzle-dazzle statistics. One of the surprising joys of reading him entails unlearning: much of what you know about population, he reveals, just isn't so.

The habits of taking something for granted, of supposing it true without proof, are called, in the vernacular, "assumptions," and it is always thrilling to discover and correct them. Last generates this thrill so often that he'll cause you to question the convictions and expectations of over a generation of demographers: No, the people of the world are not multiplying beyond excess; we aren't becoming overcrowded; we will not run out of food; we won't even run out of jobs. On the contrary, we are running out of people, if anything.

And this is bad, Last submits, because the proximate consequences of shrinking populations are war, disease, and economic stagnation. "[S]ub-replacement fertility rates," he says, "eventually lead to a shrinking of population—and throughout human history, declining populations have always followed or been followed by Very Bad Things."[41] He adds that "these grim tidings from history may be in our future, since population contraction is where most of the world is headed."[42] He doesn't provide much in the way of historical examples except to reference the Dark Ages and quote from Adam Smith, but his point is well taken.

A fertility rate of 2.1 is necessary for population numbers to remain steady. The American fertility rate is at 1.93. The rates for other industrialized countries, especially in Europe, are lower. Even the so-called Third World is reproducing at lower rates than before. As Last explains, "In 1979, the world's fertility rate was 6.0; today it's 2.52. From a current population of 6.9 billion, the United Nations and others predict that world population will peak somewhere between 10 billion and 12 billion in the next 85 years and then begin the long, inexorable process of shrinking back down."[43] Thomas Friedman would have been better off, it seems, saying that the world was "shrinking," not flat.

In America, Hispanic women are having the most babies, followed by African American women. American whites are having the fewest babies. The ethnic composition of America is bound to change over the next generations, but even minority populations are having fewer children. Last claims that the overall decline is due to America's "One-Child Policy," which is unofficial, unlike the Chinese One-Child Policy, which is official. He puts it this way: "As a result of One-Child, the fertility rate in China is roughly 1.54. In America, the fertility rate for white, college-educated women—we'll use them because they serve as a fair proxy for our middle class—is 1.6. In other words, America has created its very own One-Child Policy. It's soft and unintentional, the result of accidents of history and thousands of little choices. But it has been just as effective."[44]

America's One-Child Policy is a cultural symptom, not a direct government mandate. I say "direct" because certain government mandates—seat belt and car seat laws, for instance—have affected population numbers, and other factors for declining birth rates are indirectly related to government policies. Such factors include birth control and abortion, women in the workforce, financial burdens brought on by Social Security and Medicare, and the astronomical costs of raising children. Not only is there a "baby industry" bubble, reflected by the high prices of baby furniture, clothes, accessories, and toys, there is also a tuition bubble as education costs have escalated at all levels from preschool to college.

Last estimates that the costs of raising a single child in America exceed, on average, $1.1 million. Despite the enormous financial sacrifices parents have made, their children—there was a time when college students were "adults," but Last includes them in the category of "children"—nevertheless fritter away their twenties by binge-drinking, hooking up, smoking dope, borrowing massive federal loans to finance their lavish lifestyles, voting Democratic, cohabiting, and, in some ironic cases, hating their parents for obsessing over money.

American households today have more pets than children. Not that there is anything wrong with pets; it's just that pet culture has displaced the culture and recreation of traditional families. There are restaurants and hotels for dogs and cats. If you want your pet groomed, you can take her to a beauty salon to get her a perm or a manicure. Gentrified parks have sprung up for dog owners, who detest any child trying to use the doggy playground, which, after all, was not made for kids. A recent bill before Congress contemplated tax breaks for—get this—pet-care expenses. We have, it seems, begun to disregard the important theological, philosophical, and scientific distinctions between humans and animals, and the result has been to reduce our population and degrade our concept of the family unit.

The fuss in the 1960s and 1970s was all about how population was exploding and how government could not keep up. It appeared everyone was worried that the planet was at maximum capacity with no sign that humans were reducing their reproduction rates. Call it divine plan or intervention, evolution, spontaneous order, or whatever—there appears to be a regulating power beyond our control that has reined us back in and slowed us down. We just aren't making babies like we used to.

Last views decreasing population not so much as a crisis, but as something to be deeply concerned about. Last is in favor of facts, and too often our cultural elites have ignored facts about population and sustainable societies in favor of an ideology of individual self-fulfillment and liberation. It can be very pleasant, for some, to live at the end of a cultural era; but it is nevertheless an end. Last is concerned that we fully understand the implications of what we as a culture have done, and not believe progress in one field means progress in all others. Yes, education, for example, is a good, and it is also good that more people now have access to it. But that also has meant more time is spent being educated than creating families, and that has negative consequences for a society that should be recognized along with the good consequences.

Aristotle, that sober champion of moderation, indicated in *The Politics* that the population of a polis should not be so big or small that a government cannot carry out civic functions with ease and utility. All citizens, he said, should know each other personally. A polis of this scale is nothing like the Leviathan we have today. "The greatest surveyable number required for achieving a life of self-sufficiency"—that is how Aristotle describes the optimum standard of population. Perhaps we're moving in the right direction after all. Although in light of Last's observations about culture—the pet idolatry, abortions on demand, cohabitations, costs of raising children, delayed maturity, and so on and so forth—we seem to be moving in that direction for unhealthy and in many cases immoral reasons.

If Aristotle is wrong about the optimum standard of population, then surely we are getting what we deserve and suffering the consequences of bad decisions, unethical policies, and narcissistic attitudes. But even if he is right, as I believe he is, then it is too late for us to enjoy the pleasures and comforts of a smaller, more fitting scale of human life, for an optimum society must be virtuous, not just moderate in size, and virtuous we are not.

Ideas Make Us Rich

If it's true that Wayne Booth inspired Deirdre McCloskey's interest in the study of rhetoric, then it's also true—happily, in my view—that McCloskey has refused to mimic Booth's programmatic, formulaic methods and boorish insistence on prosaic succinctness. *Bourgeois Equality* is McCloskey's third volume in a monumental trilogy that began with *The Bourgeois Virtues* (2006) and *Bourgeois Dignity* (2010), each published by the University of Chicago Press. The last of these volumes is a Big Book, alike in kind but not in theme to Jacques Barzun's *From Dawn to Decadence* (2000), Camille

Paglia's *Sexual Personae* (1990), or Herald Berman's *Law and Revolution* (1983) and *Law and Revolution II* (2006). It is meandering and personal, blending scholarship with an essayistic style that recalls Montaigne or Emerson.

McCloskey's elastic arguments are shaped by informal narrative and enlivened by her plain and playful voice. At times humorous, rambling, and deliberately erratic, she gives the distinct impression that she is simply telling a story, one that happens to validate a thesis. She's having fun. Imagine Phillip Lopate articulating economic history. McCloskey is, in this regard, a latter-day Edward Gibbon, adopting a mode and persona that's currently unfashionable among mainstream historians, except that she's more lighthearted than Gibbon, and unashamedly optimistic.

Writing with an air of confidence, McCloskey submits, contra Thomas Piketty, that ideas and ideology—not capital accumulation or material resources—have caused widespread economic development. Since 1800, worldwide material wealth has increased and proliferated; the quality of life in poor countries has risen—even if it remains unequal to that of more prosperous countries—and the typical human being now enjoys access to the food, goods, services, medicine, and healthcare that, in earlier centuries, were available to only a select few in the richest parts of the globe. The transition from poverty to wealth was occasioned by shifting rhetoric that reflected an emerging ethical consensus. The rhetorical-ethical change involved people's "attitudes toward other humans,"[45] namely, the recognition of shared experience and "sympathy," as Adam Smith stated in *The Theory of Moral Sentiments*. Attributing human progress to ideas enables McCloskey to advocate the norms and principles that facilitated economic growth and social improvement (e.g., class mobility and fluidity) while generating extensive prosperity. Thus, her project is at once scholarly and tendentious: a study of the conditions and principles that, in turn, she promotes.

She argues that commercialism flourished in the 18th century under the influence of ideas—such as "human equality of liberty in law and of dignity and esteem"[46]— that were packaged in memorable rhetoric and aesthetics. "Not matter, mainly, but ideas"[47] caused the Great Enrichment. In other words, "[t]he original and sustaining causes of the modern world [...] were ethical, not material,"[48] and they included "the new and liberal economic idea of liberty for ordinary people and the new and democratic social idea of dignity for them."[49] This thesis about liberty and dignity is clear and unmistakable if only because it is repetitive. McCloskey has a habit of reminding readers—in case you missed her point the first, second, or fifty-seventh time around—that the causes of the Industrial Revolution and the Great Enrichment were ideas, not "narrowly economic or political or legal changes."[50] She maintains, to this end, that the Scottish Enlightenment succeeded in combining the concepts of liberty and dignity into a desirable form of equality—not equality of outcomes, of course, but of opportunity and treatment under the law. And the Scottish model, to her mind, stands in contradistinction to the French example of centralized, top-down codification, command, planning, and design.

A perennial villain lurks in the pages of her history: the "clerisy," which is an "appendage of the bourgeoisie"[51] and often dubbed "the elite" in regular parlance. McCloskey calls the clerisy "the sons of bourgeois fathers"[52] and "neo-aristocratic."[53] The clerisy includes those "artists, intellectuals, journalists, professionals, and bureaucrats" who resent "the commercial and bettering bourgeoisie."[54] The clerisy seeks, in different ways at different times, to extinguish unfettered competition with exclusive, illiberal, irrevocable grants and privileges that are odious to free society and offensive to the rights of average consumers. "Early on," says McCloskey, referring to the period in Europe after the revolutionary year 1848, "the clerisy began to declare that ordinary people are misled in trading, and so require expert protection and supervision."[55] The clerisy since then has been characterized by paternalism and a sense of superiority.

Because the clerisy is shapeshifting, assuming various forms from time to time and place to place, it's a tough concept to pin down. The word "clerisy" does not appear in the book's index to permit further scrutiny. By contrast, McCloskey's general arguments are easy to follow because the book is separated into parts with questions as their titles; subparts consisting of one-sentence headings answer those questions.

In a massive tour de force such as this, readers are bound to take issue with certain interpretive claims. Historians will find McCloskey's summaries to be too breezy. Even libertarians will accuse her of overlooking manifest wrongs that occurred during the periods she surveys. My complaints are few but severe. For instance, McCloskey is, I believe, either careless or mistaken to announce that, during the 19th and early 20th century, "under the influence of a version of science," in a territory that's never specifically identified, "the right seized upon social Darwinism and eugenics to devalue the liberty and dignity of ordinary people, and to elevate the nation's mission above the mere individual person, recommending, for example, colonialism and compulsory sterilization and the cleansing power of war."[56]

Let's hope that it's innocent negligence rather than willful distortion that underlies this odd, unqualified, categorical assertion. Adam Cohen's *Imbeciles* (2016) and Thomas C. Leonard's *Illiberal Reformers* (2016) describe how, in the United States, social Darwinism and eugenics were adopted primarily, though not exclusively, by the Left, not the Right. These recent books come on the heels of several scholarly treatments of this subject: Thomas M. Shapiro's *Population Control Politics* (1985), Philip R. Reilly's *The Surgical Solution* (1991), Joel Braslow's *Mental Ills and Bodily Cures* (1997), Wendy Kline's *Building a Better Race* (2001), Stefan Kuhl's *The Nazi Connection* (2002), Nancy Ordover's *American Eugenics* (2003), Christine Rosen's *Preaching Eugenics* (2004), Christina Cogdell's *Eugenic Design* (2004), Gregory Michael Dorr's *Segregation's Science* (2008), Paul A. Lombardo's edition *A Century of Eugenics in America* (2011), and Alexander Minna Stern's *Eugenic Nation* (2016). These represent only a small sampling.

Is McCloskey unaware of these texts? Probably not: she reviewed Leonard's book for Reason, although she did so after her own book reached press. At any rate, would she have us believe that Emma Goldman, George Bernard Shaw, Eugene Debs, Marie Stopes, Margaret Sanger, John Maynard Keynes, Lester Ward, and W. E. B. Du Bois were eugenicist agitators for the political Right? If so, she should supply her definition of "Right," since it would go against commonly accepted meanings. On the matter of colonialism and war, self-identified members of the Old Right such as Albert Jay Nock, John Flynn, and Senator Robert Taft advocated precisely the opposite of what McCloskey characterizes as "Right." These men opposed, among other things, military interventionism and adventurism. The trouble is that McCloskey's muddying of the signifiers "Left" and "Right" comes so early in the book—in the "Exordium"— that readers may lose trust in her, question her credibility, and begin to suspect the labels and arguments in her later chapters.

Other undefined terms only make matters worse, ensuring that Mc-Closkey will alienate many academics, who, as a class, are already inclined to reject her libertarian premises. She throws around the term "Romanticism" as if its referent were eminently clear and uncontested: "a conservative and Romantic vision";[57] "science fiction and horror fiction [are] ... offshoots of Romanticism";[58] "[Jane Austen] is not a Romantic novelist ... [because] [s]he does not take Art as a model for life, and does not elevate the Artist to a lonely pinnacle of heroism, or worship of the Middle Ages, or adopt any of the other, antibourgeois themes of Novalis, [Franz] Brentano, Sir Walter Scott, and later Romantics";[59] "Romanticism around 1800 revived talk of hope and faith and a love for Art or Nature or the Revolution as a necessary transcendent in people's lives";[60] "Romantic candor";[61] "the late eighteenth-century Romantic literary critics in England had no idea what John Milton was on about [sic], because they had set aside the rigorously Calvinist theology that structured his poetry";[62] "the nationalist tradition of Romantic writing of history";[63] "Romantic ... hostilities to ... democratic rhetoric";[64] "[i]n the eighteenth century ... the idea of autonomy triumphed, at any rate among the progressive clerisy, and then became a leading Romantic idea, á la Victor Hugo";[65] and "the Romantic conservative Thomas Carlyle."[66]

To allege that the clerisy was "thrilled by the Romantic radicalism of books like *Mein Kampf* or *What Is to Be Done*"[67] is also recklessly to associate the philosophies of, say, Keats or Coleridge or Wordsworth with the exterminatory fantasies of Hitler and Lenin. McCloskey might have guarded against this misleading conflation by distinguishing German idealism or contextualizing Hegel or by being more vigilant with diction and definition. Her loose language will leave some experts (I do not profess to be one) scratching or shaking their heads and, more problematic, some non-experts with misconceptions and misplaced targets of enmity. One imagines the overeager and well-meaning undergraduate, having read *Bourgeois Equality*, setting out to demonize William Blake or destroy the reputation of Percy Shelly, about whom Paul Cantor has written judiciously. Wouldn't originality, imagination, creativity, and individualism—widely accepted markers of Romanticism—appeal to McCloskey? Yet her unconditionally derogatory treatment of Romanticism—which she portrays as a fixed, monolithic, self-evident thing—undermines aspects of that fluctuating movement, period, style, culture, and attitude that are, or seem to be, consistent with her Weltanschauung.

But I protest too much. These complaints should not diminish what McCloskey has accomplished. Would that we had more grand studies that mapped ideas and traced influences across cultures, communities, and eras. McCloskey takes the long view, as we all should. Her focus on rhetoric is crucial to the future of liberty if, given the technological advances we have made, the "work we do will be more and more about decisions and persuading others to agree, changing minds, and less and less about implementation by hand."[68] Equally significant is her embrace of humanomics—defined as "the story [of] a complete human being, with her ethics and language and upbringing"[69]—which materializes in casual references to Henrik Ibsen's plays, challenges to the depiction of John Milton "as a lonely poet in a garret writing merely to the starry heavens,"[70] analyses of Jane Austen's novels, and portrayals of Elizabethan England. Her historical and narrative arc enables us to contextualize our own moment, with all of its troubles and possibilities.

Best of all, her book is inspiring and exhilarating and brimming with rousing imperatives and moving calls to action. "Let us, then," she says at one point, "not reject the blessings of economic growth on account of planning or pessimism, the busybody if well-intentioned rationalism of some voices of the French Enlightenment or the adolescent if charming doubts of some voices of the German Romantic movement, fashionable though both attitudes have long been among the clerisy. As rational optimists, let us celebrate the Great Enrichment, and the rhetorical changes in freer societies that caused it."[71] At another point she encourages her audience to guard against "both cynicism and utopianism,"[72] and elsewhere to heed "trade-tested cooperation, competition, and conservation in the right mix."[73] These little nudges lend her credibility insofar as they reveal her true colors, as it were, and demonstrate that she is not attempting—as is the academic wont—to hide her prejudices and conceal her beliefs behind pretended objectivities.

Poverty is relative and, hence, permanent and ineradicable, despite McCloskey's claim that we can "end poverty."[74] If, tomorrow, we woke up and the wealth of each living person were magically to multiply twentyfold—even fiftyfold—there would still be people at the bottom. The quality of life at the bottom, however, would be vastly improved. The current manifestation of global poverty shows how far we as a species have advanced in the last few centuries. McCloskey is right: We should pursue the ideas that accelerated and achieved human flourishing, that demonstrably brought people out of distress and destitution. Hard sciences and mathematical models are insufficient in themselves to convey the magnitude and splendor of these ideas and their accomplishments. Hence we should welcome and produce more books like McCloskey's that undertake a "rhetorical-ethical Revaluation" to both examine and celebrate "a society of open inquiry," one which not only "depends on rhetoric in its politics and in its science and in its economy," but which also yields intellectual creativity and political freedom.[75] In McCloskey's approach, economics and the humanities are not mutually exclusive; rather, they are mutually illuminating and, in fact, indispensably and inextricably tied. An economics that forsakes the dignity of the human person and his capacity for creativity and aesthetics does so at its own peril and to its own disgrace. All economics is, at its core, humanomics. We could do without the latter term if we understood the former.

The Dirty Business of Government Trash Collection

It's been many years since *The Wall Street Journal* profiled the Mises Institute and claimed that Auburn was an ideal spot for studying libertarian ideas and the Austrian tradition. I don't know how much has changed since then, but I arrived in Auburn expecting a free-market sanctuary, a veritable haven where the ideas of Menger and Mises and Hayek were in the air and imbibed by the majority of people who weren't members of the Auburn faculty, and even by some who were.

Once settled in Auburn, I realized I'd been quixotic and naïve. Even before national media picked up on a recent story about an officer who spoke out against his department's ticket and arrest quotas, even before the city of Auburn squeezed out Uber with severe licensing regulations, even before Mark Thornton highlighted the Skyscraper Curse in town, there was the matter of my trash bin.

I bought my house from a relocation company, the previous owner having been assigned a new position in another city. He was, this owner, in a hurry to move. Before he left town, he and his family rolled their trash bin to the side of the home, away from the street, where the garbage collector refused to retrieve it. They had stuffed the bin with garbage: food, paper, cardboard boxes, dirty diapers, and other junk. There was so much trash in the bin that the lid wouldn't fully close. It looked like a yawning mouth. The house was on the market for approximately eight months before I purchased it, and I assume the bin had been sitting there, at the side of the house, the entire time. Naturally it had rained during the last eight months, so, with its half-open lid, the bin was flooded with soupy garbage and untold parasites. And it reeked.

The City enjoys a virtual monopoly on garbage collection; it tacks its fees onto the City's water and sewage bill. The few private garbage-collection companies in town service mostly restaurants and businesses: entities that simply cannot wait a week for garbage pickup and need a service provider capable of emptying whole dumpsters full of trash. The City does allow residents to opt out of their collection services, but this only masks soft coercion with an illusion of consumer choice.

Government opt-out clauses are malicious precisely because of the impression that they're harmless if not generous. Contract law is premised on the principles of mutual assent and voluntary agreement. Government opt-out clauses, however, deprive consumers of volition and bargaining power. They distort the natural contracting relationship by investing one party, the government, with power that the other party cannot enjoy. Not contracting for services is not an option, and government is the default service provider that sets the bargaining rules; the deck is stacked against the consumer before negotiating can begin.

The onus, moreover, is on the consumer to undo a contract that he's been forced into, rather than on the government to provide high-quality services at competitive rates in order to keep the consumer's business. Opt-out clauses make it difficult for the consumer to end his relationship with the government provider, and they force potential competitors to operate at a position of manifest disadvantage.

My wife and I took turns calling the City to ask about getting a new trash bin. No amount of cleaning and sterilization could rid the current bin of its stench. We couldn't keep the bin inside our garage because of the oppressive odor. We left voicemails with different people in different departments at the City, begging for a new bin and explaining our situation, but our calls weren't returned. There was no customer service of the kind a private company would have. After all, there was little danger of losing our business: the City was the service provider for nearly every neighborhood in town because of the difficulty private companies had breaking into a market controlled by government. We were, for now, stuck with the City's inefficiencies and unresponsiveness. With much persistence my wife was eventually able to speak to an employee of the City. She was informed, however, that we could not get a new trash bin unless ours was broken or stolen. That stunk.

I learned in time about other drawbacks to our government-provided garbage service. During the holidays, collection schedules changed. When my wife and I lived in Atlanta and used a privately owned garbage company, our collection schedules never changed. Our collections were always on time. Our garbage collectors were kind and reliable because, if they weren't, I could hire new collectors who would materialize in my driveway the next morning with shining smiles on their faces.

It's simple enough to follow an altered holiday schedule, so that's what we did in Auburn, only the collectors declined to follow that schedule themselves. After Thanksgiving, when trash tends to pile up, we placed our trash bin out on the street according to schedule. So did our neighbors. Yet nobody picked up our trash. Our entire street tried again the next week, on the appointed day, and once again nobody picked up the trash. A concerned neighbor called the City, and we were able to remedy the now-messy situation, but not without spending time and energy that could have been channeled toward better things.

When I was a child my brother and I were tasked each year with clearing trees, weeds, and shrubs that were growing along the pond in our backyard. We would pile sticks and sawed-up tree trunks and other debris on the curb of our driveway, along with bags of grass clippings, and our garbage collectors, who worked for a private company, would always pick up these items without question or complaint. We were so grateful that sometimes we'd leave them envelopes with extra cash to express our thanks.

In Auburn, however, I was once unable to squeeze an additional garbage bag into our trash bin, which was full, so I rolled the bin to the street and placed the additional bag beside it. I then lumbered inside for my morning coffee, when all of a sudden the garbage collector drove up and parked beside my bin. I watched from the window as he descended from his truck, shook his head, climbed back into his truck, picked up a pad and paper, and began scribbling with his pen. The next thing I knew he was issuing a yellow citation for an alleged infraction. It turned out to be a mere warning, but it indicated, right there in bold letters, that the next time we did something so egregious as putting our trash out for collection without using the bin, some repercussion—I forget what—would visit us.

When I think about the things the garbage collectors would remove from our driveway in Atlanta—an old door, a broken toilet, a malfunctioning lawnmower—I marvel that the City requires you to purchase tags at the Revenue Office if you wish to place things like dryers, water heaters, refrigerators, or microwaves on the street for garbage collection. Yet I remain optimistic, and not only because Joseph Salerno has come to town to hold the newly endowed John V. Denson II chair in the Department of Economics at Auburn University.

I'm optimistic because I see some positive change. We recently organized a garage sale and came to discover, two days before the big day, that the City required a permit for such events. This time when we called the City to ask about the mandatory permit for garage sales, we received good news: those permits were no longer required as long as we conducted the sale in our own driveway. However minor, that's progress. Perhaps it'll spill over into other sectors of our little local community. Until then, War Eagle!

Make America Mobile Again

This 2016 election season proved that, regardless of who becomes the Democratic or Republic nominee for president, the American political landscape has been reshaped. Candidates expected to have a smooth path to their party's nomination have met, instead, a bumpy road. The rise of Donald Trump and Bernie Sanders as viable candidates reflects the growing feeling among ordinary Americans that the system is rigged, that they're stuck in conditions enabled and controlled by an amorphous cadre of elites from Washington and Wall Street.

Income inequality is higher today than it's been in nearly a century. Middle- and lower-class citizens of other First World countries enjoy more economic mobility than do middle and lower-class Americans. The United

States has fallen behind managerial and quasi-socialist governments in Europe in empirical rankings of economic freedom. The gap between the so-called 1% and the rest of America is growing, and recent college graduates, saddled with student loan debt and poor job prospects, are financially behind where their parents were at the same age.

Things don't look promising. But one law professor, F. H. Buckley of the freshly named Antonin Scalia Law School at George Mason University, outlines ways to repair structural, systemic burdens on the American economy. His book, *The Way Back* provocatively advocates for socialist ends by capitalist means.

Although the word socialism recalls revolution, stifled competition, attacks on private ownership, abolition of the price-system and sound economic calculation, hunger, mass-murder, off-brand goods and low-quality services, among other demonstrable horribles, Buckley has something less vicious in mind. By socialism, he does not mean a centralized government that replaces the market system with economic planning and state control of the means of production. His "socialism" is not socialism at all.

Leaving socialism undefined, he suggests that free-market economics (a term he avoids but implies) and the dismantling of the regulatory state will do more than actual socialism and its variants to lift people out of poverty and maximize their quality of life. The Left, in short, has asked the right questions about income inequality and economic mobility but supplied the wrong answers or solutions. "Sadly," Buckley complains, "those who loudly decry income disparities often support policies which make things worse."[76]

It's the aristocratic elites, in Buckley's view, who benefit from mass bureaucracy, the welfare state, a broken immigration and public-school system, trade barriers, a flawed tax code, and a general decline in the rule of law. These unjust institutions, policies, and conditions, with their built-in advantages for a select few, cause and sustain economic immobility. They solidify the place of aristocrats—what Buckley also calls the New Class—at the top of the social stratum. Those with high levels of wealth game the system through special favors, government grants, shell companies, complicated tax schemes, offshore banking, and other loopholes designed to ensure that the 1% are excluded from the regulatory barriers imposed and administered by government at the expense of the 99%.

The aristocracy that Buckley targets is not the natural aristocracy celebrated by certain American Founders for its virtue and political disinterestedness. It's an artificial aristocracy that has little to do with merit or talent. The Founders—probably all of them—would have been appalled by the likes of Bill and Hillary Clinton: figures who became multi-millionaires through partisan politics. The Clintons embody the new artificial aristocracy. They amassed their wealth by championing programs that have slowed economic mobility while purporting to do the opposite. The Founders, by contrast, believed that benevolent aristocrats would be free from economic pressure and thus would not succumb to temptations to use government positions or privileges for personal gain.

The Founders would have cringed to learn that public service has become a vehicle to riches. For all his many faults, Donald Trump, when he was a candidate, appealed to disenfranchised Americans because he declared he'd financed his own campaign and admitted that a rigged system—exemplified by our federal bankruptcy laws—worked in his favor. He knows the government system is unfair and claims he wants to change it.

"America was a mobile society for most of the twentieth century," Buckley says, citing statistics and substantiating his claim with charts and graphs.[77] Trump's supporters no doubt long for those days of economic mobility that Buckley locates in the exuberant 1950s.

When Trump announces that he wants to make America great again, people stuck at the bottom of the rigid class divide respond with enthusiasm. On a subterranean level, they seem to be hoping that America can once again become a mobile society, a place where a lowly pioneering frontiersman like Abraham Lincoln (Buckley's favored symbol of social and economic mobility) can rise from humble beginnings to become the President of the United States. Buckley believes that "the central idea of America, as expressed in the Declaration [of Independence], became through Lincoln the promise of income mobility and a faith in the ability of people to rise to a higher station in life."[78]

Class structure is more settled in America than in much of Europe. Yet America has always defined itself against the European traditions of monarchy, aristocracy, dynasty, and inherited privilege. Buckley states that "America and Europe have traded places."[79] The trope of the American Dream is about rising out of your received station in life to accomplish great things for yourself and your posterity. What would it mean if U.S. citizens were to envy, instead, the European Dream? What if America is now the country of privilege, not promise? If the American financial and economic situation remains static, we'll learn the answers to these questions the hard way.

Perhaps the most interesting and unique feature of Buckley's book is his embrace of Darwinian theory—including the genetic study of phenotypes and kin selection—to explain why American aristocrats combine to preserve their power and restrain the middle and lower classes. In short, people are hard-wired to ensure the survival of their kind, so they pass on competitive advantages to their children. "American aristocrats," Buckley submits, "are able to identify each other through settled patterns of cooperation called reciprocal altruism."[80] People organize themselves into social groups that maximize the genetic fitness of their biological descendants. If certain advantages are biologically heritable, then "a country would have to adopt punitive measures to handicap the gifted and talented in order to erase all genetic earnings advantages."[81]

Eugenics measures were popular during the Progressive Era, before we learned about the horrors of Nazi genocide, but surely the Left does not want to return to such inhumane and homicidal practices to realize their beloved ideal of equality. Yet Buckley reveals—more subtly than my summary suggests—that biological tampering is the only way for egalitarians to transform their utopian fantasies into a concrete reality.

To those who might point out that Buckley, a tenured law professor living in the handsome outskirts of D.C., is himself a member of this self-serving aristocracy, Buckley declares that he's a traitor to his class. Without bravado or boast, he presents himself as the rare altruist who recognizes the net gains realized through reasonable cooperation among disparate groups.

Trump and Ted Cruz might have held Buckley's book on hand as they made their final case to the electorate in 2016. Buckley explains why conservatives, libertarians, and Republicans alike should care about economic mobility and inequality. By ignoring the problem of economic disparity, he warns, "the Republican establishment has handed the Democrats a hammer with which to pound it."[82] Buckley identifies the types of cronyism and economic barriers to entry that have caused social immobility and inequality. To resolve our troubles, he advocates "easy pieces of useful and efficient legislation" that he dubs his "wish list."[83]

He describes this "wish list" and sketches what Americans can do to reinvigorate their economy and make their country mobile again. By facilitating educational choice and charter schools, streamlining the immigration system, curtailing prosecutorial overreach and the criminalization of entrepreneurship, and cutting back on the financial regulations, tax loopholes, and corporate laws that are calculated to benefit rather than police those at the top, Americans can bring back the conditions necessary for the proliferation of individual liberty and prosperity—or, in Buckley's words, restore the promise of America.

Pragmatists versus Agrarians?

John J. Langdale's *Superfluous Southerners* paints a magnificent portrait of Southern conservatism and the Southern Agrarians, and it will become recognized as an outstanding contribution to the field of Southern Studies. It charts an accurate and compelling narrative regarding Southern, Agrarian conservatism during the 20th century, but it erroneously conflates Northern liberalism with pragmatism, muddying an otherwise immaculate study.

Langdale sets up a false dichotomy as his foundational premise: progressive, Northern pragmatists versus traditionalist, Southern conservatives. From this premise, he draws several conclusions: that Southern conservatism offers a revealing context for examining the gradual demise of traditional humanism in America; that Northern pragmatism, which ushered in modernity in America, was an impediment to traditional humanism; that "pragmatic liberalism" (his term) was Gnostic insofar as it viewed humanity as perfectible; that the man of letters archetype finds support in Southern conservatism; that Southern conservatives eschewed ideology while Northern liberals used it to present society as constantly ameliorating; that Southern conservatives celebrated "superfluity" in order to preserve canons and traditions; that allegedly superfluous ways of living were, in the minds of Southern conservatives, essential to cultural stability; that Agrarianism arose as a response to the New Humanism; and that superfluous Southerners, so deemed, refined and revised established values for new generations.

In short, his argument is that Southern conservatives believed their errand was to defend and reanimate a disintegrating past. This belief is expressed in his discussion of the work of six prominent Southern men of letters spanning two generations: John Crowe Ransom, Donald Davidson, Allen Tate, Cleanth Brooks, Richard Weaver, and M. E. Bradford.

Langdale ably demonstrates how the Southern Agrarians mounted an effective and tireless rhetorical battle against organized counterforces, worried that scientific and industrial progress would replace traditional faith in the unknown and mysterious, and fused poetry and politics to summon forth an ethos of Romanticism and chivalry. He sketches the lines of thought connecting the earliest Agrarians to such later Southerners as Weaver and Bradford. He is so meticulous in his treatment of Southern conservatives that it is surprising the degree to which he neglects the constructive and decent aspects of pragmatism.

Careful to show that "Agrarianism, far from a monolithic movement, had always been as varied as the men who devised it,"[84] he does not exercise the same fastidiousness and impartiality towards the pragmatists, who are branded with derogatory labels throughout the book even though their ideas are never explained in detail. The result is a series of avoidable errors.

First, what Langdale treats as a monolithic antithesis to Southern conservatism is a multifaceted philosophy marked by only occasional agreement among its practitioners. C. S. Peirce was the founder of pragmatism, followed by William James, yet Peirce considered James's pragmatism so distinct from his own that he renamed his philosophy "pragmaticism." John Dewey reworked James's pragmatism until his own version retained few similarities with James's or Peirce's. Oliver Wendell Holmes Jr. never identified himself as a pragmatist, and his jurisprudence is readily distinguishable from the philosophy of Peirce, James, and Dewey. Each of these men had nuanced interpretations of pragmatism that are difficult to harmonize with each other, let alone view as a bloc against Southern, traditionalist conservatism.

Second, the Southern Agrarians espoused ideas that were generally widespread among Southerners, embedded in Southern culture, and reflective of Southern attitudes. By contrast, pragmatism was an academic enterprise rejected by most Northern intellectuals and completely out of the purview of the average Northern citizen. Pragmatism was nowhere near representative of Northern thinking, especially not in the political or economic realm, and it is hyperbolic to suggest, as Langdale does, that pragmatism influenced the intellectual climate in the North to the extent that traditionalist conservatism influenced the intellectual climate in the South.

Third, the pragmatism of Peirce and James is not about sociopolitical or socioeconomic advancement. It is a methodology, a process of scientific inquiry. It does not address conservatism per se or liberalism per se. It can lead one to either conservative or liberal outcomes, although the earliest pragmatists rarely applied it to politics as such. It is, accordingly, a vehicle to an end, not an end itself. Peirce and James viewed it as a technique to ferret out the truth of an idea by subjecting concrete data to rigorous analysis based on statistical probability, sustained experimentation, and trial and error. Although James occasionally undertook to discuss political subjects, he did not treat pragmatism as the realization of political fantasy. Pragmatism, properly understood, can be used to validate a political idea, but does not comprise one.

The Southern Agrarians may have privileged poetic supernaturalism over scientific inquiry; it does not follow, however, that pragmatists like Peirce and James evinced theories with overt or intended political consequences aimed at Southerners or traditionalists or, for that matter, Northern liberals. Rather than regional conflict or identity, the pragmatists were concerned with fine-tuning what they believed to be loose methods of science and epistemology and metaphysics. They identified with epistemic traditions of Western philosophy but wanted to distill them to their core, knowing full well that humans could not perfect philosophy, only tweak it to become comprehensible and meaningful for a given moment. On the other hand, the Southern Agrarians were also concerned with epistemology and metaphysics, but their concern was invariably colored by regional associations, their rhetoric inflected with political overtones. Both Southern Agrarians and pragmatists attempted to conserve the most profitable and essential elements of Western philosophy; opinions about what those elements were differed from thinker to thinker.

Fourth, Langdale's caricature (for that is what it is) of pragmatism at times resembles a mode of thought that is alien to pragmatism. For instance, he claims that "pragmatism is a distinctly American incarnation of the historical compulsion to the utopian and of what philosopher Eric Voegelin described as the ancient tradition of 'gnosticism.'"[85] Nothing, however, is more fundamental to pragmatism than the rejection of utopianism or Gnosticism. That rejection is so widely recognized that even Merriam-Webster lists "pragmatism" as an antonym for "utopian."

Pragmatism is against teleology and dogma; it takes as its starting point observable realities rather than intangible, impractical abstractions and ideals. What Langdale describes is more like Marxism: a messianic ideology with a sprawling, utopian teleology regarding the supposedly inevitable progress of humankind. Given that pragmatism is central to his thesis, it is telling that Langdale never takes the time to define it, explain the numerous differences between leading pragmatists, or analyze any landmark pragmatist texts.

Landgale's approach to "superfluity" makes *Superfluous Southerners* the inverse of Richard Poirier's 1992 *Poetry and Pragmatism*: whereas Langdale relates "superfluity" to Southern men of letters who conserve what the modern era has ticketed as superfluous, Poirier relates "superfluity" to Emerson and his literary posterity in Robert Frost, Gertrude Stein, Wallace Stevens, T. S. Eliot, William Carlos Williams, and Ezra Pound. Both notions of superfluity contemplate the preservation of perennial virtues and literary forms; one, however, condemns pragmatism while the other applauds it. For both Langdale and Poirier, "superfluity" is good. It is not a term of denunciation as it is usually taken to be. Langdale cites Hungarian sociologist Karl Mannheim to link "superfluity" to traditionalists who transform and adapt ideas to "the new stage of social and mental development,"[86] thus keeping "alive a 'strand' of social development which would otherwise have become extinct."[87]

Poirier also links superfluity to an effort to maintain past ideas. His notion of "superfluity," though, refers to the rhetorical excesses and exaggerated style that Emerson flaunted to draw attention to precedents that have proven wise and important. By reenergizing old ideas with creative and exhilarating language, Emerson secured their significance for a new era. In this respect, Emerson is, in Poirier's words, "radically conservative."

Who is right? Langdale or Poirier? Langdale seeks to reserve superfluity for the province of Southern, traditionalist conservatives. Does this mean that Poirier is wrong? And if Poirier is right, does not Langdale's binary opposition collapse into itself?

These questions notwithstanding, it is strange that Langdale would accuse the Emersonian pragmatic tradition of opposing that which, according to Poirier, it represents. Although it would be wrong to call Emerson a political conservative, he cannot be said to lack a reverence for history. A better, more conservative criticism of Emerson—which Langdale mentions in his introduction—would involve Emerson's transcendentalism that promoted a belief in innate human goodness. Such idealism flies in the face of Southern traditionalism, which generally abides by the Augustinian doctrine of innate human depravity and the political postures appertaining thereto.

What Langdale attributes to pragmatism is in fact a bane to most pragmatists. A basic tenet of pragmatism, for instance, is human fallibilism, which is in keeping with the doctrine of innate human depravity and which Peirce numbers as among his reasons for supporting the scientific method. Peirce's position is that one human mind is imperfect and cannot by itself reach trustworthy conclusions; therefore, all ideas must be filtered through the logic and experimentation of a community of thinkers; a lasting and uniform consensus is necessary to verify the validity of any given hypothesis. This is, of course, anathema to the transcendentalist's conviction that society corrupts the inherent power and goodness of the individual genius.

Langdale's restricted view of pragmatism might have to do with unreliable secondary sources. He cites, of all people, Herbert Croly for the proposition that, in Croly's words, "democracy cannot be disentangled from an aspiration toward human perfectibility." The connection between Croly and pragmatism seems to be that Croly was a student of James, but so was the politically and methodologically conservative C. I. Lewis. And let us not forget that the inimitable Jacques Barzun, who excoriated James's disciples for exploiting and misreading pragmatism, wrote an entire book—*A Stroll with William James*—which he tagged as "the record of an intellectual debt."

Pragmatism is a chronic target for conservatives who haven't read much pragmatism. Frank Purcell has written in *Taki's Magazine* about "conservatives who break into hives at the mere mention of pragmatism." Classical pragmatists are denominated as forerunners of progressivism despite having little in common with progressives. The chief reason for this is the legacy of John Dewey and Richard Rorty, both proud progressives and, nominally at least, pragmatists.

Dewey, behind James, is arguably the most recognizable pragmatist, and it is his reputation, as championed by Rorty, that has done the most to generate negative stereotypes and misplaced generalizations about pragmatism. Conservatives are right to disapprove of Dewey's theories of educational reform and social democracy, yet he is just one pragmatist among many, and there are important differences between his ideas and the ideas of other pragmatists.

In fact, the classical pragmatists have much to offer conservatives, and conservatives—even the Southern Agrarians—have supported ideas that are compatible with pragmatism, if not outright pragmatic. Burkean instrumentalism, committed to gradualism and wary of ideological extremes, is itself a precursor to social forms of pragmatism, although it bears repeating that social theories do not necessarily entail political action.

Russell Kirk's *The Conservative Mind* traces philosophical continuities and thus provides clarifying substance to the pragmatist notion that ideas evolve over time and in response to changing technologies and social circumstances, while always retaining what is focal or fundamental to their composition. The original subtitle of that book was "From Burke to Santayana," and it is remarkable, is it not, that both Burke and Santayana are pragmatists in their own way? Santayana was plugged into the pragmatist network, having worked alongside James and Josiah Royce, and he authored one of the liveliest expressions of pragmatism ever written: *The Life of Reason*. Although Santayana snubbed the label, general consensus maintains that he was a pragmatist. It is also striking that Kirk places John Randolph of Roanoke and John C. Calhoun, both Southern conservatives, between these pragmatists on his map of conservative thought. There is, in that respect, an implication that pragmatism complements traditionalism.

Langdale relies on Menand's outline of pragmatism and appears to mimic Menand's approach to intellectual history. It is as though Langdale had hoped to write the conservative, Southern companion to *The Metaphysical Club*. He does not succeed because his representation of pragmatism is indelibly stamped by the ideas of Rorty, who repackaged pragmatism in postmodern lexica. Moreover, Langdale's failure or refusal to describe standing differences between the classical pragmatists and neo-pragmatists means that his book is subject to the same critique that Susan Haack brought against Menand.

Haack lambasted Menand for sullying the reputation of the classical pragmatists by associating pragmatism with nascent Rortyianism—"vulgar

Rortyianism," in her words. Langdale seems guilty of this same supposition. By pitting pragmatism against Southern conservatism, he implies that Southern conservatism rejects, among other features, the application of mathematics to the scientific method, the analysis of probabilities derived from data sampling and experimentation, and the prediction of outcomes in light of statistical inferences. The problem is that the Agrarians did not oppose these things, although their focus on preserving the literary and cultural traditions of the South led them to express their views through poetry and story rather than as philosophy. But there is nothing in these methods of pragmatism (as opposed to the uses some later pragmatists may have put them to) that is antithetical to Southern Agrarianism.

Superfluous Southerners is at its best when it sticks to its Southern subjects and does not undertake comparative analyses of intellectual schools. It is at its worst when it resorts to incorrect and provocative phrases about "the gnostic hubris of pragmatists"[88] or "the gnostic spirit of American pragmatic liberalism."[89] Most of its chapters do a remarkable job teasing out distinctions between its Southern conservative subjects and narrating history about the Southern Agrarians' relationship to modernity, commitment to language and literature, and role as custodians of a fading heritage. Unfortunately, his book confounds the already ramified philosophy known as pragmatism, and at the expense of the Southern traditionalism that he and I admire.

Socialism: World's Greatest Generator of Poverty

If you're looking for a short introduction to socialism that rewards rereading, Thomas DiLorenzo's *The Problem With Socialism* is it. Perhaps your son or daughter has returned from college talking about collective control of the means of production and sporting Bernie Sanders t-shirts. Perhaps you're a political novice looking for informed guidance.

Perhaps you're frustrated with America's economic decline and deplorable unemployment rates. Perhaps you listened with bewilderment as some pundit distinguished democratic socialism from pure socialism in an attempt to justify the former.

Whoever you are, and whatever your occasion for curiosity, you're likely to find insight and answers from DiLorenzo. A professor of economics at

Loyola University Maryland, DiLorenzo opens his book with troubling statistics: 43% of millennials, or at least those between ages 18 and 29, view socialism more favorably than capitalism, and 69% of voters under 30 would vote for a socialist presidential candidate. Socialism—depending on how it's defined in relation to communism—may have killed over 100 million people and impoverished countless others over the course of the 20th century.

So why have the youth (full disclaimer: I'm a millennial myself) welcomed this ideology that's responsible for mass killings, organized theft, war crimes, forced labor, concentration camps, executions, show trials, ethnic cleansing, disease, totalitarianism, censorship, starvation, hyperinflation, poverty, and terror?

Why have death, destruction, and abject destitution become so hip and cool? Because of effective propaganda and utopian promises of "free" everything.

The problem is, as anyone who's ever studied economics knows, there's no such thing as free stuff. Somebody pays at some point.

"What socialists like Senator Sanders should say if they want to be truthful and straightforward," DiLorenzo thus avers, "is not that government can offer citizens anything for free, but that they want healthcare (and much else) to become a government-run monopoly financed entirely with taxes. Taxes hide, but do not eliminate, the cost of individual government programs."[90] And these programs are far more expensive to society than they would be on the free market.

The predicable rejoinder to such a claim—repeated ad nauseam by television personalities—is that socialism works, nay thrives, in, say, Sweden. DiLorenzo corrects the record: "Socialism nearly wrecked Sweden, and free market reforms are finally bringing its economy back from the brink of disaster."[91]

Strong language, but DiLorenzo maps the history and supplies the data to back it up. "The real source of Sweden's relatively high standard of living," he explains, has "everything to do with Sweden avoiding both world wars and jumping into the industrial revolution when its economy was one of the freest, least regulated, and least taxed in Europe."[92]

Other common binary assumptions are reversed in these pages: socialism causes pollution whereas capitalism protects the environment; socialism leads to war whereas capitalism is peaceful; socialism consolidates power among an elite few whereas capitalism decentralizes and disperses power, which ultimately resides with individual consumers making small economic adjustments based on their particular needs.

Even socialized medicine proves more inequitable than market-based alternatives. Proponents of Canadian-style healthcare ignore the fact that "Canadian health care is actually far more expensive, and the quality far less than it would be if doctors and hospitals had to compete for patients on the basis of quality and price."[93]

Coloring his analysis with references to the Austrian economists Ludwig von Mises, Friedrich Hayek, and Murray Rothbard, DiLorenzo undertakes a variety of other issues implicated by socialism: egalitarianism, fascism, income taxation, wage and price controls, monopolies, public schooling, and more.

Had I been his publisher, I would have insisted that he also include disturbing, graphic, and gruesome images of real, dead human bodies stacked on real, dead human bodies, of ransacked churches, and of confiscated property—alarmingly tangible consequences and horrifying illustrations of pure, realized socialism.

Senator Sanders and most of his followers mean well, of course, and genuinely and in good faith advocate policies they believe to be in the best interests of the United States. Yet the history of the cause they champion is fundamentally at odds with their desired goals.

DiLorenzo has the courage to call socialism what it is: "the biggest generator of poverty the world has ever known."[94] For young students especially, his concise primer could make the difference between feeling the Bern, and getting burned.

The Antiwar Tradition in American Letters

James Carroll, the novelist and Christian man of letters who has won numerous accolades over a long, distinguished career, sets the tone for this fine edition, *War No More*, in his short foreword. "Wars," he says, "have defined the nation's narrative, especially once the apocalyptic fratricide of the Civil War set the current running in blood—toward the Jim Crow reenslavement of African Americans, further genocidal assaults against native peoples, imperial adventures abroad, a two-phased World War that permanently militarized the American economy and spawned a bifurcated imagination that so requires an evil enemy that the Cold War morphed seamlessly into the War on Terror."[95]

We've seen editions like this before—*We Who Dared to Say No to War*, edited by Murray Polner and Thomas E. Woods Jr. comes to mind—but the focus here is different and decidedly literary. Lawrence Rosenwald, the editor, believes the "antiwar impulse" requires a rich "vocabulary" that's "visionary, sensual, prophetic, outraged, introspective, self-doubting, fantastic, irreverent, witty, obscene, uncertain, heartbroken"—in short, that signals a range of human emotions and experiences.[96] Rosenwald promises that "[a]ll of those traits are on display here," and follows through with essays and memoirs by Ralph Waldo Emerson, Henry David Thoreau, Kurt Vonnegut, Edmund Wilson, and, among others, Norman Mailer.[97]

Rosenwald has also achieved a diversity of genre. He includes poems by Henry Wadsworth Longfellow, Stephen Crane, Adrienne Rich, Herman Melville, Robert Bly, Sara Teasdale, Edna St. Vincent Millay, George Starbuck, and Walt Whitman; short stories by Ray Bradbury and Ambrose Bierce; a genre-defying piece by Mark Twain (*"The War Prayer"*); songs by Country Joe McDonald, Ed McCurdy, and Pete Seeger and Joe Hickerson; a statement before a federal grand jury; letters and an interview; a gospel song (*"Down by the River-Side"*); a leaflet on the Vietnam War (the conflict with the most permeating presence in the book); excerpts of the prefatory articles of the Constitution of the Iroquois Confederacy; and more.

Women as a class are underrepresented in Rosenwald's selections. I count 104 men and 35 women among the contributors. Are there fewer women involved in the antiwar movement throughout American history? Or did Rosenwald ignore females because of his preference for particular writers and writings? We may never know because he does not address the gender disparity. If antiwar writers are, in fact, disproportionally male, then further study of that curious fact—or at least some speculation about it—seems warranted.

Multiple traditions merge in these pages: John Woolman, Benjamin Rush, and Reinhold Niebuhr speak as Christians; Eugene V. Debs, Jane Addams, Arturo Giovannitti, and Howard Zinn as proxies for the Left; and Andrew Bacevich as a representative of the Right. Figures like Randolph

Bourne cut across trite political labels. Writers associated with certain styles and forms demonstrate their versatility with other kinds of writing. For instance, Robert Lowell, known for his poetry, shows his mastery of the epistolary form in his letter to President Franklin D. Roosevelt.

Rosenwald proves to be far more astute than Jonah Goldberg in his assessment of William James's "The Moral Equivalent of War." Whereas Rosenwald submits that this essay is "intended as oppositional" to war,[98] Goldberg, a senior editor at *National Review*, treats it as fascist and accuses it of presenting "militarism as a social philosophy" that was not only "a pragmatic expedient" but also the basis for "a workable and sensible model for achieving desirable ends."[99] Of course, Goldberg has been wrong before.

Given that Rosenwald purports to have featured the writing of "pacifists," the inclusion of John Kerry and Barack Obama is deplorable. True, Kerry's statement against the Vietnam War is notable as a work of peace activism, but Kerry also voted in 2002 to authorize President Bush's use of force to disarm Saddam Hussein, advocated U.S. military involvement in Syria, and appears at least partially responsible for the U.S. backing of Saudi-led bombings in Yemen.

If opposition to the Vietnam War is now the measure of pacifism, then most Americans today are pacifists, there being, as of the year 2000, just 30% of Americans who believe that that war was not a mistake, according to a Gallup poll. Thus, Kerry is hardly unique in such opposition. Nicholson Baker, in his energetic essay for this volume, seems more attuned than Rosenwald to Kerry's foreign-policy prescriptions, castigating Kerry for inciting military involvement in Gaddafi's Libya.

President Obama, for his part, oversaw regular bombings throughout the Middle East, including in Pakistan, Yemen, Iraq, and Somalia; ordered U.S. military intervention in Libya; increased U.S. troop levels in Afghanistan and escalated U.S. military operations there; and urged Americans to support U.S. military involvement in Syria. These positions are ironic in light of his warning, in his piece in this collection, against traveling "blindly" down "that hellish path" to war.[100]

Rosenwald's brief, personal introductions (he recalls hearing James Baldwin speak in the Cathedral of St. John the Divine in New York, for instance, and mentions a tribute he wrote for Daniel Berrigan) to each chapter engender an autobiographical feel. One senses that this book represents a patchwork of accumulated memories, that Rosenwald has recounted and repurposed old reading experiences for present political needs. Inviting Carroll to pen the foreword, moreover, was entirely appropriate and wise. As this review opened with Carroll's eloquent words, so it closes with them.

"Because the human future, for the first time in history, is itself imperiled by the ancient impulse to respond to violence with violence," Carroll intones, "the cry 'war no more!' can be heard coming back at us from time ahead, from the as yet unborn men and women—the ultimate voices of peace—who simply will not come into existence if the essential American soul does not change."[101] But all is not lost; Carroll remains optimistic. "The voices of this book, a replying chorus of hope," he says, "insist that such change is possible."[102]

Glory and Indignity

"I am an aristocrat. I love liberty, I hate equality."[103] Thus spoke John Randolph of Roanoke (1773–1833), one of the most curious, animated figures ever to grace American soil. That David Johnson's biography of Randolph is the first of its kind since Russell Kirk published *John Randolph of Roanoke* in 1951 suggests how deteriorated American memory and education have become. Randolph ought to be studied by all American schoolchildren, if not for his politics then for the vital role he played in shaping the nation's polity. Dr. Kirk declared that in writing about Randolph, he was summoning him from the shades. If so, Johnson has gone a step farther and brought Randolph into the sunshine to reveal just how spectacular a man he really was.

Kirk's biography of Randolph was in fact his first book. Kirk dubbed the colorful Virginian a "genius," "the prophet of Southern nationalism," and the "architect of Southern conservatism."[104] In *The Conservative Mind*, Kirk treated Randolph as a necessary link between George Mason and John C. Calhoun and proclaimed that Randolph should be remembered for "the quality of his imagination."[105] Randolph enabled the proliferation and preservation of the conservative tradition in America. He became an icon for decentralization and localism.

Why would a scandalous, sickly, go-it-alone, riotous rabble-rouser appeal to the mild-mannered Dr. Kirk? The answer, in short, is that Randolph was as conservative a politician as America has ever produced, and he was, despite himself, a gentleman and a scholar. Eccentric though he appeared and often acted, Randolph celebrated and defended tradition, championed small government and agrarianism, sacrificed careerism and opportunism for unwavering standards, professed self-reliance and individualism, took pains to preserve the rights of the states against the federal government, delighted in aristocratic tastes and manners, read voraciously the great works of Western civilization, cultivated the image of a statesman even as he attended to the wants and needs of his yeomen constituents, discoursed on weighty topics with wit and vigor, and adhered to firm principles rather than to partisan pandering. Admired by many, friend to few, he made a prominent display of his wild personality and unconditional love for liberty, and he devoted himself, sometimes at great cost, to the ideals of the American Revolution, which had, he claimed, marked him since childhood.

Remembered chiefly (and, in the minds of some progressives, unfortunately) for his contributions to states' rights doctrines and to the judicial hermeneutics of strict constructionism, Randolph was responsible for so much more. The son of a wealthy planter who died too young, Randolph became the stepson of St. George Tucker, a prominent lawyer who taught at the College of William and Mary and served as a judge on the Virginia General District Court and, eventually, on the Virginia Court of Appeals, the United States District Court for the District of Virginia, and the United States District Court for the Eastern District of Virginia. A cousin to Thomas Jefferson, Randolph studied under George Wythe and his cousin Edmond Randolph. A boy who was forced to flee his home from the army of Benedict Arnold, Randolph later played hooky from college to watch the orations of Fisher Ames, the stout Federalist from New York, and Madison. He served in the U.S. House of Representatives as well as the U.S. Senate, and was, for a brief time, Minister to Russia. A supporter of Jefferson before he became Jefferson's tireless adversary, he criticized such individuals as Patrick Henry, Washington, Madison, Monroe, John Adams, Henry Clay, and Daniel Webster. He was sickened by the Yazoo Land Scandal, opposed the War of 1812 in addition to the Missouri Compromise, and promoted nullification.

Many conservatives, Kirk among them, have tended to overlook the more unpalatable aspects of Randolph's life, whether personal or political. For instance, Randolph was, more than Jefferson, enthralled by the French Revolution and supportive of its cause. He manufactured a French accent, used a French calendar, and called his friends "Citizens." In his twenties, he referred to himself as a deist "and by consequence an atheist," and he acquired, in his own words, "a prejudice in favor of Mahome-danism," going so far as to proclaim that he "rejoiced in all its [Islam's] triumphs over the cross."[106] One might excuse these infelicities as symptoms of youthful indiscretion and impetuosity, but they do give one pause.

Not for lack of trying, Randolph could not grow a beard, and although he spoke well, his voice was, by most accounts, awkward, piping, off-putting, and high-pitched. His critics have painted him as a villain of the likes of Shakespeare's Richard III: resentful, obstinate, loudmouthed, and as deformed in the mind as he was in the body. Yet Randolph cannot be made into a monster. More than others of his station in that time and place, Randolph was sensitive to the problems of slavery, which had only inten-sified rather than diminished since the Founding. He freed his slaves in his will, granted them landholdings in Ohio, and provided for their heirs. Slav-ery was incompatible with liberty, and Randolph, despite being a product of his time, appears to have worried much about the paradox of a nation conceived in liberty but protective of institutional bondage. Randolph as-serted, in some way or another, repeatedly, that his politics were based on a presumption of liberty, which was (and is) the opposite of slavery and governmental tyranny.

Ten years in the making, Johnson's biography was well worth the wait and cannot be accused of historical amnesia or selective telling. It presents Randolph in all his glory and all his indignity. Johnson's Randolph is as much a man of letters, taste, and refinement as he is a grudge-holding, fin-ger-wagging scoundrel. As biographies go, this is surely one of the best in a long time. That holds for any biography of any individual—a tall claim to be sure, but one this volume meets. Johnson's prose is impeccably paced and free of jargon. His two Appendices—one displaying Randolph's family tree and the other profiling prominent individuals of Randolph's time—make for useful references. This book will benefit students and teachers alike, and all readers will find here an accessible, exciting account of early American politics.

Would that we had a conservative movement today that resurrected gentility and culture as indispensable values of leadership. Ever cognizant of the interests of the landed gentry, bookish and proudly eloquent, steeped in Latin and Greek, fearful of taxation, Randolph would, no doubt, be frowned upon today, and the neglect of his memory is perhaps the backhanded tribute paid to him by the left-leaning educational establishment. Our politicians no longer relish Shakespeare, as Randolph did, and it is doubtful that they have read seriously from Virgil or Horace, Milton or Chaucer. Add to these the works of Cervantes, Plutarch, Pope, Defoe, Swift, Fielding, Ovid, Livy, Xenophon, Cicero, Hume, Beattie, and Blackstone, and one begins—but only just begins—to get a sense of the wide breadth of Randolph's knowledge.

Having wandered from William & Mary to Princeton to Columbia, Randolph discovered that he despised the academy in no small part because he was more intelligent than anyone there. Later, as one of the most preeminent if not the most storied Antifederalist spokesmen, he established himself as a man of consistency and principle. One knew where he stood, and when he pontificated about the dangers of government and its various manifestations throughout history, he did so as one who was fully, impressively informed.

Johnson makes the case for Randolph's continued relevance by citing such recent misfortunes as the government bailouts, undeclared wars, judicial supremacy, and out-of-control spending. These events, the direct consequences of rapid centralization of power, bloated bureaucracy, and vulgar political gamesmanship, would have horrified Randolph, who called for small government, tax elimination, debt reduction, and repeal of those laws tending to inflate government. Randolph griped that he "would not die in Washington" where he would "be eulogized by men I despise, and buried in the Congressional Burying Ground."[107] He more or less got what he wanted; although magnificent in life, he left this world unceremoniously, his burial unremarkable. In a way, this seems appropriate. From his legacy, we are reminded that there is much greatness in what is small, and much smallness in what is great. At a mere 233 pages— excluding notes, acknowledgments, and appendices—the same could be said of this book.

Dixie Bohemia

John Shelton Reed's *Dixie Bohemia* is difficult to classify. It's easier to say what it isn't than to say what it is.

It isn't biography. It isn't documentary. It isn't quite history, although it does organize and present information about a distinct class of past individuals interacting and sometimes living together in a unique, definable space.

It isn't quite sociology either, although Reed is, by training and profession, a sociologist, and sociology does, every now and then, sneak its way into the pages.

Maybe it's best to suggest that the book is a bit of each of these, but it's also an annotated edition of *Sherwood Anderson and Other Famous Creoles: A Gallery of Contemporary New Orleans*. Written and compiled by William Spratling and William Faulkner, whom Reed affectionately dubs the "Two Bills," *Sherwood Anderson and Other Famous Creoles*, first published in 1926, was something of a joke: its oft-rambunctious subjects weren't really Creoles, but simply friends of the authors, and most weren't, by most measurable standards, famous.

Reed's stated goal, one of them at least, is to provide an "introduction to a Bohemian crowd of artists, writers, journalists, musicians, poseurs, and hangers-on found in the French Quarter in the mid-1920s."[108] This eclectic and creative crowd comprises what Reed calls a social circle, or, in more academic parlance, a "loose network of relationships linked by friends in common," "by association with the same institutions," and "by common interests."[109]

Reed explains that social circles, by nature, "have no formal leaders, but they may have their notables,"[110] and they have their cores, too. The leader of the so-called "famous Creoles" is Sherwood Anderson, and the core, as you might have guessed, is the French Quarter.

Tulane University, with all its energy, entertainers, and eccentrics, enabled and sustained the circle that produced the local arts, literature, and culture. The area and its residents gained a national, indeed international, reputation. As Meigs Frost, a reporter who made the cut as a famous Creole, put it, "So many of us here are internationally famous locally."[111]

Reed's subtly sociological introductory chapters place his subjects, which were also the two Bills' subjects, into their historical context—and what a wild, exotic, and at times erotic context it is. His comprehensive research is delivered with such wit and enthusiasm that one forgets that this work is scholarship written by a former professor and published by a university press. His occasional use of the first person and confessional, qualifying asides— "as far as I know,"[112] "Some may find it easier than I do,"[113] "to my mind artists should not be judged on what prejudiced observers see in their work,"[114] "It is difficult to discuss this,"[115] "I have mentioned,"[116] "I know of someone,"[117] "it's fair to say,"[118] "It's hard to imagine"[119]—will let you know, or let you guess at, where he stands on an issue or acknowledges an assumption on his part. Such delicate humility—or is it just honest collo-quialism?—is rare for a person who made his career in the university, and it would be a shame if readers neglected to notice it.

Peopled with absinthe-drinking, music-loving debauchers, 1920s New Orleans was a place where madams and brothels were as common as jam-balaya and gumbo; where music poured into the streets, which smelled of spices, sex, and booze; where bootleggers (this was the Prohibition Era, re-member) set up shop next to cops (who were customers of the brothels and the bootleggers); where the only limit on free love, it seemed, was the stul-tifying effect of alcohol; where parties—especially costume balls—were con-sidered failures if nobody got naked; and where vivacious theater, daily newspapers, and edgy literary periodicals flourished.

If this milieu seemed excessive, radical, intemperate, even libertine, it was also in a way conservative: there was among its dwellers a ubiquitous impulse to preserve and maintain. History, both that being made and that made already, was important to the artists and writers. The districts, the streets, the homes, the buildings, the sidewalks—all of it required and re-ceived care and protection and underwent systematic revitalization. The literati, as conservationists, were afraid that the world they had inherited, and to some extent made, was endangered.

Fans of Reed have come to expect certain things: the informal idioms and plain speech he uses while dissecting, with surgeon-like precision, com-plex people and institutions; the surprising clarity he brings to understudied topics; and the delightful, conversational prose with which he arrests your attention, transports you into another world, and then releases you back into your own world.

In this, he does not disappoint. As always, he delivers—and in so doing provides telling insights into a minor renaissance in American literary history. His discussions of race and sexuality will inspire (or provoke) future study, but more importantly he has addressed some of the least known phases of some of the most known American litterateurs.

Reed doesn't need my endorsement. But he's got it.

Buckley for the Masses

Overly committed as he was to supposedly universal political ideals and the spread of American liberal democracy throughout the world, William F. Buckley Jr. was not my kind of conservative. He could be tactless and cruel, as when he wrote in an obituary for Murrary Rothbard that "Rothbard had defective judgment" and "couldn't handle moral priorities." Buckley then trumpeted some unflattering anecdotes about Rothbard before likening him to David Koresh. Yet despite his tantrums and vendettas, something in the way he conducted himself—his showy decorum, flaunted manners, and sophisticated rhetoric—appeals to me.

Carl T. Bogus, an American law professor, seems to share my qualified respect for Buckley, despite disagreeing with him on important political and theoretical issues. "I should tell the reader up front," Bogus warns, "that I am a liberal and thus critical—in some instances, highly critical—of Buckley's ideology."[120] Yet Bogus admires William F. Buckley Jr. "enormously."[121]

Unlike bobble-headed television personalities and think-tank sycophants, Bogus does justice to his subject, treating Buckley's ideas evenhandedly. "Disheartened by the present state of partisan animosity," he argues that one solution "is to take opposing ideas seriously."[122] Indeed, Bogus not only takes Buckley seriously but credits him for having changed America's political realities.

The book focuses on what Bogus deems the "creation of the modern conservative movement"[123]—namely, the years between 1955 and 1968— but attends as well to events before 1955 that served as formative influences on Buckley. Hence Bogus devotes much space to explaining the characteristics of the conservative movement before the rise of *National Review* to suggest that Buckley transformed the movement into something new and dynamic. Toward that end, he assesses the significance of William Howard Taft and Sen. Robert Taft, publications such as *The American Mercury*, and journalists like H. L. Mencken. All of this is good by way of introduction, if a little humdrum for those already familiar with the subject.

At points Bogus lapses into cliché, as when he declares that "Conservatism today is a three-legged stool . . . based upon libertarianism, religious conservatism, and neoconservatism."[124] The average American "conservative," informed by FOX News and the late Rush Limbaugh, will, as a matter of course, have developed odd notions about who represents which category in this triad. But Bogus leads the reader to believe that the meaning of such terms is not fraught with confusion or highly contested.

Bogus's claim that "Buckley was himself a libertarian, a religious conservative, and a neoconservative" will come as news to libertarians and admirers of Buckley alike.[125] The terms may overlap, but the political beliefs they represent consist of too many ideas that are mutually exclusive. Conservatives with an historical sense will be annoyed by Bogus's frequent grandiose claims—for example, that James Burnham was "the first neoconservative,"[126] or that the "conservative movement was born on November 19, 1955."[127] That remark, besides being silly, would seem to undermine the very meaning of the word conservative, as it is impossible for the birth of a political philosophy to entail preservation or restoration. To make matters worse, Bogus overstates the friction between Buckley and Russell Kirk. "Though Buckley admired Kirk," Bogus explains, "Kirk surely understood that he could never prevail within the councils of *National Review* for the simple reason that Buckley was a libertarian."[128] This opinion is repeated elsewhere: "Kirk championed a form of conservatism that Buckley quite distinctly did not favor. Buckley was himself a libertarian, even if he had not yet so described himself."[129]

Buckley was hardly a libertarian, however liberally the word is defined, let alone an advocate for "hard-edged libertarianism."[130] (Bogus bases this claim on the title of Buckley's recklessly named book *Happy Days Were Here Again: Reflections of a Libertarian Journalist.*)

Buckley did, it is true, have trouble recruiting Kirk to *National Review*, in part because, as Bogus points out, Buckley had unfavorably reviewed Kirk's *Academic Freedom* in another publication just before the launch of *NR*. Buckley and Kirk also disagreed, often vehemently, about matters of public policy. Yet the two men got along, and not just because their relationship was "symbiotic," the adjective Bogus uses to suggest that they benefited financially from their professional association. In fact, Russell

Kirk and William Buckley, appreciating a cultivated intellect, respected each other. Whatever differences existed between them were not so extreme as to harden into insurmountable disdain or contempt. Modern conservatism required both the scholarship of Kirk and Buckley's animated spokesmanship, and both men knew it.

Without Kirk, there would be no conservative movement; without Buckley, no animated spokesmen for conservatism. And without the threat of communism and the Cold War, there would be no motive for collective action for any who might have considered themselves champions or defenders of conservatism. That is the standard narrative of the conservative movement, and Bogus more or less sticks to it. The notable exception is the attention paid to Buckley's obsessive purges, his relentless attempts to narrow the scope of conservatism to fit his own constricted definition. Bogus discusses at length the concerted efforts of *National Review* editors to stigmatize Ayn Rand and the Objectivists, Robert Welch and the Birchers, and, of course, Rothbard and other libertarian purists. Bogus ignores the paleoconservatives altogether.

Although fair in its treatment of an ideological rival, Buckley is neither an original nor an instructive book, through it is ultimately saved by William Buckley himself, a delightful and intriguing figure—sometimes a blowhard, sometimes a dandy—who makes up in charisma what Bogus lacks in meticulousness. Yet Bogus's book deserves its audience: the politically unsophisticated, whose understanding of conservatism derives from Republican politicians and the media.

In Search of Fascism

The term "fascism" is employed with such regular enthusiasm by everyone from political activists to celebrities and academics that our pundits could be forgiven for assuming that fascists lurk behind every corner and at every level of government. MSNBC host Keith Olbermann accused the Bush administration of fascism. Thomas Sowell has called President Obama a fascist. A quick online search yields accusations that Donald Trump and Hillary Clinton are fascists. The term "Islamofascism" circulates widely, and groups as dissimilar as campus Social Justice Warriors and the leaders of the National Rifle Association have been dubbed fascist.

It's clear why fanatics or dogmatists would label their opponents with the f-word: rhetorical play scores political points. But is there ever any truth behind the label?

Paul Gottfried enters the semantic fray with a clarifying and elucidating book, *Fascism: The Career of a Concept*. His study is not based on new archival finds. It's not narrative history. It's instead a comparative study of different treatments of fascism in which Gottfried discloses his preferred methodologies and favorite historians. Despite the prevalence of allegations of fascism, Gottfried submits that the only indisputable example of fascism in practice is Mussolini's interwar Italy.

The term fascism, as it has gained currency in our radio-television lexicon, lacks a clear referent. Its use reveals more about the speaker than about the signified phenomenon: the context in which the term is used can determine the speaker's place on the left-right spectrum. "Fascism" has become a pejorative and disparaging marker for views a speaker dislikes; it's a name that relegates the named to pariah status, provoking censorship and shaping basic notions about political figures and policies. "Fascism now stands," Gottfried says, "for a host of iniquities that progressives, multiculturalists, and libertarians all oppose, even if they offer no single, coherent account of what they're condemning."[131]

Gottfried is frustrated by the vagaries and false analogies resulting from the use of "fascism" as rhetorical weaponry. He criticizes "intellectuals and publicists" who are nominally antifascist yet "feel no obligation to provide a historically and conceptually delimited definition of their object of hate."[132]

Tracing the evolution of the meanings and representations of this political ideology in the works of numerous researchers, Gottfried's study can seem, at times, like an amalgam of book reviews or bibliographical essays— or like several synopses strung together with his own comparative evaluations. Academics more than casual readers will appreciate these efforts to summarize the field, although anyone wishing to acquire a surface-level knowledge of this deep subject will come away edified.

So what exactly is fascism? This question, Gottfried insists, "has sometimes divided scholars and has been asked repeatedly ever since Mussolini's followers marched on Rome in October 1922."[133] Gottfried presents several adjectives, mostly gleaned from the work of others, to describe fascism:

reactionary, counterrevolutionary, collectivist, authoritarian, corporatist, nationalist, modernizing, and protectionist. These words combine to form a unified sense of what fascism is, although we may never settle on a fixed definition because fascism has been linked to movements with various distinct characteristics. For instance, some fascists were Christian (e.g., the Austrian clerics or the Spanish Falange) and some were anti-Christian (e.g., the Nazis). There may be some truth to the "current equation of fascism with what is reactionary, atavistic, and ethnically exclusive,"[134] Gottfried acknowledges, but that is only part of the story.

"The initial momentum for locating fascism on the counterrevolutionary Right," writes Gottfried, "came from Marxists, who focused on the struggle between fascists and the revolutionary Left and the willingness of owners of forces of production to side with the fascists when faced by revolutionary threats."[135]

Fascism is not necessarily a creature of the counterrevolutionary right, however. Gottfried maps an alternative tradition that describes fascism as a leftist collectivist ideology. Fascism promoted welfare policies and thrived on revolutionary fervor. In the United States in the 1920s and '30s, the progressives more than self-identified members of the right celebrated and admired European fascism. FDR praised and imitated Mussolini. Such details seem to substantiate the claim that fascism was intrinsically leftist, at least in the eyes of U.S. citizens who were contemporaries of interwar fascism. But, Gottfried notes, "Fascism drew its strength from the attempt to oppose the Left while taking over some of its defining characteristics."[136]

Gottfried's book may not be intended as an antidote for the less rigorous and nakedly polemical *Liberal Fascism*. Unlike the author of that work, Jonah Goldberg, who seemed genuinely surprised by his discovery of what was in fact a well-documented connection between fascism and the left, Gottfried is characteristically measured and careful as he compares research rather than selectively and pugnaciously repurposing it. Gottfried is taken seriously by those who reject his own paleoconservatism—including those on the left who find his views unpalatable or downright offensive—because he doesn't smear opponents or resort to knee-jerk, grandiose claims to shock or surprise.

Gottfried concludes that fascism is right-wing after all, not left-wing, even if its concrete manifestations have been more militant than traditional conservatism. Like traditional conservatives, fascists did not believe that government programs could alter human nature, and they saw little value in the human-rights mantras extolling the individual's capacity for self-government.

Today the managerial state carries out leftist projects on behalf of equality and diversity, but that was not true for interwar European governments. Fascism was a product of the 20th century in which conservative adoration for aristocratic hierarchy seemed anachronistic and pragmatically useless as a political stratagem. Without an established aristocracy in their way, fascists constructed an artificial hierarchy to control the populace: a mythical and symbolic hierarchy attracted to the aesthetics of high modernism. The interwar fascists colored brute force with nationalist iconography and aestheticized violence as a cathartic and regenerative force against decadence.

Probably all treatments of "fascism" as a cohesive, homogeneous philosophy held together by likeminded adherents are wrong, incomplete, careless, or dishonest. Gottfried believes that the term "fascism" has undergone unwarranted manipulation since the German historian Ernst Nolte conflated fascism and Nazism in a manner that enabled less astute critics on "the multicultural Left" to justify "their attack on their opponents as Nazis and not simply generic fascists."[137]

The failure or refusal to distinguish between totalizing, exterminatory Nazism and other, less extreme forms of fascism may signal the intentional propagation of a political agenda. Gottfried cautions against such politicization of history. "History," he warns, "is of immediate practical interest to political partisans, and this affinity has allowed a contentious activity to be sometimes grossly abused."[138]

The popular embrace of incorrect or highly contested notions of fascism has generated media sensationalism about an ever-imminent fascist threat that must be eradicated. The media trope of looming fascism has provoked demands for the kinds of censorship and authoritarianism that, ironically, characterize the very fascism that supposedly needs to be eliminated. Gottfried's study is too particular, nuanced, and multifaceted to be reduced to simple correctives for these mass-media trends. It is, however, a model for the type of work that can earn a hearing from more attentive audiences. Critiques of fascism from the right must follow Gottfried's lead, not Goldberg's, to attain credibility.

The Conservative Mindset

The harsh, uncouth rhetoric of professional politicians stands in marked contrast to the writings of Russell Amos Kirk, a founding father of modern American conservatism.

Books on Kirk exist, but they're few. Fellow conservatives, many of them friends or colleagues of Kirk—T. S. Eliot, William F. Buckley, Barry Goldwater, F. A. Hayek, Eric Voegelin, and Leo Strauss—have received more attention. Kirk is the victim of his virtues: he was less polarizing, celebrated by followers and detractors alike for his measured temperament and learned judgments. He did earn numerous adversaries, including Hayek and Frank Meyer, who in retrospect appear more like ambivalent friends, but the staying power of Kirk's congeniality seems to have softened objections to his most resolute opinions.

Bradley J. Birzer, a professor at Hillsdale College who holds a chair named for Kirk, filled a need with his lucid and ambitious biography of Kirk, *Russell Kirk: American Conservative*. Birzer is the first researcher to have been granted full access to Kirk's letters, diaries, and draft manuscripts. He has avoided—as others haven't—defining Kirk by his list of accomplishments and has pieced together a comprehensive, complex account of Kirk's personality, motivations, and influences.

Birzer offers five themes in Kirk's work, and less so his private life, which Birzer only touches on: his intellectual heritage, his ideas of the transcendent, his Christian humanism, his fiction, and the reach and implications of his conservatism. Kirk isn't a dull subject. One need not identify as a conservative to appreciate his polished charm and idiosyncrasies. A plump, bespectacled gentleman who feigned disdain for technology, Kirk was something of a spiritualist with a penchant for the weird. He considered himself a Stoic before he had converted to Catholicism, a regeneration that makes sense in light of the relation of Stoic to Pauline thought.

As a young man Kirk spent four years in the military. His feelings about this experience were conflicted. He suffered from a blend of ennui and disenchantment but occupied his free time with reading, writing, and studying. He was horrified by the use of atomic bombs in Hiroshima and Nagasaki, where the United States had decimated the most flourishing Western cultural and religious centers in the Japanese Empire, just as he was by the internment of Japanese Americans.

The tremendous violence of the 20th century, occasioned by the rise of Nazism, communism, and fascism, impressed upon Kirk a sense of tragedy and fatalism. He came to despise totalitarianism, bureaucracy, radicalism, and "ideology" as leveling systems that stamped out the dignity and individuality of the human person. Hard to place along the left-right spectrum, he was as critical of big corporations and the military as he was of big government and labor.

When Kirk inserted himself into political debates he supported Republican politicians, becoming temporarily more interventionist in his foreign policy before returning to a form of Taftian isolationism, but he always remained more worried about reawakening the moral imagination than in having the right candidates elected to office. His was a long view of society, one without a fixed teleology or secular eschatology, and skeptical of utopian thought. Kirk advocated a "republic of letters," a community of high-minded and profoundly sensitive thinkers devoted to rearticulating perennial truths (such as the need to pacify human violence, temper human urges for power, and cultivate human longing for the transcendent or divine) and preserving humanist institutions.

Kirk's politics were shaped by imaginative literature and characterized by a rich poetic vision and vast cultural literacy. Fascinated by such disparate figures as Edmund Burke, Irving Babbitt, Paul Elmer More, T. S. Eliot, Sir Walter Scott, George Santayana, and most of the American Founders, Kirk was also versed in the libertarianism of Albert Jay Nock and Isabel Paterson, whose ideas he admired as a young man but vehemently rejected throughout his mature years. Burke and Babbitt, more than any other men, shaped his political philosophy. And his irreducible imagination made room for mysticism and a curious interest in ghosts.

Kirk's debt to Burke cannot be overstated. "Like the nineteenth-century liberals," Birzer says, "Kirk focused on the older Burke, but he countered their dismissal of Burke's ideas as reactionary and exaggerated."[139] Kirk also downplayed Burke the Whig, who championed the cause of the American Revolution, which Kirk considered to be not a revolution but a conservative restoration of ancient English liberties. Kirk was wary about the Enlightenment, as was Burke, because the scientism of that period tended to oversimplify inherently complex human nature and behavior. Kirk also thought the Enlightenment philosophes had broken too readily from the tested traditions of the past that shaped human experience.

Kirk appealed to American patriotism—which he distinguished from reckless nationalism—in *The American Cause* (1957) (which he later renounced as a "child's book"), *The Roots of American Order* (1974), and *America's British Culture* (1993), drawing attention to what he saw as the enduring customs and mores that guard against utopian conjecture. Yet American patriotism was, in Kirk's mind, heir to the patrimony of Athens, Jerusalem, Rome, and London. From the mistakes and successes of these symbolic cities Americans could learn to avoid "foreign aid" and "military violence," as well as grandiose attempts to "struggle for the Americanization of the world."[140]

Disillusioned with academia after his graduate work at Duke, Kirk was offered a position, which he turned down, at the University of Chicago. Kirk fell in love with the University of St. Andrews, however, where he took his doctorate and wrote a lengthy dissertation on Edmund Burke that would later become his magnum opus, *The Conservative Mind*. Kirk revised *The Conservative Mind* throughout his life, adding new permutations and nuances to ensure the continued resonance of his cultural mapping.

The almost instant success of *The Conservative Mind* made Kirk an unlikely celebrity. The book featured sharply etched portraits of men Kirk considered to be representatives of the conservative tradition. Regrettably, and perhaps tellingly, Kirk tended to ignore the contributions of women, passing over such apposite figures as Julian of Norwich or Margery Kempe, with whom he, as a mystic Catholic anglophile, had much in common. Kirk shared more with these women, in fact, than he did with Coleridge or Thomas Babington Macaulay, who appear in *The Conservative Mind*.

Kirk was also woefully misguided about American pragmatism. He overlooked Burke's influence on, and compatibility with, pragmatism. (As Seth Vannatta ably demonstrates in *Conservatism and Pragmatism*, Burke "is a model precursor of pragmatism because he chose to deal with circumstances rather than abstractions.")[141] Kirk failed to see the pragmatic elements of Santayana, whom he adored, and he seemed generally unaware of the work of C.S. Peirce. Kirk's breezy dismissal of William James, Santayana's teacher and later colleague, suggests he hadn't read much of James's oeuvre, for Kirk lumped the very different James and Dewey together in a manner that proved that Kirk himself was susceptible to the simplification and reduction he decried in others.

Conservatism, for Kirk, consisted of an attitude or mindset, not an explicit or detailed political program. Enumerating vague "canons" of conservatism that Kirk tweaked from edition to edition, *The Conservative Mind* was a "hagiographic litany,"[142] a genealogy of the high-minded heroes of ordered liberty and convention. Kirk didn't intend the book to be model scholarship. It was something more—an aestheticized bricolage cannibalized from Burke and Eliot and others, with inspirational and ritualistic value. It has never gone out of print.

Kirk is sometimes accused of being contradictory, holding simultaneously incompatible positions, in part because he lauded apparent antagonists such as John C. Calhoun and Abraham Lincoln. "Kirk found something to like in each man," Birzer says of Calhoun and Lincoln, "for each, from [Kirk's] perspective, embodied some timeless truth made sacramentally incarnate."[143]

Tension between rivaling conservative visions is reconciled in Kirk's desire never "to create an ideology out of conservatism, a theology at the quick and the ready with which one could easily beat one's opponents into submission."[144] Ideology, Kirk believed, was a symptom of totalitarianism, and as such was the common denominator of fascism and communism. Kirk believed his own philosophy was not an ideology, because he, like Burke, preferred "a principled defense of justice and prudence" to any specific faction or agenda.[145] He recognized that change was necessary, but thought it should be guided by prudence and historical sensitivity.

For a history buff, Kirk could be positively ahistorical and uncritical, ignoring the nuances and particularities of events that shaped the lives of his heroes. He ignored Calhoun's commitment to the peculiar institution, and with a quick wave of the hand erased slavery from Calhoun's political calculus, adding that "Calhoun defended the rights of minorities,"[146] which is true in the sense of a voting bloc but confusing in light of the racial and ethnic connotations of "minority" in contemporary usage. (Kirk clarified in subsequent pages that by "minorities" he meant "numerical minorities, or economic or sectional or religious or political."[147]) Kirk made clumsy caricatures out of his assumed enemies, calling men like Emerson "perhaps the most influential of all American radicals."[148] Emerson had met

Coleridge, whose Romanticism partially inspired Emerson's transcendentalism. Yet Kirk loathed Emerson and praised Coleridge and saw no inconsistency in doing so.

Kirk was not alone during the 1950s. The decade witnessed a renaissance of conservatism, exemplified by the publication of not only Kirk's *The Conservative Mind*, but also Robert Nisbet's *The Quest for Community*, Strauss's *Natural Right and History*, Ray Bradbury's *Fahrenheit 451*, Eliot's *The Confidential Clerk*, Voegelin's *New Science of Politics*, Gabriel Marcel's *Man against Mass Society*, Christopher Dawkins's *Understanding Europe*, C. S. Lewis's *Mere Christianity*, Whittaker Chambers's *Witness*, and Buckley's *God and Man at Yale*. It was *The Conservative Mind*, however, that "gave one voice to a number of isolated and atomized voices."[149] It also lent intellectual substance and credibility to the activist groundswell surrounding such politicians as Goldwater a decade later.

When Kirk joined Buckley's *National Review*, the manner of his writing changed. Previously he had contributed to literary and scholarly journals, but, as Birzer points out, his "contributions to the *National Review* slowly but surely crowded out his output to other periodicals."[150] Working for *National Review* also drew Kirk into personality conflicts that passed as theoretical disagreements. Kirk sided with Buckley, for instance, in banishing from the pages of *National Review* any writers associated with the John Birch Society. Kirk despised the egoism of Ayn Rand, scorned the label neoconservative, and did not take kindly to the doctrines of Irving Kristol. Yet Kirk held Leo Strauss in high regard, in no small part because of Strauss's scholarship on Burke and natural rights.

Strauss is sometimes treated as the fount of neoconservativism, given that his students include, among others, Allan Bloom, Harry Jaffa, and Paul Wolfowitz. But Kirk never would have considered the esoteric and conscientious Strauss to be in a league with neoconservative provocateurs like Midge Decter and Norman Podhoretz, who indicted Kirk for anti-Semitism after Kirk, in a speech before the Heritage Foundation, stated that some neoconservatives had mistaken Tel Aviv for the capital of the United States—a tactless comment that was blown out of proportion.

"Kirk never sought conformity with those around him," Birzer argues, "because he never wanted to create a sect or a religion or a cult of personality."[151] Kirk labored for the sake of posterity, not self-promotion. "The idea of creating 'Kirkians,'" as there are Straussians, Misesians, Randians, and Rothbardians, "would have horrified [Kirk] at every level of his being";[152] Birzer insists that Kirk "desired only to inspire and to leaven with the gifts given him," adding that "[h]e did well."[153] "I hope," Birzer concludes, "I have done at least half as well" in writing Kirk's biography.[154]

Bringing Kirk into renewed focus during the contentious election season of 2016, as the term conservatism was bandied about, contested, and abused by commentators as varied as David Brooks and Phyllis Schlafly, Megyn Kelly and Rush Limbaugh, Karl Rove and Michael Savage, Birzer reminded us—and reminds us today—that conservatism, properly understood, is a "means, a mood, an attitude to conserve, to preserve, and to pass on to future generations the best of the humane tradition rather than to advocate a particular political philosophy, party, or agenda."[155]

One wonders, watching the campaign stops and debate spectacles, the ominous political advertisements and alarmist fundraising operations, what's left of this humane tradition in our current political discourse. When our politicians lack a responsible and meaningful awareness of the residual wisdom of the ages, we get the leadership and politics we deserve. Would that we had more Russell Kirks around to remind us of the enduring things that, in times like these, are hard to find and difficult to believe in.

Sanctifying the Individual

Academics often write for themselves. Chasing tenure, promotion, and the fleeting approval of their peers, they author books that no one reads. Hyperspecialized and boring, jargon-laden and politically ineffectual, these works fail to account for the big questions that interest the educated public and inspire young students.

Larry Siedentop, an emeritus fellow of Keble College, Oxford, is not so insular or pedantic. In *Inventing the Individual*, he advances a grand concept of "the West," a totalizing signifier that has lost currency in recent decades because it implies a monolithic territory with a shared culture and linear history at odds with its turbulent, complicated past. He rejects the notion of a static or essentialized Western civilization and conventional history as written by professional historians. Instead, he outlines periods or eras according to their sociological developments. Doing so allows him to define historical figures and phases by their treatment of family, religion, property, law, government, and philosophy.

Siedentop chides that as a consequence of following professional historians and academic trends, "we no longer have a persuasive story to tell ourselves about our origins and developments."[156] He sets out to tell just that kind of story, resting on two assumptions:

1. "If we are to understand the relationship between beliefs and social institutions ... then we have to take a very long view."[157]
2. "Beliefs are ... of primary importance" to the progress or regress of civilization, as demonstrated by Marxism's infiltration of "liberal thinking" during the 20th century.[158]

Siedentop recognizes that the world is a battleground of ideas—a proposition that seems obvious in light of the rise of Islamic fundamentalism and the "transmuting of Marxist socialism into quasi-capitalism in the world's largest country, China."[159] He traces arguably the most lasting and significant idea of Western liberalism—that of the individual—from its roots in Greek and Roman antiquity to its proliferation during the Middle Ages and finally to its current manifestation in secularism. Siedentop argues that contrary to common beliefs, the Renaissance was not central to the displacement of ancient values and that "as an historiographical concept the Renaissance has been grossly inflated."[160] Evidence of modernity, he submits, percolated much earlier: during the 10th century.

Boldly abridging the centuries into neat conjectural paradigms, Siedentop nevertheless captures depth and detail while presenting a magisterial and impressive narrative that is also coherent, perhaps too coherent for those who believe history is anything but tidy. Siedentop disputes that Greek and Roman antiquity were, unlike their Christian posterity, characterized by political freedoms and the prizing of reason and inquiry. Antiquity was marked by a different kind of religion, rooted in kin and tribe. The distinction between public and private had not yet developed; the demarcation was instead between public and domestic.

In this time before Christianity, inequality was an unchallenged virtue, an ultimate good; all morality vested in the paterfamilias, the keeper of the clan. There were no rights as such, not even to life, at least not outside the hierarchical family unit. All human agency was directed toward the preservation and glorification of the household and the lineage of its members, in particular the dominant male hero. Devotion to the family shaped rules about property and ownership; dutiful sexual reproduction and close ties between relatives led to the growth of families and eventually to the corporate associations that, with their shared domestic practices and mores, became nascent cities.

Siedentop's chief contribution is to show that, throughout Western history, liberty has not entailed a rejection of Christianity; there's no historical basis for the allegation that Christianity is inherently authoritarian, statist, or illiberal. To the contrary, Christianity created the conditions necessary for economic and political liberalism to flourish, first by threatening the aristocratic models of the ancient citizen class, and second by redirecting human curiosity toward the individual soul and its afterlife. "Liberal thought is the offspring of Christianity,"[161] Siedentop asserts, because "liberalism rests on the moral assumptions provided by Christianity."[162]

The teachings of Jesus of Nazareth undermined the ancient patriarchal family of the Greek and Roman models by emphasizing the moral agency of individuals and their correlative responsibilities. "For I am come to set a man at variance against his father, and the daughter against her mother, and the daughter in law against her mother in law," Jesus declared, adding that "a man's foes shall be they of his own household." Such a statement would have appalled and baffled the ancients with their ancestor worship and their consecration of hearth and home.

The Apostle Paul broadened Jesus's lessons and instructions to encompass a wider notion of justice grounded in moral equality. He championed a collaborative social order that would support, nourish, and discipline its members separately and on a case-by-case basis. Individuals, not groups, were admitted into heaven based on their personal beliefs and inner convictions. Society thus needed to motivate individual sanctification.

The gift of grace was available to anyone who chose to accept it; consequently, everyone possessed a basic dignity that legal institutions had to recognize. "The quality of individual will or disposition," explains Siedentop, "was becoming the Christian leitmotiv. Paul's imagery of depth had fostered the sense of a realm of conscience that demanded respect. Individual agency and divine agency were now understood as parts of a continuum."[163]

Siedentop's narrative of the spread of reason and rationality and his portrayal of the doctrine of free will that gained credence within the early Christian church represent the theoretical antithesis to Nietzsche's genealogy of morals. Whereas Nietzsche chastised Christianity for its celebration of meekness and mildness—ethics of self-negation that he considered sickly—Siedentop details the early church fathers' strong defense of rights of conscience and freedom of worship. Whereas Nietzsche located a virile individualism in nobility and aristocracy, Siedentop sees in monasticism the emergence of consensual market associations and exchanges subject to a definite rule of law. Whereas Nietzsche characterized Christianity as a form of "slave morality" marked by *ressentiment*, Siedentop reveals that the competition between church and state inadvertently brought about the shifting jurisdictions, fluid boundaries, and vying claims of authority that enabled market liberalism to expand. Unlike Nietzsche, Siedentop is neither tendentious nor polemical, but the point remains: his depiction of Christian liberty is incompatible with Nietzsche's rendering of Christians as evil and immoral, duplicitous and envious.

We are the sum of our past, the product of our combined labors through the several generations. We have inherited customs and beliefs often unwittingly and in different forms. Having survived political unrest, ideological opposition, social experimentation, and technological progress, these customs and beliefs have proven their fitness and credibility over time. The title *Inventing the Individual* implies that humans have created rather than constituted individuals. The concept of the individual is not natural, timeless, universal, permanent, unchanging, or eternal; it's a construct that needed growth and cultivation. The idea of the individual remains the West's most defining, enduring contribution to humankind. It's also, perhaps, the most fragile and endangered.

We forget that the ideas and values we uncritically accept were unimaginable to many of our predecessors, even in the West. Without understanding how we came to assess and promote the individual—to such an extent that we now build laws and institutions to protect our inalienable rights— we risk taking those rights for granted and losing them. Siedentop puts this profound question to his readers: "If we in the West do not understand the moral depth of our own tradition, how can we hope to shape the conversation of mankind?"[164]

How indeed. All times and places are matters of turmoil and confusion until they have passed; then they become, in the pens of historians, inevitable. Not so with Siedentop, who puts our own moment into perspective by bringing us closer to the turmoil and confusion that created us. He helps us to appreciate why and how we do what we do and think what we think.

Illiberal Arts

A diversity of thought and a variety of perspectives are necessary to facilitate competition among ideas. Such competition selectively eliminates the bad from the good, the true from the false, and the practical from the impractical. Opposing viewpoints must enter into this more constructive contest so that the struggle does not move into the arena of physical violence. Thus, toleration of dissenting and controversial opinions is fundamental to peaceful discourse, intellectual progress, and human liberty.

These ideas about freedom of speech and expression have been passed down in different forms from Milton to Mill to Locke and made their way into the First Amendment of the United States Constitution. They are now under threat in the most unlikely of places: university campuses.

Greg Lukianoff's *Unlearning Liberty* addresses this phenomenon. Lukianoff opens this book with the curious case of Ronald Zaccari, the former president of Valdosta State University who single-handedly facilitated the "administrative withdrawal" of a student who publicly challenged the university's plans to construct two parking garages on campus. Lukianoff suggests that this case may seem extreme, "but it isn't all that exceptional."[165]

Each chapter documents several strange and excessive punitive measures implemented by universities. For instance, the disciplining of a Jewish student for using a benign Hebrew colloquialism to tell another group of students to pipe down while he tried to study; the student found guilty of racial harassment for reading a history book criticizing the Klan, while passersby saw only the cover of the book that displayed a photograph of a Klan rally; the student newspaper threatened with penalties for poking fun at the administration of a prominent business school.

Lukianoff's long, big-picture catalogue of university abuses might seem like an absurd or purely fictional parade of horribles, but every alarming incident detailed here is all too real. *Unlearning Liberty* is more surprising than enjoyable to read because its message is so disconcerting: In Lukianoff's words, "the world of higher education today is harming American discourse and increasing polarization."[166]

This book should leave you outraged and indignant at the illiberal, systemic, systematic, and bewildering suppressions of speech and association taking place on campuses across America. But its target is broader than that. It also criticizes the astronomical costs of higher education, the inflated salaries of university presidents and administrators, the bloated education bureaucracy, and the flagrant disregard by universities for legal processes and protocols that have developed out of centuries of trial-and-error: due process, fair hearings, trial by jury, and the opportunity of the accused to confront his accusers.

Lukianoff is a self-proclaimed Democrat, environmentalist, atheist, activist, lawyer, and the president of the nonprofit Foundation for Individual Rights in Education (FIRE). His work cuts across simple labels like "conservative" or "liberal" as he champions freedom of speech, individual rights, religious liberty, freedom of conscience, and equal protection under the law. Lukianoff himself is a trailblazing defender of the First Amendment and the Bill of Rights against universities that seek to train students and faculty into silent acceptance of bad policies, frightened acquiescence to abuses of authority, and docile submission to rampant corruption and discrimination. He and FIRE are famous—and, in some circles, infamous—for drawing attention to the arbitrary, selective enforcement of administrative policies against particular groups or individuals for political or retaliatory purposes.

I personally have fought against concerted attempts by faculty and administrators to silence criticisms of bad university policies. As one example, when a certain university ordered one of its students to remove a Ron Paul banner from his dorm room window, although other dorm room windows displayed an array of banners, I wrote an op-ed for the local newspaper challenging the university's selective enforcement of its policy. As a doctoral candidate at the university, where I had a long family history, I was concerned as much for the university as I was for the student. In response, one renowned faculty member with an endowed chair dashed off the following email to me:

I saw your letter in the Montgomery paper, and it sounds as if you are unaware of the contribution to the deaths and injuries of students because of banners and posters over windows at the university in New Jersey a few years back. As I learned in my own youth, "Ready, Fire, Aim" is not a good mode of conduct, and you are now in a program that, we hope, produces research-oriented people.

The irony here is the implication that I had failed to do my research while this professor had not failed to do hers: I wasn't criticizing the university policy per se, but the application of the policy to only one student, apparently for his political beliefs. As someone who had earned two law degrees and was currently practicing law (even though I was also a doctoral student in her program), I was not demonstrating a "Ready, Fire, Aim" mode of conduct, but she was. Reading *Unlearning Liberty* reminds me that I was never alone.

Universities ought to place a premium on free inquiry and the kind of unfettered intellectual exchange promoted and represented by the republicanism of America's Founders. Instead, universities have begun to discourage healthy disagreement and have become echo chambers in which certain members seek to enforce a rigid orthodoxy and to promote complacent groupthink. Even worse is the bullying "political correctness" that crushes ideological diversity and the discursive competition necessary for intellectual progress. Speech codes are a form of censorship. Rather than accomplishing their stated goal of reducing offensive language and behavior, they more often protect the power of administrators and prevent the exposure of embarrassing but true facts about university blunders and the application of stringent legalisms. As universities have brazenly abdicated their traditional role as guardians of communicative liberties and civilized debate, no new institutions have filled the void.

Without some special differentiation among rivaling opinions that are articulated freely within a community of thinkers, ideas and the society based on them cannot advance. It's time for universities to expand rather than compress the range of discursive options, and to multiply rather than decrease the chances for open dialogue. Doing so would aid in restoring universities to their proper role: searching for knowledge. Lukianoff's excellent book compiles a list of abuses. Now it's time for us to do something about them.

Ron Paul's Education Revolution

Former Texas congressman Ron Paul has been a track star, flight surgeon, obstetrician, author, political theorist, and presidential candidate. He's also written a book about American education. What motivated him to do so, and when did he develop an interest in curriculum, education technology, and pedagogy?

The answer, he explains in his preface to *The School Revolution*, is rooted in his personal experience as a young student in the 1940s and 50s. Dr. Paul was educated in a small public school in a suburb of Pittsburgh. He explains that he grew up when the "federal government was not yet endowed with the authority to keep us safe from ourselves,"[167] which is to say, when the messianic character of American education had not yet set out to secularize the youth, condition them to accept the ideals and principles of Statism, and divorce them from the canons and foundations of Western Civilization. The young Paul was instructed in prayer and the Bible and never saw his peers use drugs or commit crimes more serious than skipping recess or gym class.

Paul excelled in math and would finish assignments before the other students could. "The sooner I finished," he remarks, "the longer I could loaf while waiting for everyone to catch up, all the while probably making noise and interrupting others."[168] The hours he spent waiting on his peers caused him, later in life, to realize that "it would have been better for the school to adapt the teaching scenario to each student's ability—something now well understood in homeschooling."[169]

Dr. Paul's book is not an autobiography, despite what its opening pages might suggest. It is, rather, as its title declares, nothing less than a call to revolution. Dr. Paul says as much: "Because I see my work for liberty as extending far beyond politics, and because I see that freedom is not divisible, I offer this book as the second phase of the revolution."[170] The first phase of the revolution, to which he dedicated his career, was political (see, for instance, his 2008 book *The Revolution*), but this second phase is educational and, in that sense, foundational—for one must be educated in liberty before one may become an ambassador for liberty.

Government schools cannot cultivate the wisdom and freethinking necessary to achieve such education, for their very existence is antithetical to liberty. Against government schooling, which seeks always to validate its powers and hence to authorize the taxation and spending that sustain it, Dr. Paul presents "a libertarian view of education, from kindergarten through high school and college."[171] He submits that the stakes are higher in education than in taxation because "future voters are trained in the principles of who should decide on taxes."[172] In other words, one must learn to be aware of organized State theft (taxation) before one can effectively oppose organized State theft; however, one cannot, or cannot easily, learn about the dangers of the State from a State-sponsored system that seeks to train students into unthinking worship of the State.

Government schooling is premised on the false notion that every child can achieve the same level of success if only increased funding and nationalized curricula were mandated. This ideal and its cult of followers, the most ingenuous, well-meaning of whom are decent and moral yet misguided and indoctrinated teachers and parents, have only served to delay the maturity and personal responsibility of the youth while instilling in students a dangerous sense of entitlement: when students fail, the teachers are at fault; when students cannot complete their homework, the homework is too difficult; when books are too long, the authors failed to account for their readers' attention span.

The cumulative effect of these pedagogical errors is that students come to college with no plans for their future and with little appreciation for, or understanding of, the costs of their education. Once they incur student loan debts, they turn to the State to bail them out through "loan forgiveness" programs based on "civil" or "public" service. The predatory State thereby ensures and expands its power by making perpetual, infantilized dependents of the youth, who in turn pass along inculcated values of Statism to the next generation.

Only in the hands of the central planners, those elite missionaries for Statism, could this massive, bureaucratic deformation and ideological transformation come about. "[T]he modern welfare state," Dr. Paul says on this score, "is premised on the view that individuals are not fully responsible for their actions, and therefore they do not deserve extensive liberty."[173] He adds that the "welfare state winds up treating adults as if they were children," for just as "children are not granted a great deal of liberty of action by their parents, so the modern welfare state constantly expands its authority over the lives of individuals."[174] The more massive and more paternalistic the government education system becomes, the less mature the students become, and the further behind they fall in their competition with students of other nations.

By contrast, Dr. Paul proclaims, "[l]iberty is inescapably associated with responsibility."[175] Therefore, he reasons, "as individuals mature, they must accept greater personal responsibility for their actions."[176] Indeed, "there can be no extension of liberty without an accompanying extension of personal responsibility."[177] If modernity taught us anything, it was that the "most meaningful way to improve the world is to free up the creativity of individuals."[178] Too often our textbooks depict the history of Western Civilization as progressing in intelligence and creativity when humans were liberated from the constraints of the church—Stephen Greenblatt's *The Swerve: How the World Became Modern* comes to mind, although it isn't a textbook—but something quite different is the case: the sciences and the arts flourish when they are disentangled from State interference. Even the most memorable and talented preachers, saints, and theologians thrived when the church was liberated from the corruption and oversight of government.

If Dr. Paul had limited his commentary in this book to the descriptive—that is, to the cataloguing and categorizing of failures in the government education system—then readers would be in for a gloomy account. Yet he recommends exciting, profound alternatives to Statist education and advocates for rigorous leadership training "grounded in a system of cause and effect that rewards productivity, as assessed by consumers, and [that] promotes voluntary transactions and associations."[179] He urges readers to support homeschooling, an increased role for Web-based technologies in the classroom, rivaling education systems in which parents choose to place their children, the restoration of family-based practices and curricula, and drastic cost-cutting or more localized funding to finance measures in keeping with community values.

No longer should parents be forced to subsidize a flawed educational system that seeks to undermine family values and capitalism that together have done more than anything else to elevate the quality of life among all classes in all places, alleviate poverty, generate innovation and creativity, develop the humanities, facilitate wider access to basic healthcare and medicine, and expand general human happiness. This book, in conjunction with the Ron Paul Curriculum, redirects us to the family and capitalism and attempts to correct decades of educational regression. As the proverb says, "Train up a child in the way he should go: and when he is old, he should not depart from it." *The School Revolution* offers the children a direction in which they should go. Now let us train them.

No One Knows What "Change" and "Equality" Mean

Politicians today have weaponized two principles that are now prevailing orthodoxies on college campuses, in the mass media, and among activist blatherskites: change and equality.

Change and equality sound nice in theory, but what, exactly, do these words mean? The eminent thinker and man of letters Russell Kirk provides key insights into the nature and limitations of change and equality.

Is change always for the better? Isn't there regress, deterioration, degeneration, and decay? Wouldn't we need a conservative disposition—an understanding of history in its immeasurable complexity—to know the difference between change that's good and change that's bad?

"When a society is progressing in some respects," Kirk warns, "usually it is declining in other respects."[180] The French Revolution certainly brought changes: widespread violence, corruption, the beheading of innocents, the massacring of clergy, looting, chaos, food shortages, and the destruction of churches. The Russian Revolution promised change and delivered it in the form of war, mass murder, riots, starvation, and dictatorship. The Chinese Communist Revolution successfully instituted changes that resulted in tens of millions of deaths.

If you want change for the sake of something different, the object is transformation itself, not a definitive outcome. What do you achieve? The creed of change implies that you can never get things right: the only correct state is that of perpetual flow and flux.

"You're on the wrong side of history," we're told by those who demand change. They value progress as the *summum bonum*, as though the past were devoid of good people and useful data, as if it were a monolithic evil from which you must flee and hide your eyes. But you should not move forward—you should not change—without the past to guide you.

We must be mindful of the debts we owe our ancestors, without whom, after all, we wouldn't have the ideas, luxuries, technologies, and freedoms we enjoy. Kirk exemplifies a proper attitude toward change in his *Concise Guide to Conservatism*: "Change is essential to a good society," but it must take place "within the framework of tradition."[181] He adds that "progress is possible only so long as it is undertaken upon the sure footing of permanence."[182]

I like asking progressives what society would need to look like for them to become conservatives. What is their teleology, their ultimate goal for culture and governing institutions? What achievement would they preserve and defend?

Change can be dangerous. The wisdom of generations—the taking of the long view—acts as a check against those radical changes that lead to loss of life and violations of the dignity and bodily integrity of every human person.

Equality raises the questions: Equal to what? Equal in what sense? But this means it is a signifier without a signified. There's no such thing as equality in the tangible, phenomenal world. Every lawyer knows on some level that differentiations between people are inevitable.

"Civilized society requires that all men and women have equal rights before the law," Kirk writes, "but that equality should not extend to equality of condition: that is, society is a great partnership, in which all have equal rights—but not to equal things."[183]

Why? Because justice, in Kirk's view, demands "sound leadership, different rewards for different abilities, and a sense of respect and duty."[184] Moreover, "In the name of equality, the collectivist establishes a political and economic order which subjects a great mass of individuals to the will and whim of a new managerial elite."[185]

The law categorizes us: citizen and noncitizen, parent and child, minor and adult, alive and dead, employer and employee, buyer and seller, debtor and creditor, single and married, majority and minority, donor and donee, plaintiff and defendant, prosecution and defense, innocent and guilty, solvent and insolvent, offeror and offeree, payer and payee, promisor and promisee, landlord and tenant, agent and principal.

Nobody escapes labels under the law: human, mother, father, child, spouse, brother, sister, niece, nephew, cousin, aunt, uncle, descendant, heir, client, guardian, bystander, driver, owner, resident, patient, insured, devisee, witness, litigant, student, taxpayer, guest, signatory, broker, trustee, volunteer, testator, mortgagor, investor, author, licensee, victim, subscriber, decedent—the list goes on.

Everyone fits within more than one of these classifications, which are not necessarily hierarchical. The flesh-and-blood people to whom they refer, however, are not treated equally in all circumstances. They cannot be because no one can occupy an identical position in society, nor hold the exact same provisions in the exact same settings within the exact same jurisdiction.

We have different jobs, careers, ages, obligations, goals, talents, and familial statuses. The law treats people differently because of their different roles and responsibilities in specified contexts. Taxonomical differences are natural and inevitable, flowing from the diversity of human experience.

Laws by definition discriminate: they state who may or may not do something, who possesses or protects rights, who creates or enforces rules, who must or must not act in particular situations, which acts are proper or improper in light of unique circumstances. Discrimination is inevitable. The operative question, then, is *on what basis* laws discriminate. Some bases are acceptable whereas others are not.

Aristotle maintained that the telos, or the purpose, of the law is to achieve goodness and virtue. Accordingly, laws discriminating on the grounds of race are presumptively invalid because they have no bearing upon human intent or action, on the *pursuit* of goodness or virtue. Rather, they involve an immutable characteristic, a trait people cannot help, an unchosen quality of the human body.

Goodness and virtue, by contrast, involve *choices*. A person acts morally by selecting one course of action over another. The law incentivizes good behavior and punishes crime or mischief. It shouldn't penalize people for acts they didn't or couldn't commit, for properties they are incapable of changing or affecting.

Except in the eyes of God, absolute equality, true equality, doesn't exist. Attempts to attain it necessitate coercion, perhaps even the annihilation of certain people or the destruction of certain places and things. Yet I wouldn't expect the government forcibly to remove someone else's good lung to replace my bad lung to equalize our conditions. Besides, no two lungs are alike.

Equality, as a concept, is the enemy of another concept the left purports to champion: diversity. Every human being is unique. Every person has distinct skills, aptitudes, weaknesses, and temptations. Diversity involves differences. It is real, not an ideal like equality.

"Variety and diversity are the characteristics of a high civilization," Kirk says.[186] "Uniformity and absolute equality are the death of all real vigor and freedom in existence."[187]

We should celebrate the fact that no two people are alike, that our variety as a species makes us wonderful and marvelous. We're in awe when musicians produce sounds we *cannot* produce, when artists render images we *cannot* render, when athletes leap or jump or run in ways foreign to our bodies, when writers arrange words on a page with a facility we lack.

Diversity is good and beautiful; seeking to eliminate it in the name of equality is cruel and misguided. We rightly fear societies in which one group uses political power and the apparatus of government to deprive individuals of their wealth and property in pursuit of hypotheticals like equality. Kirk reminds, after all, that the "aim of the collectivistic state is to abolish classes, voluntary associations, and private rights, swallowing all these in the formless blur of the 'general will' and absolute equality of condition—equality, that is, of everyone except the clique which rules the state."[188]

Understandably, we focus on policy during election seasons. But maybe we should quiz candidates on their philosophical moorings. If we do, we might find that progressives have embraced quixotic concepts that lead, in practice, to violence and coercion rather than their intended outcomes.

Kirk cautioned against the siren songs of change and equality. We should listen.

Learning What We Don't Know

I begin with a trigger warning. What follows contains references that could evoke strong feelings about the nature and purpose of literature, a manifestly dangerous field of human creativity consisting of stories about, and representations of, highly sensitive and potentially upsetting subjects, including but not limited to racism, rape, classism, war, sex, violence, imperialism, colonialism, religious persecution, suicide, and death. Those who find discussions or descriptions of such demonstrably timeless elements of human experience unpalatable or offensive should consult medical professionals before reading my comments about Robert P. Waxler's *The Risk of Reading*. Readers are encouraged not to engage any aspect of this book that might provoke hurtful memories, grave discomfort, or existential angst.

Reading is precarious enough as it is, without having to introduce concepts or narratives about complex perennial themes, fictional renderings of plausible and fantastic events, or the contingencies of everyday life. Therefore, if you feel you must avoid material that elicits a passionate or emotional response derived from the inevitably discomforting features of both lived and imagined experience, then you must not only bypass *The Risk of Reading* but also lock yourself in a closet, plug your ears with your fingers, and shout "la la la la la" until you're no longer aware of your subjective self and the sometimes painful, sometimes joyous ubiquity of reality.

Enough of that. If you're still reading, you agree to hold harmless this reviewer, Robert Waxler, and the publishers of this book for any claims or damages resulting from serious discussions of literature. You're hereby warned: reading is risky—hence the title of Waxler's book. Not just reading, but deep reading, is risky, according to Waxler, because it teaches us "about who we are and where we are located in the midst of complexities in the world."[189]

Deep reading disturbs the satisfying complacency of both ignorance and certitude. It can make you unhappy, challenge your most cherished presuppositions, and force you to think rigorously and laboriously about the nature of human relations and our place in the world. A life without reading isn't so risky, at least for those who prefer not to be bothered with inconvenient narrative or exposed to different points of view. Knowing you're right without working for understanding is easy. Why get distraught? Why not simply "know" without having to exert yourself in contemplation, without exercising your imaginative powers?

My generation, the millennials, will take shameless offense at Waxler's notion that we are situated, temporal beings with definite bounds and limitations, little insignificant persons in a vast web of human history, near-nothings within a cosmic totality who are destined to suffer the fate of every living thing. This may be overstating, if not misrepresenting, Waxler's presiding themes, but the anti-egoist premise is implicit in his chapters. It is an irrefutable premise at odds with my generation's prized assumption that the knowing self is fluid and permeable, subject to the malleable constructions of choice and chance, always appropriable and appropriated—never fixed, never closed, never immutable, never assigned.

For my generation, the anything-goes-except-standards generation, slow reading—deep reading—is anathema, the kind of tedious exercise rendered unnecessary by hypertext and the rhyzomatic Internet. A studied appreciation for nuanced story and linguistic narrative has been replaced by an insatiable craving for instant gratification, by trite sound bites and fragmented data, by graspable bullet points and ready access to reduced testimony. We've got information at our hands, this generation of mine, but no wisdom or knowledge in our heads.

Although he does not come right out and say so explicitly, Waxler seems to have my generation in mind. I, like the character Lenny Abramov in Gary Shteyngart's *Super Sad True Love Story*, am "someone who grew up with books but now finds himself surrounded by screens, consumer sensation, data streams, [and] the spectacle of electronic circuitry masquerading as public transparency."[190] A child today cannot avoid these technological distractions. Waxler's not an old fogey intent on bemoaning new media for the sake of the cozy familiar or Luddite quixotism; rather, he's worried about what is happening to reading as much as to readers when the rhetorical medium incentivizes rank inattentiveness and scattered interest.

Reading properly, in Waxler's view, teaches us how much we do not know, not how much we know, about our mysterious universe and human interaction. Consequently and paradoxically, he maintains, reading improves and expands our tacit knowledge about the quotidian things that shape our lives and inform our decisions, the subtle things we might overlook or misapprehend if we aren't attentive. And we're not attentive, most of the time—at least that's what Waxler appears to mean by his emphasis on "the distraction of each flickering instant" in which "information and data pull us away from ourselves, set themselves up as sovereign, as if they are all-knowing gods."[191]

Having paid homage to deep reading in his introductory chapter, Waxler puts his deep reading, or the fruits of his deep reading, on display. He examines nine texts in as many chapters: Genesis (the creation account),

Frankenstein, Alice in Wonderland, Heart of Darkness, The Old Man and the Sea, Catcher in the Rye, One Flew over the Cuckoo's Nest, Fight Club, and *The Sense of an Ending.* Then there's a brief concluding chapter on the future of linguistic narrative—not a prediction or prophecy but a call to pensive action. These books have it all—sex, violence, death, sin, rebellion. They are risky.

Waxler encourages us to face our vulnerabilities and insecurities by reading deeply and widely, ever mindful of the nuances and possibilities of language and story. His subjects proceed chronologically, Genesis being the oldest text and The Sense of Ending, which was published just four years ago, the most recent. These subjects have little in common save for the high regard in which they're held by a critical mass of readers. It's premature to say whether some of these books are canonical—as in classics—but all of them are difficult and stirring: candidates for canonicity if they can prove their fitness over time.

All you need to know about Waxler's thesis resides in his title—and subtitle. He submits that his subjects are "risky" or "dangerous"—terms laced with sarcasm and irony—because they help us to make sense of other people and our surroundings, which together amount to culture and experience. Understanding our concrete phenomenal surroundings, via literature, enables us to make sense of what Whitman called the "Me Myself," or the "I" that was, for Descartes, the starting-point of metaphysics and epistemology—or so Waxler would have us believe.

Waxler's thesis may be right—who can deny such broad claims?—but it doesn't always play out as agreeably as it might in his analyses. Too much summary and synopsis presupposes a reader who hasn't undertaken the primary text. Waxler's local points are more interesting than his general conclusions about the worth of reading well and wisely—conclusions that, it must be said, are sufficiently apparent to go without saying, although they form the only discernable through-line in this exposition of disparate authors, texts, and time periods, and thus serve a vital function.

Waxler is not attempting to imbue his readers with cultural literacy; rather, he's trying to teach them how to read deliberately. He echoes Kenneth Burke by suggesting that literature is equipment for living. We shouldn't fail to recognize the skill with which Waxler dissects texts. The problem is that such dissection removes the strangeness of the reading

212

experience, deprives the unseasoned reader of his chance to luxuriate in the sublime power of language and story. Waxler's critical commentary simply cannot do what the literary works themselves do: provoke, inspire, move, awe, stimulate, anger, shock, and hurt. Therefore, a sense of repetition and banality settles over Waxler's arguments: the biblical account of creation teaches truths regardless of whether it "happened"; Mary Shelley raises unanswerable questions about restraints on human ambition; Lewis Carroll's Alice finds meaning in a meaningless world; Joseph Conrad's Marlow and Kurtz help us "locate our own ongoing journey that defines us, each in our own way"; Hemingway's portrayal of Santiago at sea instills understanding about "the truth of the achievement, the accomplishment, and the loss"; and so on. You get the gist: readers are vicarious participants in the stories they read; thus, the stories are instructive about the self. Again, unoriginal—but also undeniable.

Conservatives will be surprised at the manner in which Waxler enlists men of the left to make some traditionalist-seeming points. He mentions Lacan and Foucault—known in conservative circles for French Theory, poststructuralism, jargon, pseudoscience, and psychobabble, among other things—for the proposition that literature transmits virtues and values that constructively guide human activity and orient moral learning. Such references implicitly warn about the risk and short-sightedness of closing individuals within ideological boxes that can be stored away without consequence—or perhaps they demonstrate how creative thinkers can use just about anyone to make the points they want to make.

By all means read Waxler's book. But, *sooth to sayne*, if you really want a risk, if you really want to live dangerously, which is to say, as a self-aware, contemplative being, then you should—trigger warning, trigger warning!— read the books Waxler discusses rather than Waxler himself. I'm confident the risky Waxler would urge the same course. He's just that dangerous.

Acknowledgments

The essays, articles, and reviews in this book originally appeared as follows:

"Richard Posner: The Federal Court Maverick Turns Detractor." Review of Richard Posner's *The Federal Judiciary* (Harvard University Press, 2017) in *Los Angeles Review of Books* (December 15, 2017) [available at https://lareviewofbooks.org/article/richard-posner-the-federal-court-maverick-turns-detractor/].

"Richard Posner is a Monster." *Los Angeles Review of Books* (December 1, 2016) [available at https://lareviewofbooks.org/article/richard-posner-is-a-monster/#!].

"Judges and Dons." Review of Richard Posner's *Divergent Paths: The Academy and the Judiciary* (Harvard University Press, 2016). Review in *The University Bookman* (Winter 2016) [available at http://www.kirkcenter.org/index.php/bookman/article/judges-and-dons/].

"The Sad Career of Justice Stephen Breyer." *The Imaginative Conservative* (April 5, 2016) [available at http://www.theimaginativeconservative.org/2016/04/sad-career-justice-stephen-breyer.html].

"Consistently Inconsistent: On Oliver Wendell Holmes Jr." *Los Angeles Review of Books* (August 27, 2019) [available at https://lareviewofbooks.org/article/consistently-inconsistent-on-oliver-wendell-holmes/].

"The Greatest Judge in American History?" *Athenaeum Review*. Issue 2 (Spring / Summer 2019), pp. 52–55.

"The Court's Supreme Injustice." Review of Paul Finkelman's *Supreme Injustice* (Harvard University Press, 2018) in *Los Angeles Review of Books* (May 24, 2018) [available at https://lareviewofbooks.org/article/the-courts-supreme-injustice/].

"What Is the Rule of Law, Anyway?" *The Intercollegiate Review* (Spring 2017) [available at https://home.isi.org/what-rule-law-anyway].

"Love and the Law Professors." *The University Bookman* (February 19, 2017) [available at http://www.kirkcenter.org/index.php/bookman/article/love-and-the-law-professors/].

"Our Real Constitution—And What Happened to It." *The University Bookman* (January 8, 2017) [available at http://www.kirkcenter.org/index.php/bookman/article/our-real-constitution-and-what-happened-to-it/].

"The Moral Case for Property Rights." Review of Adam MacLeod's *Property and Practical Reason* (Cambridge University Press, 2015). Review in the *Law & Liberty* (January 18, 2016) [available at http://www.liberty-lawsite.org/book-review/the-moral-case-for-property/].

"Nomocracy and Oliver Wendell Holmes, Jr." *Nomocracy in Politics: Liberty, Prudence, Imperfection, and Law* (September 30, 2013) [available at http://nomocracyinpolitics.com/2013/09/30/nomocracy-and-oliver-wendell-holmes-jr/].

"The Power of Dissent." Review of Melvin Urofsky's *Dissent and the Supreme Court: Its Role in the Court's History and the Nation's Constitutional Dialogue* (Pantheon Books, 2015). Review in *The Alabama Lawyer*. Vol. 77, No. 3 (May 2016), pp. 170-71.

"The 'Great Writ': The Power of Habeas Corpus in America." Review of Anthony Gregory, *The Power of Habeas Corpus in America: From the King's Prerogative to the War on Terror* (Cambridge University Press, 2013). Review in *The Freeman*, Vol. 64, No. 6 (July/August 2013), pp. 41–43 [available at http://www.fee.org/the_freeman/detail/the-great-writ#axzz2VXnkFiyl].

"A Word for Christian Lawyers: Remember Russell Kirk." *The Christian Lawyer*. Vol. 6, No. 3 (Summer 2010), pp. 6–9.

"Children Once, Not Forever: Harper Lee's *Go Set a Watchman* and Growing Up." *Indiana Law Journal Supplement*. Vol. 91, No. 6 (2015), pp. 6–4.

Review of Marja Mills's *The Mockingbird Next Door: Life With Harper Lee* (New York: The Penguin Press, 2014). Review in *Southern Literary Review* (2014) [available at http://southernlitreview.com/reviews/the-mockingbird-next-door-by-marja-mills.htm].

"The Circuitous Path of Papa and Ezra." *The American Conservative*. Vol.

16, No. 2 (March / April 2017), pp. 52–55 [available at http://www.theamericanconservative.com/articles/the-circuitous-path-of-papa-and-ezra/].

"Redeeming the Debauched Falstaff." *The American Conservative* (October 26, 2017) [available at http://www.theamericanconservative.com/articles/redeeming-the-debauched-falstaff/].

"Harold Bloom's American Sublime." Review of Harold Bloom's *The Daemon Knows: Literary Greatness and the American Sublime* (Spiegel & Grau, 2015). Review in *The American Conservative* (May 28, 2015) [available at http://www.theamericanconservative.com/articles/harold-blooms-american-sublime/].

Review of Casey Cep, *Furious Hours: Murder, Fraud, and The Last Trial of Harper Lee* (New York: Alfred A. Knopf, 2019). Review in *The Alabama Lawyer*. Vol. 80, No. 6 (2019), pp. 462–64.

"The Humanistic Tradition in Literature." Review of James Seaton's *Literary Criticism from Plato to Postmodernism: The Humanistic Alternative* (New York: Cambridge University Press, 2014). Review in *The University Bookman* (Summer 2014) (posted online on June 21, 2014) [available at http://www.kirkcenter.org/index.php/bookman/article/the-humanistic-tradition-in-literature/].

"Why the Union Soldiers Fought." Review of Gary Gallagher, *The Union War* (Cambridge, Massachusetts: Harvard University Press, 2011). Review in *The University Bookman* (Fall 2011) (posted online on October 16, 2011) [available at http://www.kirkcenter.org/index.php/bookman/article/why-the-union-soldiers-fought/].

Review of Michael Kreyling's *A Late Encounter With the Civil War* (University of Georgia Press, 2014). Review in *Southern Literary Review* (2015) [available at http://southernlitreview.com/reviews/a-late-encounter-with-the-civil-war-by-michael-kreyling.htm].

Review of Coleman Hutchison, *Apples and Ashes: Literature, Nationalism, and the Confederate States of America* (Athens, Georgia: University of Georgia Press, 2012). Review in *Southern Literary Review* (2012) [available at http://southernlitreview.com/reviews/apples-ashes-by-coleman-hutchison.htm].

Review of Gilbert Allen's *The Final Days of Great American Shopping* (Columbia, South Carolina: University of South Carolina Press, 2016). Review in *Southern Literary Review* (2016) [available at http://southernlitreview.com/reviews/final-days-great-american-shopping-gilbert-allen.htm].

"Paul Cantor: Model Mentor." *The Ludwig von Mises Institute Canada Emerging Scholar Article* (September 23, 2014) [available at http://mises.ca/posts/blog/paul-cantor-model-mentor/].

"Phantoms of Terror." Review of Adam Zamoyski's *Phantom Terror* (New York: Basic Books, 2015). Review in *Taki's Magazine* (April 29, 2015) [available at http://takimag.com/article/phantoms_of_terror_allen_mendenhall/print#disqus_thread].

"Donald Trump the Cowboy." *The Daily Caller* (January 30, 2017) [available at http://dailycaller.com/2017/01/30/donald-trump-and-the-image-of-the-cowboy/].

"Teaching Humbly and Without Malice." *Law & Liberty* (July 25, 2019) [available at https://www.lawliberty.org/2019/07/25/teaching-humbly-and-without-malice-russell-kirk/].

"Sex With the Dead." *The Smart Set* (Drexel University) (January 14, 2019) [available at https://thesmartset.com/sex-with-the-dead/].

"Flourishing and Synthesis." *The Journal of Ayn Rand Studies*. Vol. 11, No. 2 (Issue 22, December 2011), pp. 249–53.

"Debunking the Demographers." Review of Jonathan V. Last, *What to Expect When No One's Expecting: America's Coming Demographic Disaster* (New York: Encounter Books, 2013). Review in *The University Bookman* (Spring 2013) (posted online on April 1, 2013) [available at http://www.kirkcenter.org/index.php/bookman/article/debunking-the-demographers/].

"Book Review: *Bourgeois Equality: How Ideas, Not Capital or Institutions, Enriched the World*. Deirdre McCloskey. University of Chicago Press." *Quarterly Journal of Austrian Economics*. Vol. 19, No. 2 (Summer 2016), pp. 214–22 [available at https://mises.org/system/tdf/Review%20of%20Bourgeois%20Equality.pdf?file=1&type=document].

"The Dirty Business of Government Trash Collection." *Mises Daily* (October 14, 2015) [available at https://mises.org/library/dirty-business-government-trash-collection].

"Make America Mobile Again." Review of F. H. Buckley's *The Way Back: Restoring the Promise of America* (Encounter Books, 2016). Review in *The American Spectator* (April 28, 2016) [available at http://spectator.org/make-america-mobile-again/].

"Pragmatists versus Agrarians?" Review of John J. Langdale, *Superfluous Southerners: Cultural Conservatism and the South, 1920–1990* (University of Missouri Press, 2012). Review in *The University Bookman* (Spring 2013) (posted online on June 1, 2013) [available at http://www.kirkcenter.org/index.php/bookman/article/pragmatists-versus-agrarians/].

"Book Review: The Problem With Socialism." Review of Thomas DiLorenzo's *The Problem With Socialism* (Regnery Publishing, 2016). Review in *The Daily Caller* (August 17, 2016) [available at http://dailycaller.com/2016/08/17/book-review-the-problem-with-socialism/].

"The Antiwar Tradition in American Letters." Review of War No More: Three Centuries of American Antiwar and Peace Writing, edited by Lawrence Rosenwald (The Library of America, 2016). Review in *Antiwar.com* (July 13, 2016) [available at http://original.antiwar.com/mendenhall/2016/07/12/antiwar-tradition-american-letters/].

"Glory and Indignity." Review of David Johnson, *John Randolph of Roanoke* (Baton Rouge: Louisiana: Louisiana State University Press, 2012). Review in *The University Bookman* (Fall 2012) (posted online on October 16, 2012) [available at http://www.kirkcenter.org/index.php/bookman/article/glory-and-indignity/].

"October Read of the Month: *Dixie Bohemia*, by John Shelton Reed." Review of John Shelton Reed, *Dixie Bohemia: A French Quarter Circle in the 1920s* (Baton Rouge, Louisiana: Louisiana State University Press, 2012). Review in *Southern Literary Review* (2012) [available at http://southernlitreview.com/reviews/october-read-of-the-month-dixie-bohemia-by-john-shelton-reed.htm].

"Buckley for the Masses." *Chronicles: A Magazine of American Culture*. Vol. 36, No. 7 (2012), pp. 28–29.

"In Search of Fascism." Review of Paul Gottfried's *Fascism: The Career of a Concept* (Northern Illinois University Press, 2016). Review in *Swarajya*

(July 2, 2016) [available at http://swarajyamag.com/books/in-search-of-fascism]. Originally published in *The American Conservative*. Vol. 15, No. 3 (May/June 2016), pp. 55–57.

"The Conservative Mindset: Allen Mendenhall on *Russell Kirk: American Conservative*." Review of Bradley J. Birzer's *Russell Kirk: American Conservative* (University of Kentucky Press, 2015). Review in *Los Angeles Review of Books* (March 19, 2016) [available at https://lareviewofbooks.org/review/the-conservative-mindset].

"Sanctifying the Individual." Review of Larry Siedentop's *Inventing the Individual: The Origins of Western Liberalism* (Belknap Press of Harvard University Press, 2014). Review in *The Freeman* (January 22, 2015) [available at http://fee.org/freeman/detail/sanctifying-the-individual?utm_source=Foundation+for+Economic+Education+Current+Contacts&utm_campaign=062ace3858-In_Brief_1_22_2015&utm_medium=email&utm_term=0_77ef1bd48e-062ace3858-13799910].

"Illiberal Arts." Review of Greg Lukianoff's *Unlearning Liberty: Campus Censorship and the End of the American Debate* (New York: Encounter Books, 2014). Review in *The Freeman* (April 18, 2014) [available at http://www.fee.org/the_freeman/detail/illiberal-arts].

"Ron Paul's Education Revolution." Review of Ron Paul's *The School Revolution: A New Answer for Our Broken Education System* (New York and Boston: Grand Central Publishing, 2013) *LewRockwell.com* (October 28, 2013) [available at http://www.lewrockwell.com/2013/10/allen-mendenhall/ron-pauls-homeschool-revolution/].

"No One Knows What 'Change' and 'Equality' Mean." *The Intercollegiate Review* (October 1, 2019) [available at https://isi.org/intercollegiate-review/russell-kirk-change-equality/].

"Learning What We Don't Know." Review of Robert P. Waxler's *The Risk of Reading: How Literature Helps Us to Understand Ourselves and the World* (Bloomsbury, 2014). Review in *The University Bookman* (Summer 2015) [available at http://www.kirkcenter.org/index.php/bookman/article/learning-what-we-dont-know/].

Endnotes

Part I: Law

1   See Robert H. Bork, *The Tempting of America: The Political Seduction of the Law* (New York: Touchstone, 1990) 6, 45–48, and 248.

2   William H. Rehnquist, "The Notion of a Living Constitution," *Texas Law Review*, Vol. 54 (1976) 704–05.

3   Thomas Sowell, *A Conflict of Visions* (New York: William Morrow, 1987) 38, 51–52, 55, 116, 162–63, 168, 175–77, 179, 181, 186–87, 201–02, 258 n. 55.

4   "Showcase Panel IV: An Examination of Substantive Due Process and Judicial Activism." A debate between J. Harvie Wilkinson, III; Steven G. Calabresi; Mark Tushnet; William H. "Chip" Mellor; Walter E. Dellinger, III; and Nelson R. Lund and moderated by Edith H. Jones. The Federalist Society 2012 National Lawyers Convention. *Texas Review of Law & Politics*, Vol. 17, No. 2 (2013) 323. Calabresi refers to Holmes as "Judge Wilkinson's hero." Ibid., 326.

5   See Sheldon M. Novick, "Introduction," *The Collected Works of Justice Holmes: Complete Public Writings and Selected Opinions of Oliver Wendell Holmes* (Sheldon M. Novick, ed., 1995) 115–17, 121, and 134 nn. 178–90.

6   Felix Frankfurter, "The Constitutional Opinions of Justice Holmes," *Harvard Law Review*, Vol. 29 (1916) 698.

7   Forrest McDonald, "Forward," in M. E. Bradford, *Original Intentions on the Making of the United States Constitution* (Athens: The University of Georgia Press, 1993) 16.

8   Marshall L. DeRosa, *The Ninth Amendment and the Politics of Creative Jurisprudence: Disparaging the Fundamental Right of Popular Control* (New Brunswick, New Jersey, and London: Transaction Publishers, 1996) 151–52.

9   Thomas Sowell, "Obama and the Supreme Court/'Empathy' vs. law," *Twin Cities Pioneer Press* (May 7, 2009) [available at https://www.twincities.com/2009/05/07/thomas-sowell-obama-and-the-supreme-courtempathy-vs-law/].

10   Ibid.

11   Ibid.

12   Letter from Oliver Wendell Holmes, Jr. to John T. Morse (Nov. 28, 1926),

quoted in Louis Menand's *The Metaphysical Club* (New York: Farrar, Straus and Giroux, 2001) 67.

13 Oliver Wendell Holmes, Jr., "Ideals and Doubts," *Illinois Law Review*, Vol. 10 (1915) 3.

14 *Tyson & Bro.-United Theatre Ticket Offices, Inc. v. Banton*, 273 U.S. 418, 446 (1927) (Holmes, J., dissenting).

15 Letter from Oliver Wendell Holmes, Jr. to Harold Laski (March 4, 1920), in *Holmes-Laski Letters: The Correspondence of Mr. Justice Holmes and Harold J. Laski, 1916–1925*, Vol. 1 (Mark DeWolfe Howe, editor, 1953) 249.

16 *Giles v. Harris*, 189 U.S. 475, 488 (1903).

17 *Bartels v. Iowa*, 262 U.S. 404, 412 (1921) (Holmes, J., dissenting).

18 Frankfurter, supra note 6, 686.

19 Thomas Grey, "Holmes's Language of Judging—Some Philistine Remarks." *St. John's Law Review*, Vol. 70, No. 5 (1996) 7.

20 261 U.S. 86 (1923). This case arose out of a race riot. Holmes authored the majority opinion, which held that federal courts may review *habeas corpus* petitions raising discrimination claims in state courts.

21 237 U.S. 309, 345–50 (1915). Holmes dissented on the grounds that federal courts may review state court rulings as to due process violations.

22 281 U.S. 586, 595 (1930) (Holmes, J., dissenting).

23 *Truax v. Corrigan*, 257 U.S. 312, 344 (1921) (Holmes, J., dissenting).

24 Ibid.

25 198 U.S. 45 (1901).

26 Robert H. Bork, *The Tempting of America: The Political Seduction of the Law*, supra note 1, 44.

27 *McDonald v. City of Chicago*, 130 S.Ct. 3020, 3058 (2010) (Scalia, J., concurring); *City of Chicago v. Morales*, 527 U.S. 41, 85 (1999) (Scalia, J., dissenting).

28 *Lochner*, 75.

29 Ibid.

30 *Stack v. New York R.R. Co.*, 58 N.E. 686, 687 (Mass. 1900).

31 Oliver Wendell Holmes, Jr., *The Collected Legal Papers* (Mineola, New York: Dover Publications, 2007) 239.

32 Ibid.

33 Oliver Wendell Holmes, Jr., *The Common Law* (Boston: Little, Brown & Co., 1881) 35.

34 Oliver Wendell Holmes, Jr., "Book Notices." *American Law Review*. Vol. 14 (1880) 234.

35 Holmes, *The Common Law*, supra note 30, 1–2.

36 256 U.S. 345, 349 (1921).

37 Holmes, *The Common Law*, supra note 30, 37.

38 *Buck v. Bell*, 247 U.S. 200, 207 (1927) (Holmes, J., dissenting).

39 Stephen Budiansky, *Oliver Wendell Holmes: A Life in War, Law, and Ideas* (W. W. Norton & Company, 2019), 105–06.

40 Allen Mendenhall, *Oliver Wendell Holmes Jr., Pragmatism, and the Jurisprudence of Agon* (Bucknell University Press, 2017), 98, 101, 116.

41 Budiansky at 130.

42 Oliver Wendell Holmes Jr., "The Path of the Law," *Harvard Law Review*, Vol. 10 (1897) 461.

43 Budiansky at 185–86.

44 *The Pragmatism and Prejudice of Oliver Wendell Holmes Jr.* Seth Vannatta, Editor. Lexington Books, 2019. 1. (For this author's contribution to that volume, see Allen Mendenhall, "The Natural Law Theorist," *The Pragmatism and Prejudice of Oliver Wendell Holmes Jr.* Seth Vannatta, Editor. Lexington Books, 2019. 87–115.)

45 Louis Menand. *The Metaphysical Club.* (New York: Farrar, Straus and Giroux, 2001) 4.

46 Budiansky at 461.

47 Oliver Wendell Holmes, Jr. "Natural Law." *Harvard Law Review*, Vol. 32 (1918–19) at 40.

48 Ibid.

49 "The Path of the Law," Address at the Dedication of the New Hall of the Boston University School of Law (Jan. 8, 1897), in *Harvard Law Review*, Vol. 10 (1897) 460–61.

50 Holmes, "The Natural Law," *Harvard Law Review*, Vol. 32 (1918–19) 43.

51 Ibid., 44.

52 *S. Pac. Co. v. Jensen*, 244 U.S. 205, 222 (1917) (Holmes, J., dissenting).

53 Holmes, "The Natural Law," supra note 37, 41.

54 Ibid., 43.

55 Robert H. Bork, *A Time to Speak: Selected Writings and Arguments* (Wilmington, Delaware: ISI Books, 2008) 272.

56 Ibid., 311.

57 *Towne v. Eisner*, 245 U.S. 418, 425 (1918).

58 Max Lerner, *The Mind and Faith of Justice Holmes: His Speeches, Essays, Letters, and Judicial Opinions* (New Brunswick, New Jersey: Transaction Publishers, 1989) 222.

59 *Lochner v. N.Y.*, 198 U.S. 45, 75 (1903) (Holmes, J., dissenting).

60 *U.S. v. Johnson*, 221 U.S. 488 (1911).

61 278 U.S. 41 (1928).

62 *Compania General De Tabacos De Filipinas v. Collector of Internal Revenue*, 275 U.S. 87, 100 (1927) (Holmes, J., dissenting).

63 Richard Posner, *The Federal Judiciary* (Harvard University Press, 2017), xi.

64 Posner, *The Federal Judiciary*, 11.

65 Ibid.

66 Ibid., 5.
67 Ibid., 139
68 Ibid., 410.
69 Ibid., 411.
70 Ibid., 141
71 Ibid., x.
72 Ibid., ix.
73 Ibid., 386.
74 Ibid., 7.
75 Ibid., 12.
76 Ibid., 28.
77 Ibid., 127.
78 Ibid.
79 Ibid., 238.
80 Ibid., 412.
81 Ibid., 393.
82 Ibid., x.
83 Ibid., 40.
84 William Domnarski, *Richard Posner* (Oxford University Press, 2016), 1.
85 Ibid., 151.
86 Ibid., 95.
87 Ibid., 17.
88 Ibid.
89 Ibid.
90 Ibid.,146.
91 Ibid., 255.
92 Ibid.,1.
93 Ibid., 248.
94 Ibid., 247.
95 Ibid., 248.
96 Ibid., 127.
97 Richard Posner, *Divergent Paths: The Academy and the Judiciary* (Harvard University Press, 2016), x.
98 Ibid.
99 Ibid.
100 Ibid., 17.
101 Ibid., xii.
102 Ibid.
103 Ibid., xii, 73, 372.
104 Ibid., 8.
105 Ibid., 9.
106 Ibid., 8.

107 Ibid., 3.

108 Ibid., 9, 13.

109 Ibid., 9.

110 Ibid., 10.

111 Ibid., 121.

112 Ibid., 127.

113 Ibid., 121, 122, 127.

114 Ibid., 127.

115 Ibid.,

116 Ibid., 11.

117 Ibid., 1.

118 Ibid., 74.

119 Stephen Breyer, *The Court and the World: American Law and the New Global Realities* (Alfred A. Knopf, 2015), 8.

120 Breyer, *The Court and the World*, 8.

121 I do not mean this as an insult. Breyer himself encourages others "to find better and specific responses" than he can offer from his limited vantage point as a justice on the United States Supreme Court. Breyer, *The Court and the World*, 8.

122 Breyer, *The Court and the World*, 281.

123 Breyer can be impressively subtle with his advocacy. For example, when he asserts that "our federal courts may eventually have to take account of their relationships with foreign institutions just as they now take account of their relationships with state courts and other American federal and state legal institutions," he appears, in context and in light of his arguments throughout the book, to mean that federal courts ought to take account of their relationships with foreign institutions. Ibid., 7. The vague verbal construction "take account of" begs the question: What does Breyer have in mind? To "take account of" something seems innocuous and not quite the same as "utilizing," "following," or "employing." The argument that courts ought to "pay attention to" foreign law is not remarkable. It becomes clear, however, as Breyer lays out his argument, that "take account of" means something more like the deliberate implementation and incorporation of foreign laws and norms in the American legal system, a far more controversial notion than simply to notice or observe foreign law with objective distance.

124 Ibid., 4.

125 Ibid., 235.

126 Ibid., 284.

127 Ibid., 7.

128 Ibid., 4.

129 Ibid.

130 Ibid.

131 Ibid. 81.

132 Ibid., 13.

133 132 S. Ct. 1421, 566 U.S. ___, 182 L. Ed. 2d 423 (2012).

134 299 U.S. 304, 318–19 (1936).

135 323 U.S. 214, 221–22 (1944). Of this holding, Breyer states, "So what happened to civil liberties? How could the Court have reached such a decision? The question is a fair one, particularly since the majority included Justices Black, Douglas, Frankfurter, and Reed, all of whom later joined the unanimous Brown v. Board of Education decision, striking down racial segregation as unconstitutional. The most convincing, or perhaps charitable, explanation that I can find is that the majority, while thinking the government wrong in Korematsu itself, feared that saying so would only lead to other such cases in which the government was right, and that the Court would have no way of telling one kind from the other. Someone has to run a war. In this case, it would either be FDR or the Court. Seeing the folly of the latter choice, the Court elected not to question the President's actions. This is an argument, baldly put, for broad, virtually uncheckable war powers. But as we have seen, it resembles what many presidents may actually have thought in time of war." Breyer, *The Court and The World*, 36.

136 317 U.S. 1, 63 S. Ct. 1 (1942) (ruling in advance of a full opinion); 317 U.S. 1, 24–29, 63 S. Ct. 2 (1942) (ruling with full opinion).

137 In Breyer's words, "the Steel Seizure case, even if read narrowly, represents a major change in the Court's approach to the President's emergency powers. Occasionally a prior case … had pointed to court-enforced limits. But in the Steel Seizure case, the Court both held that limits existed and analyzed the matter in detail. Its conclusion: better the indeterminacy of Pharaoh's dreams than a judicial ratification of presidential emergency power without limits." Breyer, *The Court and The World*, 63.

138 Ibid., 61.

139 Ibid.

140 542 U.S. 466 (2004).

141 542 U.S. 507 (2004).

142 548 U.S. 557 (2006).

143 553 U.S. 723 (2008).

144 Breyer, *The Court and The World*, 80.

145 Ibid., 81.

146 Ibid., 80.

147 Ibid., 13.

148 Breyer concludes Part I by stating: "Interdependence means that, when facing subsequent cases like those discussed so far, the Court will increasingly have to consider activities, both nonjudicial and judicial, that take place abroad. As to the former, the Court will have to understand in some detail foreign

circumstances—that is, the evolving nature of threats to our nation's security, and how the United States and its partners are confronting them—in order to make careful distinctions and draw difficult lines. This need for expanded awareness will require the Court to engage with new sources of information about foreign circumstances, in greater depth than in the past. Indeed, by agreeing to decide, rather than avoiding or rubber-stamping, cases involving national security, the Court has implicitly acknowledged a willingness to engage with the hard facts about our national security risks." Ibid., 81.

149 Ibid., 81.

150 Ibid., 80.

151 Ibid., 91–92, 96–97.

152 Ibid., 132.

153 Ibid., 92.

154 Ibid., 91.

155 Ibid., 96–97.

156 Ibid., 168.

157 Ibid.

158 Ibid.

159 Ibid., 169.

160 That Breyer devotes considerable space to his concerns about treaty powers in relation to other constitutional provisions, such as the Supremacy Clause, shows he is alive to this distinction; his concerns also suggest that, under the Constitution, with regard to treaties, there remain open questions among reasonable thinkers about the limits and proper application of the separation-of-powers doctrine. See generally ibid., 228–35. See also *Sanchez-Llamas v. Oregon*, 548 U.S. 331 (2006); *Medellín v. Texas*, 552 U.S. 491 (2008); *Bond v. United States*, 572 U.S. ___ (2014).

161 See Breyer, *The Court and the World*, 237–39.

162 Ibid., 170. See, e.g., *Abbott v. Abbott*, 130 S. Ct. 1983, 560 U.S. 1 (2010); *Lozano v. Alvarez*, 133 S. Ct. 2851 (2013).

163 Breyer, *The Court and the World*, 195–97.

164 Ibid., 180–81.

165 See *BG Group PLC v. Republic of Argentina*, 572 U.S. ___, 134 S. Ct. 1198 (2014) (discussed in Breyer, *The Court and the World*, 185, 187–92, 195).

166 Breyer, *The Court and the World*, 195.

167 Ibid., 81.

168 In his responsibly mixed review of *The Court and the World*, Akhil Reed Amar states, "Left largely unstated is Breyer's apparent premise that as American judges become more familiar with non-American legal sources …, these very same American jurists will just naturally begin to think globally and to ponder foreign legal materials even in plain-vanilla cases of American constitutional law that do not directly involve foreign events or foreign persons." Akhil Reed

Amar, "Law and Diplomacy," *Los Angeles Review of Books* (November 24, 2015) [available online at https://lareviewofbooks.org/review/law-and-diplomacy] (last accessed January 3, 2016).

169 Breyer, *The Court and the World*, 81.

170 Jürgen Habermas, *The Lure of Technocracy*, trans. Ciaran Cronin (Cambridge, United Kingdom: Polity Press, 2010), 3–28.

171 "Death Penalty," Amnesty International Website, "What We Do" (last accessed January 3, 2016).

172 "Countries," Amnesty International Website, "A-Z Countries and Regions" (last accessed January 3, 2016).

173 Breyer submits the following: "When judges from different countries discuss different substantive approaches to legal problems, compare procedures, and evaluate the efficacy of judicial practices, they are not only exchanging ideas about specific tools of the trade. There is more. The underlying, but often unspoken, theme of any such meeting is the sustained struggle against arbitrariness. If the objective is ambitious, it has been so since the time of Hammurabi. The enterprise is not without setbacks. Often, like Penelope's weaving, what we create during the day is undone at night. But the effort is worthwhile. Civilization has always depended upon it. It still does. And now, to an ever greater extent, jurists from many different countries engage in that effort together." Breyer, *The Court and the World*, 280.

174 Ibid., 7.

175 Ibid., 5.

176 Richard Brookhiser, *John Marshall: The Man Who Made the Supreme Court* (Basic Books, 2018), 1.

177 Ibid., 263.

178 Ibid., 33.

179 Ibid., 1.

180 Ibid., 19.

181 Ibid., 264.

182 Ibid., 30.

183 Ibid., 12.

184 Ibid., 20.

185 Ibid., 22.

186 Ibid., 45.

187 Ibid., 151.

188 Ibid.

189 Ibid., 219.

190 Paul Finkelman, *Supreme Injustice: Slavery in the Nation's Highest Court* (Harvard University Press, 2018), 37.

191 Paul Finkelman, *Supreme Injustice*, 26.

192 Brookhiser, *John Marshall*, 20.

193 Ibid., 207.

194 Ibid., 229.

195 Ibid., 229.

196 Ibid., 4.

197 Paul Finkelman, *Supreme Injustice*, 34.

198 Brookhiser, *John Marshall*, 232.

199 Ibid., 143.

200 Ibid., 229.

201 Ibid., 276.

202 Ibid., 277.

203 Finkelman, *Supreme Injustice*, 1.

204 Ibid., 26.

205 Ibid., 36.

206 Ibid., 37.

207 Ibid., 48.

208 Ibid., 123.

209 Ibid., 129.

210 Ibid., 121, 124.

211 Ibid., 170.

212 Ibid., 191.

213 Ibid.

214 Ibid., 25.

215 Ibid., 58.

216 Adam Liptak, "Donald Trump Could Threaten U.S. Rule of Law, Scholars Say," *New York Times* (June 3, 2016) [available at https://www.nytimes.com/2016/06/04/us/politics/donald-trump-constitution-power.html] (last accessed December 1, 2020).

217 "Will the 'rule of law' survive under Trump." MSNBC.com [available at https://www.msnbc.com/all-in/watch/will-the-rule-of-law-survive-under-trump-867194947932] (last accessed December 1, 2020).

218 Shikha Dalmia, "The Immoral 'Rule of Law' Behind Trump's Deportation Regime." *Reason* (March 7, 2017) [available at https://reason.com/2017/03/07/the-immoral-rule-of-law-behind-trumps-de/] (last accessed December 1, 2020).

219 Shikha Dalmia, "How today's pro-immigrant activists are adopting the tactics of abolitionists," *The Week* (March 2, 2017) [available at https://theweek.com/articles/676729/how-todays-proimmigrant-activists-are-adopting-tactics-abolitionists] (last accessed December 1, 2020).

220 A.V. Dicey, *The Law of the Constitution*, edited by J. W.F. Allison (Oxford University Press, 2013) (1885), 233.

221 A. V. Dicey, *The Law of the Constitution*, 233.

222 Ibid.

223 F. A. Hayek, *The Constitution of Liberty*, edited by Ronald Hamowy (University of Chicago Press, 2011) (1960), 297.

224 Hayek, *The Constitution of Liberty*, 318.

225 John Hasnas, "The Myth of the Rule of Law," *Wisconsin Law Review* 199, Vol. 1995 (1995), 201.

226 Thomas Paine, *Common Sense* in *The Writings of Thomas Paine, Vol. 1 1774–1779*. Edited by Moncure Daniel Conway (G. P. Putnam's Sons, 1894), 99.

227 Thomas Paine, *Common Sense*, 99.

228 Stephen B. Presser, *Law Professors: Three Centuries of Shaping American Law* (West Academic Publishing, 2017), v.

229 Presser, *Law Professors*, v-vi.

230 Ibid., 11.

231 Ibid., 63.

232 Ibid., 104.

233 Ibid., 114.

234 Ibid., 138.

235 Ibid., 156.

236 Ibid., 241.

237 Ibid., 390.

238 Ibid., 83.

239 Ibid., 86.

240 *Tyson & Bros. v. Banton*, 273 U.S. 418, 446 (1927) (Holmes, J., dissenting).

241 Oliver Wendell Holmes Jr., "Ideals and Doubts," *Illinois Law Review*, Vol. 10 (1915), 3.

242 Presser, *Law Professors*, 2, 335.

243 Bruce P. Frohnen and George Wescott Carey, *Constitutional Morality and the Rise of Quasi-Law* (Harvard University Press, 2016), 10.

244 Quoted in Frohnen and Carey, *Constitutional Morality and the Rise of Quasi-Law*, 8.

245 Ibid., 18.

246 Ibid., 49.

247 Ibid., 38.

248 Ibid., 49.

249 Ibid., 221.

250 Ibid.

251 Ibid., 238.

252 Adam J. MacLeod, *Property and Practical Reason* (Cambridge University Press, 2015), 1.

253 MacLeod, *Property and Practical Reason*, 1.

254 John Locke, *The Second Treatise of Government* (1690) (MacMillan Publishing Company, 1952), edited by Thomas P. Peardon, 17.

255 MacLeod, *Property and Practical Reason*, 5.

256 Ibid., 235

257 Ibid.,

258 Ibid., 25, 77, 119, 159, 217.

259 William Blackstone, *Commentaries on the Laws of England, Vol. III* (1892) 129.

260 Thomas Jefferson to A. H. Rowan (1798) in *The Writings of Thomas Jefferson, Vol. IV* (J. B. Lippincott & Co, 1871), edited by H. A. Washington, 257.

261 Anthony Gregory, *The Power of Habeas Corpus in America* (The Independent Institute and Cambridge University Press, 2013), 1.

262 Gregory, *The Power of Habeas Corpus in America*, 11.

263 Ibid.

264 Ibid., 4.

265 Ibid., 5.

266 Ibid.

267 Russell Kirk, *Rights and Duties* (Ed. Mitchell S. Muncy, Intro. Russell Hittinger) (Dallas, TX: Spence Publishing Company, 1997), viii.

268 Kirk, *Rights and Duties*, 3.

269 Ibid., 4.

270 Ibid., 110.

271 Ibid., 29.

272 Ibid., 31.

273 Ibid., 30.

274 Russell Hittinger, "Introduction," in Russell Kirk, *Rights and Duties* (Ed. Mitchell S. Muncy, Intro. Russell Hittinger) (Dallas, TX: Spence Publishing Company, 1997), xxvi.

275 Ibid., 131.

276 Ibid.

277 Ibid., 139.

278 Ibid., 62.

279 Ibid.

280 Ibid.

281 Ibid., 139.

282 Ibid., 143.

283 Ibid., 124.

284 Ibid.

285 Ibid., 162.

Part II: Literature

1   See my review of Cantor's *The Invisible Hand in Popular Culture* in *The Independent Review*, Vol. 18, No. 1 (Summer 2013).

2   *Literature and the Economics of Liberty*, edited by Paul A. Cantor and Stephen Cox (Auburn, AL: Ludwig von Mises Institute, 2009), x.

3   "The Poetics of Spontaneous Order" is the title of the first chapter of *Literature and the Economics of Liberty*.

4   "An Interview With Paul Cantor: Austrian Economics and Culture." *The Austrian Economics Newsletter*, Vol. 21, No. 1 (Auburn, AL: Ludwig von Mises Institute: Spring 2001), 1.

5   1 Corinthians 13:11 (American King James Version)

6   Charles Lamb, Epigraph in Harper Lee, *To Kill a Mockingbird*. (HarperCollins, 1988) (1960).

7   Jake Flanagin, Is Harry Potter to Blame for This "Go Set a Watchman" Weirdness?, Quartz (July 13, 2015), available at http://qz.com/452086/this-go-seta-watchman-business-is-weird-and-troubling/.

8   *Despite Controversial Character Changes, Harper Lee Fans Eager to Read Mockingbird Sequel*, CBS Chicago (July 14, 2015), *available at* http://chicago.cbslocal.com/2015/ 07/14/despite-controversial-character-changes-harper-lee-fans-eager-to-read-to-kill-a-mockingbird-sequel-go-set-a-watchman/.

9   Harper Lee, *To Kill a Mockingbird* 5–6 (HarperCollins, 1988) (1960) [hereinafter Lee, *Mockingbird*].

10 Ibid., 5.

11 Ibid., 99–302.

12 Ibid.,. at 208–10, 214, 250. I say "most likely" because the text insinuates but never explicitly states that Bob Ewell beats or sexually abuses Mayella Ewell.

13 Ibid., 172–77.

14 Ibid., 167.

15 Ibid., 225. Tom Robinson tells the prosecutor that he "felt right sorry" for his accuser, Mayella Ewell, to which the prosecutor retorts, "*You* felt sorry for *her*, you felt *sorry* for her?"

16 Ibid., 253.

17 Ibid., 11–16.

18 Ibid., 225.

19 Ibid., 274–75 (the "Negro cabins" are separate from other homes and near the dump).

20 Ibid., 314–15.

21 Flanagin, supra note 3.

22 Gaby Wood, *Go Set a Watchman, Review: 'An Anxious Work in Progress,'* Telegraph (July 13, 2015), http://www.telegraph.co.uk/culture/books/bookreviews/11735560/harper-lee-go-set-a-watchman-review.html.

23 Michiko Kakutani, *Review: Harper Lee's 'Go Set a Watchman' Gives Atticus Finch a Dark Side*, N.Y. Times (July 10, 2015), available at http://www.nytimes.com/2015/07/11/books/review-harper-lees-go-set-a-watchman-gives-atticus-finch-a-dark-side.html.

24 Lee, *Mockingbird, supra* note 5, at 187.

25 Ibid., 141, 253.

26 The most famous critiques of Atticus Finch came from Monroe Freedman. For a representative example, see Monroe Freedman, *Atticus Finch*, Esq., RIP, Legal Times, Feb. 24, 1992, at 20–21; see also Monroe H. Freedman, *Atticus Finch –Right and Wrong*, 45 Ala.L. Rev. 473(1994).

27 Harper Lee, Go Set a Watchman (HarperCollins, 2015), 265.

28 Charles J. Shields, *Mockingbird: a Portrait of Harper Lee* (Henry Holt and Company, 2006), 121.

29 Ibid., 120.

30 Sam Sacks, *Book Review: In Harper Lee's 'Go Set a Watchman' Atticus Finch Defends Jim Crow*, Wall St. J. (July 10, 2015), *available at* http://www.wsj.com/articles/dark-days-in-maycombto-killa-mockingbird-1436564966.

31 The notion that we should treat *Mockingbird* and *Watchman* as separate stories—two different texts, two different constructions, two different men called Atticus Finch—is supported by one important discrepancy: In *Watchman*, Tom Robinson is alleged to have been acquitted when Atticus represented him, whereas in *Mockingbird* Tom Robinson was convicted. It is also supported by the fact that Lee waited this long to publish *Watchman*.

32 Lee, *Watchman, supra* note 23, at 247–49. Jean Louise sarcastically tells Atticus, "I grew up right here in your house, and I never knew what was in your mind. I only heard what you said. You neglected to tell me that we were naturally better than the Negroes, bless their kinky heads, that they were able to go so far but so far only...." Ibid., 247.

33 This seems to be Uncle Jack's explanation of Atticus: "The law is what he lives by. He'll do his best to prevent someone from beating up somebody else, then he'll turn around and try to stop no less than the Federal Government.... [B]ut remember this, he'll always do it by the letter and by the spirit of the law. That's the way he lives." Ibid., 268.

34 "There is a natural disgust in the minds of nearly all white people at the idea of an indiscriminate amalgamation of the white and black races." *Quoted in,* Joseph R. Fornieri, *Abraham Lincoln: Philosopher Statesman* (Southern Illinois University Press, 2014), 139.

35 "I have no purpose to introduce political and social equality between the white and the black races. There is a physical difference between the two which in my judgement will probably forever forbid their living together upon the footing of perfect equality, and inasmuch as it becomes a necessity that there must be a difference, I ... am in favor of the race to which I belong, having the superior position." Quoted in *Abraham Lincoln: Speeches and Writings* 1859–1865 32 (Library of American, 1989). During the fourth Lincoln-Douglas Debate, Lincoln stated:

I will say then that I am not, nor ever have been in favor of bringing about in any way the social and political equality of the white and black races, that I am not nor ever have been in favor of making voters or jurors of ne-groes, nor of qualifying them to hold office, nor to intermarry with white people; and I will say in addition to this that there is a physical difference between the white and black races which I believe will for ever forbid the two races living together on terms of social and political equality. And inas-much as they cannot so live, while they do remain together there must be the position of superior and inferior, and I as much as any other man am in favor of having the superior position assigned to the white race.

Ibid., 636.

36   "I have no purpose directly or indirectly to interfere with the institution of slavery in the States where it exits. I believe I have no lawful right to do so and I have no inclination to do so." *Quoted in* Ibid., 32.

37   *See* Richard Hofstadter, *Social Darwinism in American Thought* 15, 176–78 (Beacon Press, 1944).

38   *See generally* Peter S. Field, *The Strange Career of Emerson and Race*, 2 American Nineteenth Century History (2001).

39   Wood, *supra* note 18.

40   Natasha Trethewey, In Harper Lee's *'Go Set a Watchman,'* a Less Noble Atticus Finch, Wash. Post. (July 12, 2015), *available at* http://www. theguardian.com/books/2015/jul/12/go-set-a-watchman-review-harper-lee-to-kill-a-mockingbird.

41   Ibid.

42   *Quoted* in James Boswell, *The Life of Samuel Johnson*, LL.D. 372 (Philidelphia: Claxton, Remsen, & Haffelfinger, 1878).

43   *See* Allen Mendenhall, *Jefferson's Laws of Nature: Newtonian Influence and the Dual Valence of Jurisprudence and Science*, 23 Can JL & Jur. (2010); *see also* Allen Mendenhall, *From Natural Law to Natural Inferiority: The Construction of Racist Jurisprudence in Early Virginia*, 23 Can JL & Jur 20–21, 27–28, 33–34 (2010).

44   Frederick Douglass, *My Bondage and My Freedom* 369–74 (New York, Miller, Orton & Mulligan 1855).

45   Mark DeWolfe Howe, 1 *Justice Oliver Wendell Holmes: The Shaping Years, 1841–1870*, 82–88, 111,136–39,296 (Belknap Press of Harvard University Press, 1957).

46   John Milton Cooper, *Woodrow Wilson: A Biography* 272 (Vintage Books, 2011).

47   *See generally* Stefan Kuhl, *Nazi Connection: Eugenics, American Racism, and German National Socialism* (Oxford University Press, 2002).

48   Sacks, *supra* note 26.

49 Lee, *Watchman, supra* note 5, at 180.

50 Kakutani, *supra note 19.*

51 Trethewey, *supra* note 36.

52 Lee, *Watchman, supra* note 5, at 238.

53 Ibid., 239.

54 Ibid., 242.

55 Ibid., 251. Jean Louise also calls African Americans "a simple people" and expressly claims that she thinks she believes in the same "ends" as Atticus.

56 Mark Lawson, *Go Set a Watchman Review – More Complex Than Harper Lee's Original Classic, but Less Compelling,* The Guardian (July 13, 2015), *available at* http://www.theguardian.com/books/2015/jul/12/go-set-a-watchman-review-harper-lee-to-kill-a-mockingbird.

57 Daniel D'Addario, *Go Set a Watchman Review: Atticus Finch's Racism Makes Scout, and Us, Grow Up,* TIME (July 11, 2015), available at http://time.com/3954581/go-set-a-watchman-review/.

58 Thomas DiPiero, *Forget the Controversies—'Go Set a Watchman' is Worth Reading,* N.Y. Post(July 12, 2015), *available at* http://nypost.com/2015/07/12/forget-the-controversies-go-set-a-watchman-is-worth-reading/.

59 Marja Mills, *The Mockingbird Next Door* (Penguin, 2015), 3.

60 Ibid., 26

61 Ibid., 25.

62 Ibid., 49.

63 Ibid.

64 Ibid., 28.

65 Ibid., 27.

66 Ibid., 35.

67 Allen Mendenhall, "Harper Lee and Words Left Behind," *storySouth*, Issue 37 (Spring 2014) [available at http://storysouth.com/stories/harper-lee-and-words-left-behind/].

68 Casey Cep, *Furious Hours* (New York: Vintage Books, 2019), 35.

69 Ibid., 36.

70 Ibid., 39.

71 Ibid., 41.

72 Ibid., 229.

73 Ibid., 109.

74 Ibid., 145.

75 Quoted in Michael Reck, *Ezra Pound: A Close-Up* (McGraw-Hill, 1967), 41.

76 Quoted in *Ernest Hemingway: Selected Letters 1917–1961,* edited by Carlos Baker (Scribner Classics, 1981), 65.

77 Ibid.

78 Quoted in John Cohassey, *Hemingway and Pound: A Most Unlikely Friendship* (McFarland & Company, 2014), 56.

79 Quoted in Noel Stock, *The Life of Ezra Pound* (Routledge, 2013), 460.

80 Quoted in J. J. Wilhelm, *Ezra Pound: The Tragic Years, 1925–1972* (The Pennsylvania State University Press, 1994), 11.

81 Quoted in *Ezra Pound in Context*, edited by Ira B. Nadel (Cambridge University Press, 2010), 216–17.

82 Ibid.

83 Quoted in John Cohassey, *Hemingway and Pound: A Most Unlikely Friendship* (McFarland & Company, 2014), 97.

84 Ibid., 114.

85 Quoted in *Ernest Hemingway: Selected Letters 1917–1961*, edited by Carlos Baker (Scribner Classics, 1981), 548.

86 Ibid., 605.

87 Ibid.

88 Ibid., 549.

89 Quoted in *Ezra Pound in Context*, edited by Ira B. Nadel (Cambridge University Press, 2010), 61.

90 Harold Bloom, *The Daemon Knows* (Oxford University Press, 2015), 4.

91 Ibid., 4.

92 Ibid.

93 Ibid.

94 Ibid.

95 Ibid.

96 Ibid., 3.

97 Ibid., 4.

98 Ibid.

99 Ibid., 175.

100 Ibid.

101 Ibid., 6.

102 Ibid., 29.

103 Ibid., 428.

104 Ibid., 11.

105 Ibid.

106 Ibid., 194.

107 Ibid., 494.

108 Ibid., 39.

109 Ibid., 19.

110 Harold Bloom, *Falstaff: Give Me Life* (New York: Scribner, 2017), 158.

111 Ibid., 1.

112 Ibid., 11.

113 Ibid., 76.
114 Ibid., 2.
115 Ibid.
116 Ibid.
117 Kate Havard, "Falstaff Revisited," *Commentary* (May 2017) [available at https://www.commentarymagazine.com/articles/kate-havard/falstaff-revisited/].
118 Bloom, *Falstaff*, 11.
119 Ibid.
120 Ibid., 29.
121 Ibid.
122 Ibid., 5.
123 Ibid.
124 Ibid., 4.
125 Ibid.
126 Ibid., 47.
127 Ibid.
128 Ibid., 1.
129 Harold Bloom, "Introduction," *William Shakespeare: Tragedies* (edited with introduction by Harold Bloom) (New York: Bloom's Literary Criticism, 2010), 12.
130 Bloom, *Falstaff*, 1.
131 James Seaton, *Literary Criticism from Plato to Postmodernism* (Cambridge University Press, 2014), 53.
132 James Seaton, *Literary Criticism from Plato to Postmodernism*, 52.
133 Ibid., 1.
134 Ibid., 19.
135 Ibid., 28.
136 Ibid., 3.
137 Ibid., 73.
138 Ibid., 83.
139 Ibid., 28.
140 Ibid., 73.
141 Ibid., 100.
142 Ibid., 157.
143 Ibid., 193.
144 Ibid., 85.
145 Ibid., 198.
146 Ibid.
147 Ibid., 112.
148 Gary W. Gallagher, *The Union War* (Harvard University Press, 2011), 4.
149 Ibid., 4.
150 Ibid., 5.
151 Ibid.

152 Ibid., 2.
153 Ibid., 44.
154 Ibid., 46.
155 Ibid.
156 Michael Kreyling, *A Late Encounter with the Civil War* (University of Georgia Press, 2013), ix.
157 Ibid., 1
158 Ibid.
159 Ibid., 6.
160 Ibid., 4.
161 Ibid., 7.
162 Ibid., 61.
163 Ibid., 64.
164 Ibid., 73.
165 Ibid., 93.
166 Coleman Hutchison, *Apples and Ashes: Literature, Nationalism, and the Confederate States of America* (The University of Georgia Press, 2012), 2.
167 Ibid., 3.
168 Ibid.
169 Ibid., 20.
170 Ibid.
171 Gilbert Allen, *The Final Days of American Shopping* (The University of South Carolina Press, 2016), 1.
172 Ibid. 3.
173 Ibid.
174 Ibid.
175 Ibid., 19.
176 Ibid., 23.
177 Ibid.
178 Ibid., 54.
179 Ibid., 47.
180 Ibid., 59.

Part III: Culture

1   Robert Zaretsky, *Boswell's Enlightenment* (The Belknap Press of Harvard University Press, 2015), 3.
2   Ibid., 3, 158.
3   Ibid., 17.
4   Ibid., 4.
5   Ibid., 18.

6   Russell Kirk, *Russell Kirk's Concise Guide to Conservatism* (1957) (Regnery Gateway, 2019), 92.

7   Ibid., 94.

8   Ibid., 84.

9   Ibid., 87.

10   Ibid.

11   Ibid.

12   Ibid., 19.

13   Ibid., 33.

14   Ibid., 71.

15   Ibid., 28.

16   Ibid., 29.

17   Ibid., 21.

18   Ibid., 10.

19   Camille Paglia, *Sexual Personae: Art and Decadence From Nefertiti to Emily Dickinson* (London and New Haven: Yale University Press, 1990), 664.

20   Ibid.

21   See O.C.G.A. § 16–6–7 (2010).

22   See, e.g., Hans-Hermann Hoppe, *A Theory of Capitalism and Socialism* (Auburn, Alabama: Ludwig von Mises Institute, 2007), 8–17.

23   Camille Paglia, *Sexual Persona*, 664.

24   Ibid.

25   Paglia, *Sexual Persona*, 498.

26   Mark Royden Winchell, *Too Good to Be True: The Life and Work of Leslie Fiedler* (Columbia and London: University of Missouri Press, 2002), 172.

27   Leslie A. Fiedler, *Love and Death in the American Novel* (New York: Criterion Books, 1960), 289.

28   Ibid. at 290.

29   Lucy B. Maddox, "Necrophilia in *Lolita*." *The Centennial Review*. Vol. 26, No. 4 (1982), 366.

30   Ibid.

31   Tyler Trent Ochoa and Christine Newman Jones. "Defiling the Dead: Necrophilia and the Law." *Whittier Law Review*, Vol. 18 (1997), 550.

32   Edward W. Younkins, *Flourishing and Happiness in a Free Society* (University Press of America, 2011), 16.

33   Ibid., 54.

34   Ibid.

35   Ibid.

36   Ibid.

37   Ibid., 21.

38   Ibid., 174.

39   Ibid., 157.

40 Ibid.
41 Jonathan V. Last, *What to Expect When No One's Expecting: America's Coming Demographic Disaster* (New York and London: Encounter Books, 2014), 27.
42 Ibid., 27.
43 Ibid., 28.
44 Ibid., 30–31.
45 Deirdre McCloskey, *Bourgeois Equality: How Ideas, Not Capital or Institutions, Enriched the World* (Chicago: University of Chicago Press, 2006), xxiii.
46 Ibid., xxix.
47 Ibid., 643.
48 Ibid., xxxi.
49 Ibid., xxxi.
50 Ibid., 470.
51 Ibid., 597.
52 Ibid., xvii.
53 Ibid., 440.
54 Ibid., xvi.
55 Ibid., 609.
56 Ibid., xviii.
57 Ibid.
58 Ibid., 30.
59 Ibid., 170.
60 Ibid., 171.
61 Ibid., 242.
62 Ibid., 334.
63 Ibid., 353.
64 Ibid., 510.
65 Ibid., 636.
66 Ibid., 643.
67 Ibid., xviii.
68 Ibid., 498.
69 Ibid., xx.
70 Ibid., 393.
71 Ibid., 146.
72 Ibid., 540.
73 Ibid., 523.
74 Ibid., 8.
75 Ibid., 650.
76 F. H. Buckley, *The Way Back: Restoring the Promise of America* (New York and London: Encounter Books), 275.
77 Ibid., 5.
78 Ibid., 42.

79 Ibid., 53.

80 Ibid., 161.

81 Ibid., 142.

82 Ibid., 62.

83 Ibid., 276.

84 John J. Langdale III, *Superfluous Southerners: Cultural Conservatism and the South 1920–1990* (Columbia and London: University of Missouri Press, 2012), 50.

85 Ibid., 12.

86 Ibid., 6–7.

87 Ibid., 7.

88 Ibid., 26.

89 Ibid., 25.

90 Thomas J. DiLorenzo, *The Problem with Socialism* (Regnery Publishing, 2016), 3.

91 Ibid., 77.

92 Ibid.

93 Ibid., 94.

94 Ibid., 5.

95 James Carroll, "Foreword," *War No More: Three Centuries of American Antiwar & Peace Writing*, edited by Lawrence Rosenwald (The Library of America, 2016), xxv.

96 Lawrence Rosenwald, "Introduction," *War No More: Three Centuries of American Antiwar & Peace Writing*, edited by Lawrence Rosenwald (The Library of America, 2016), xxvii.

97 Rosenwald, "Introduction," *War No More*, xxvii.

98 Lawrence Rosenwald, "William James," *War No More: Three Centuries of American Antiwar & Peace Writing*, edited by Lawrence Rosenwald (The Library of America, 2016), 114.

99 Jonah Goldberg, *Liberal Fascism* (New York: Doubleday, 2007), 5.

100 Barack Obama, "Weighing the Costs of Waging War in Iraq," *War No More: Three Centuries of American Antiwar & Peace Writing*, edited by Lawrence Rosenwald (The Library of America, 2016), 697.

101 Carroll, "Foreword," *War No More*, xxvi.

102 Ibid.

103 David Johnson, *John Randolph of Roanoke* (Baton Rouge: Louisiana State University Press, 2012), 6.

104 Ibid., 6, 7.

105 Ibid., 231.

106 Ibid., 35.

107 Ibid., 229.

108 John Shelton Reed, *Dixie Bohemia: A French Quarter Circle in the 1920s* (Baton Rouge: Louisiana State University Press, 2012), 3.

109 Ibid.,5.

110 Ibid.

111 Ibid., 4.

112 Ibid., 62.

113 Ibid., 63.

114 Ibid.

115 Ibid., 74.

116 Ibid., 81.

117 Ibid.

118 Ibid.

119 Ibid., 82.

120 Carl T. Bogus, *Buckley: William F. Buckley Jr. and the Rise of American Conservatism* (Bloomsbury Press, 2011), x,

121 Ibid., x.

122 Ibid.

123 Ibid., ix-x.

124 Ibid., 21.

125 Ibid.

126 Ibid., 19.

127 Ibid., 141.

128 Ibid., 17.

129 Ibid., 111.

130 Ibid., 114.

131 Paul Gottfried, *Fascism: The Career of a Concept* (DeKalb, Illinois: Northern Illinois University Press), 1.

132 Ibid., 1.

133 Ibid., 16.

134 Ibid., 24.

135 Ibid., 24–25.

136 Ibid., 41.

137 Ibid., 2.

138 Ibid.,15.

139 Bradley J. Birzer, *Russell Kirk* (University Press of Kentucky, 2015), 105.

140 Birzer, *Russell Kirk*, 270.

141 Seth Vannatta, *Conservatism and Pragmatism in Law, Politics, and Ethics* (Palgrave Macmillan, 2014), 168–69.

142 Birzer, *Russell Kirk*, 103.

143 Ibid., 100.

144 Ibid.

145 Ibid., 107.
146 Russell Kirk, *The Conservative Mind: From Burke to Eliot*, Seventh Revised Edition (1953) (Regnery Publishing, Inc., 1995), 155.
147 Ibid., 172.
148 Ibid., 244.
149 Ibid., 5.
150 Ibid.,167.
151 Ibid., 411.
152 Ibid.
153 Ibid.
154 Ibid.
155 Ibid., 5.
156 Larry Siedentop, *Inventing the Individual* (The Belknap Press of Harvard University Press, 2014), 1.
157 Ibid., 2.
158 Ibid.
159 Ibid., 1.
160 Ibid., 337.
161 Ibid., 332.
162 Ibid., 338.
163 Ibid., 68.
164 Ibid., 363.
165 Greg Lukianoff, *Unlearning Liberty* (Encounter Books, 2012), 2.
166 Lukianoff, *Unlearning Liberty*, 12.
167 Paul, *The School Revolution* (Grand Central Publishing, 2013), viii.
168 Ibid., ix.
169 Ibid.,
170 Ibid., 5.
171 Ibid., 7.
172 Ibid., 6.
173 Ibid., 19.
174 Ibid.
175 Ibid.
176 Ibid.
177 Ibid., 20.
178 Ibid., 23.
179 Ibid., 36.
180 Russell Kirk, *Russell Kirk's Concise Guide to Conservatism* (1957) (Regnery Gateway, 2019), 83.
181 Ibid., 84.
182 Ibid., 89.

183 Ibid., 3.
184 Ibid.
185 Ibid., 59.
186 Ibid., 3.
187 Ibid., 2–3.
188 Ibid., 91.
189 Robert P. Waxler, *The Risk of Reading* (Bloomsbury, 2014), 1.
190 Ibid., 171.
191 Ibid., 176.